BIBLICAL HEBREW 2
WORKBOOK
ANSWER KEY

This answer key is designed to provide the answers to exercises in the *Biblical Hebrew 2 Workbook* in the quickest, easiest, most practical way, even for parents who do not read Hebrew themselves. It reproduces the entire text of the workbook at full size with answers provided.

BIBLICAL HEBREW 2
WORKBOOK

A High School Level, Christian Course for Lifelong Learning from God's Word

KIM McKAY

ALEF PRESS
1036 Chestnut Hill Road
Cambridge, New York 12816
www.alefpress.org

ISBN: 978-0-9881738-2-8

Printed in the United States of America

TABLE OF CONTENTS

LETTERS

CHAPTER ONE

1.1 MONDAY

Get out your Alef Press *Traditional Hebrew Songs* CD and sing through it today. Make sure you have the alef-bet song (track 11) memorized.

Work on reading Psalm 1 aloud, as fluently as possible, without concentrating on word meaning. Continue to read it aloud at least once each day this week.

Remember that the Tetragrammaton, the four-letter name of the LORD, is usually shown in Scripture with vowels, but is not pronounced as written. The vowels are only reminders to substitute the title *Adonai* אֲדֹנָי. The sacred name of God appears twice in Psalm 1 and is underlined below.

אַשְׁרֵי־הָאִישׁ אֲשֶׁר לֹא הָלַךְ בַּעֲצַת רְשָׁעִים וּבְדֶרֶךְ חַטָּאִים לֹא עָמָד וּבְמוֹשַׁב לֵצִים לֹא יָשָׁב׃
כִּי אִם בְּתוֹרַת יְהוָה חֶפְצוֹ וּבְתוֹרָתוֹ יֶהְגֶּה יוֹמָם וָלָיְלָה׃ וְהָיָה כְּעֵץ שָׁתוּל עַל־פַּלְגֵי מָיִם
אֲשֶׁר פִּרְיוֹ יִתֵּן בְּעִתּוֹ וְעָלֵהוּ לֹא־יִבּוֹל וְכֹל אֲשֶׁר־יַעֲשֶׂה יַצְלִיחַ׃ לֹא־כֵן הָרְשָׁעִים כִּי אִם־כַּמֹּץ
אֲשֶׁר־תִּדְּפֶנּוּ רוּחַ׃ עַל־כֵּן לֹא־יָקֻמוּ רְשָׁעִים בַּמִּשְׁפָּט וְחַטָּאִים בַּעֲדַת צַדִּיקִים׃ כִּי־יוֹדֵעַ יְהוָה
דֶּרֶךְ צַדִּיקִים וְדֶרֶךְ רְשָׁעִים תֹּאבֵד׃

1.2 TUESDAY

1. Practice on scrap paper until you can write out the alef-bet in block letters, in order, from memory, in the space below. Include the sofit characters.

א ב בּ ג ד ה ו ז ח ט י

כּ כ ך ל מ ם נ ן ס ע פּ פ ף צ ץ

ק ר שׁ שׂ ת

2. Even if you do not plan to use the script letters, give them a try this once. Write out the alef-bet in script. Only if you plan to usually use script do you need to write from memory.

א ב בּ ג ד ה ו ז ח ט י

כּ כ ך ל מ ם נ ן ס ע פּ פ ף צ ץ

ק ר שׁ שׂ ת

3. Match syllables that sound alike.

סוּ	קִישׁ
חֶן	לָט
רֹד	שֵׁא
בּוֹ	כֵּן
לַתְ	רוֹד
כְּשׁ	ווֹע

4. What are the two most prominent Hebrew pronunciation traditions? On which one is modern Israeli Hebrew based?

Ashkenazic and Sephardic; modern Israeli Hebrew pronunciation is based on Sephardic pronunciation

1.3 WEDNESDAY

1. Study the vowel point names until you can write each by its transliterated name.

kametz ָ

chataf kametz ֳ

patach ַ

chataf patach ֲ

segol ֶ

chataf segol ֱ

chirek ִ

tzeirei ֵ

cholem ֹ ,וֹ

shurek וּ

kibutz ֻ

sheva ְ

2. List the beged kefet letters. What characteristic do they share?

ב ג ד כ פ ת

The beged kefet letters are those which once changed pronunciation with the addition of a dagesh (dot) in the middle. In modern pronunciation, only bet, pey, and kaf do.

3. What characteristic distinguishes the guttural letters? List them.

Guttural letters are (or were) pronounced in the throat. They generally do not accept a dagesh.

א ע ה ח ר

4. Spell English words with Hebrew consonants and vowels.

example: Kate קֵתְ Teacher, please see note at bottom of page 11.

knows	נֹז, נוֹז	meat	מִית, מִיט
might	מַית, מַיט	Bach	בָּח, בָּךְ, בַּח, בַּךְ, בֲּךְ, בֲּח
yet	יֶת, יֶט, יֱת, יֱט	soul	סוֹל, שֹׁל, סֹל, שׁוֹל
boy	בּוֹי	name	נֵם
debt	דֶת, דֶט, דֱת, דֱט	less	לֶשׂ, לֶס, לֱשׂ, לֱס
beets	בִּיץ	zone	זֹן, זוֹן
fee	פִּי, פִּא, פִּיא, פִּיה	quiche	קִישׁ, כִּישׁ

5. Write the transliterated vowel names by the points.

וֹ cholem

וּ shurek

◌ֲ chataf patach

◌ֳ chataf kametz

◌ֱ chataf segol

◌ִ chirek

◌ֵ tzeirei

◌ַ patach

◌ָ kametz

◌ֻ kibutz

ֶ segol

ְ sheva

1.4 THURSDAY

1. Spell English words with Hebrew characters. After writing the word in Hebrew, spell aloud your Hebrew creations using the consonant and vowel names.

example: keel כִּיל "kaf, chirek, yud, lamed"

mice	מַיס, מָישׁ, מַישְׁא, מָיסְ, מַיסְע	noon	נוּן, נֻן
shots	שָׁץ, שַׁץ, שֲׁץ	shy	שַׁי, שָׁי
seem	סִים, שִׂים, סִם, שִׂם	aid	אֵד, עֵד, אֵיד, עֵיד
teas	תִיז, טִיז	pale	פֵּל
zoo	זֻ, זוּ	eat	אִית, אִיט, אִט, עִיט, עִית, עִת, אִת, עִט
oats	אֳץ, אוֹץ, אֹץ, עֳץ, עוֹץ, עֹץ	men	מֶן, מֱן
lace	לֵשׂ, לֵס	cave	קֵב, קֵו
seats	שִׂיץ, סִיץ	bee	בִּי
air	אֵר, עֵר	let	לֶת, לֶט, לֱת, לֱט
dune	דוּן, דֻן	phone	פֹן, פוֹן
off	אָף, עָף, אַף, עַף, אֲף, עֲף	mess	מֶשְׂ, מֶס, מֱשׂ, מֱס

Teacher, please note: There are other possible spellings than the ones above if your student goes wild adding silent letters and points, as shown above for "mice." There is more than one suitable letter for several consonant and vowel sounds; those options are shown above. The student need list only one possibility.

2. In 2 Kings 4:24 below, circle or highlight each accent mark. Mark each makkef with an X. Draw an arrow to the sof pasuk.

וַתַּחֲבֹשׁ הָאָתוֹן וַתֹּאמֶר אֶל־נַעֲרָהּ נְהַג וָלֵךְ אַל־תַּעֲצָר־לִי לִרְכֹּב כִּי
אִם־אָמַרְתִּי לָךְ׃

3. Mark the stressed syllable in each word below. State the rule that guided you.
example: לֶחֶם "When segol is in the final syllable, it is usually not stressed."

מֶלֶךְ segol in final syllable	שָׂמֵחַ final חַ הַ עַ not stressed	שָׁוְא sheva syllable is never accented	קָמֵץ last syllable is usually stressed
רוּחַ final חַ הַ עַ not stressed	אֹזֶן segol in final syllable	יֵשׁוּעַ final חַ הַ עַ not stressed	הַטּוֹב last syllable is usually stressed
לָמֶד segol in final syllable	בְּרִית sheva syllable is never accented	רֶגֶל segol in final syllable	אָלֶף segol in final syllable

1.5 FRIDAY

Remember to practice fluent reading daily.

1. Write each Hebrew letter and its numerical value.

80	פ	9	ט	1	א
90	צ	10	י	2	ב
100	ק	20	כ	3	ג
200	ר	30	ל	4	ד
300	שׁ	40	מ	5	ה
400	ת	50	נ	6	ו
		60	ס	7	ז
		70	ע	8	ח

2. Gershayim do not appear with real Hebrew words. Rather, they indicate numbers or acronyms.

3. Write the numbers 28-35 with gershayim.

28	כ"ח	33	ל"ג
29	כ"ט	34	ל"ד
30	ל'	35	ל"ה
31	ל"א		
32	ל"ב		

4. Spell English words with Hebrew characters. After writing the word in Hebrew, spell aloud your Hebrew creations using the consonant and vowel names.
example: keel כִּיל "kaf, chirek, yud, lamed"

soon	שֻׁן, שׁוּן, סֻן, סוּן	red	רֶד, רֶד
cake	קֵק, כֵּק	door	דוֹר, דֹר
peel	פִּיל	cod	כָּד, כַּד, כֲּד, קָד, קַד, קֲד
movie	מֻוִי, מוּוִי, מֻבִי, מוּבִי	sheets	שִׁיץ
daisy	דֵזִי	seat	סִית, סִיט, סִט, סִת, שִׁית, שִׁיט, שִׁת, שִׁט
neat	נִט, נִת, נִיט, נִית	toes	תוֹז, טוֹז, תֹז, טֹז

Teacher, please note: As in Thursday's exercises, there are other possible spellings than the ones above if silent letters and points are added freely. There is more than one suitable letter for several consonant and vowel sounds; those options are shown above. The student need list only one possibility.

NOUNS

CHAPTER TWO

2.1 MONDAY

Each Monday from now on, except review weeks, will present vocabulary words to memorize. Use Mondays to work on them and on reading fluently the chapter's verse. Read the verse aloud at least once each day of the week, aiming for fluency by Friday.

Remember the memorization ideas from 1.1 in the text: Read the words aloud repeatedly. Write them out, pronouncing and translating them. Draw pictures for each and label in Hebrew and English. Study with a partner to quiz and encourage one another. Use Hebrew words in family conversation whenever possible. Record yourself reading the words, then play your recording back and supply translations as you listen. Print out the flashcards at www.alefpress.org onto business card stock. Run through them often. Match Hebrew cards to English translation cards. Group cards by parts of speech. Use them to play charades. Time how quickly you can correctly complete your stack, then beat your best time. Use these ideas throughout the week, as needed.

Genesis 2:24 for fluent reading practice this week:

עַל־כֵּן יַֽעֲזָב־אִישׁ אֶת־אָבִיו וְאֶת־אִמּוֹ וְדָבַק בְּאִשְׁתּוֹ וְהָיוּ לְבָשָׂר אֶחָד׃

It is not essential to consider word meaning when reading for fluency practice, but on the next page is Genesis 2:24 again with a rough word-for-word translation. Look for words you know. Examine the words and their meanings in each week's verse. By doing so, you will see new vocabulary in action, get a feel for Hebrew syntax, and have a head start on upcoming grammar lessons. Supply any blanks in the charts. Eventually, you will be able to complete the translations yourself!

on	עַל־
thus	כֵּן
will leave	יַעֲזָב־
a man	אִישׁ
(untranslatable) see 13.3 in your textbook if you can't stand the suspense	אֶת־
his father	אָבִיו
and (with same untranslatable word)	וְאֶת־
his mother	אִמּוֹ
and will hold fast	וְדָבַק
in his wife	בְּאִשְׁתּוֹ
and it will be	וְהָיוּ
to flesh	לְבָשָׂר
one	אֶחָד׃

2.2 TUESDAY

1. Distinguish common nouns, proper nouns, and pronouns. Note which are plurals.

example: Patrick Henry *a proper noun*

Paris proper noun

דָּוִד proper noun

אֶרֶץ common noun

The Oval Office proper noun

הוּא pronoun

אִשָּׁה common noun

שָׂרָה proper noun

they pronoun, plural

pickles common noun, plural

יָם common noun

הִיא pronoun

אָב common noun

אֵם common noun

us pronoun, plural

adventure common noun

אִישׁ common noun

2. Identify common nouns, proper nouns, and pronouns in these sentences. Distinguish whether they are singular or plural:

c. n., s. c. n., s. pron., s. pron., s. pron., s.

Love is patient, love is kind. It does not envy, it does not boast, it is not proud.
1 Corinthians 13:4

(possessive) pronoun (also before "entrances")

pron., pl. c. n., s. c. n., s. pron., pl. c. n., pl. c. n., pl. c. n., pl. pron., pl.

All the world's a stage, and all the men and women merely players: they have their exits and their entrances; and one man in his time plays many parts, his acts being seven ages. —William Shakespeare, *As You Like It*

c. n., pl. c. n., pl. c. n., pl. c. n., s. c. n., s. c. n., pl. c. n., pl. (possessive) pronoun (possessive) pronoun

c. n., s. p. n., s. c. n., s. c. n., s. pron., s.

The relief which Edmund felt was so great that in spite of the cold he suddenly got warm all over right down to his toes, and at the same time there came into his head what seemed a perfectly lovely idea.
—C.S. Lewis, *The Lion, the Witch, and the Wardrobe*

c. n., s. c. n., s. pron., s. c. n., pl. (possessive) pronoun c. n., s. (possessive) pronoun

3. Spell aloud this week's vocabulary words.
example: אָב "Alef, kametz, vet."

Please turn to page 20 for these answers.

2.3 WEDNESDAY

1. Match the Hebrew words with their English translations.

he	דָּוִד m.
David	שָׂרָה f.
man	הוּא m.
Sarah	אִשָּׁה f.
father	אֵם f.
land	אֶרֶץ f.
sea	הִיא f.
mother	אָב m.
she	יָם m.
woman	אִישׁ m.

2. Label the gender of the Hebrew words above with *m.* for masculine or *f.* for feminine.

3. Guess the gender of the following Hebrew nouns. Explain your rationale. Not all nouns follow the general rules, but these will.

example: sin: חַטָּאת "Feminine, because it ends with ת."

inheritance: נַחֲלָה f., ends with אָה

voice: קוֹל m., no feminine ending

time: עֵת f., ends with ת

Sabbath: שַׁבָּת f., ends with ת

bull: פַּר m., refers to something male

family: מִשְׁפָּחָה f., ends with אָה

silver: כֶּסֶף m., no feminine ending

Naomi: נָעֳמִי f., refers to female person

4. Of the words above that have multiple syllables, which would you accent on the first syllable?

silver, because of segol in final syllable

2.4 THURSDAY

1. What is the Hebrew word for *it*?

for masculine nouns: הוּא for feminine nouns: הִיא

2. Spell English words with Hebrew characters. After writing the word in Hebrew, spell aloud your Hebrew creations using the consonant and vowel names.
Example: keel כִּיל "kaf, chirek, yud, lamed"

Students need list only one Hebrew spelling option per English word.

holy	הֹלִי, הוֹלִי	year	יִר
dear	דִיר	goat	גֹת, גוֹת, גֹט, גוֹט
yacht	יָט, יַט, יָת, יֲט, יֱט, יֱת	buy	בַּי
mellow	מֶלוֹ, מֶלֹא, מֱלוֹ, מֱלֹא	meets	מִיץ, מִץ
toy	טוֹי, תוֹי	rock	רַק, רָק, רֲק
toad	תוֹד, טוֹד, תֹד, טֹד	keep	כִּפְּא, כִּיפְּא, קִיפְּא

Note that for "keep," a final silent letter is necessary because the sofit version of pey can say only an "f," rather than a "p" sound.

2.5 FRIDAY

1. How is Genesis 2:24 coming? I'm sure you recognize *man* in there; can you recognize *father* and *mother* which appear with suffixes? Have you noticed a word or two from *Biblical Hebrew: A Homeschool Primer*? Write below, in Hebrew, the words of Genesis 2:24 that are, or include, nouns.

בְּאִשְׁתּוֹ   לְבָשָׂר   אִישׁ

אִמּוֹ   אָבִיו

כֵּן was taught in the primer. Others, like "one" and "flesh" might be remembered from song lyrics.

2. How can you tell what gender a Hebrew noun is?

Nouns that are obviously female, like a girl's name, are feminine, and obviously male nouns, like "a rooster," are masculine. If a noun ends in tav or kametz-then-hey, there is a good chance it is feminine. Most nouns are masculine. Noun genders can be ascertained with certainty only by noticing the gender of words that refer to them in context or by consulting a dictionary.

3. Match Hebrew words with English translations.

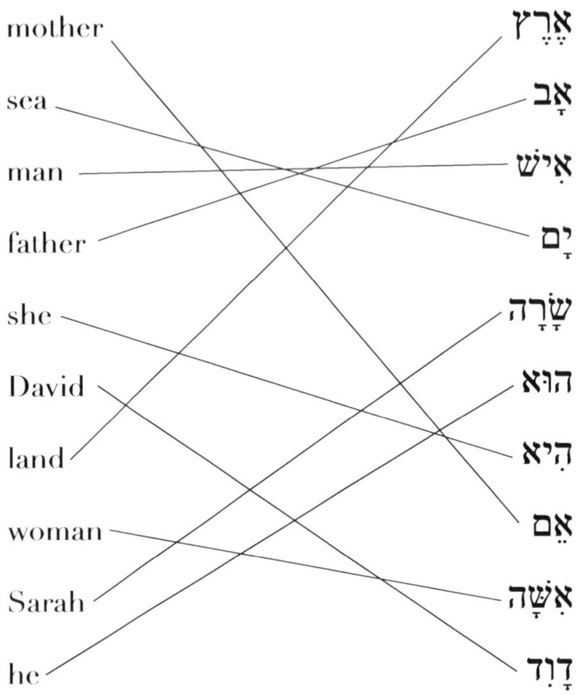

2.2.3. Exercise 3, page 17 answers:

דָּוִד	"dalet, kametz, vav, chirek, dalet"
שָׂרָה	"sin, kametz, resh, kametz, hey"
הוּא	"hey, shurek, alef"
הִיא	"hey, chirek, yud, alef"
אִישׁ	"alef, chirek, yud, shin"
אִשָּׁה	"alef, chirek, shin with dagesh, kametz, hey"
אָב	"alef, kametz, vet"
אֵם	"alef, tzeirei, mem sofit"
יָם	"yud, kametz, mem sofit"
אֶרֶץ	"alef, segol, resh, segol, tzadi sofit"

NOUN SENTENCES

CHAPTER THREE

3.1 MONDAY

Memorize this week's vocabulary words with the method that works best for you. They are all nouns and sorts of people.

The kametz in נָכְרִי is pronounced *o* as in *go*. Follow the chart in Appendix B of your textbook to see why.

Practice reading 2 Samuel 7:3 aloud:

וַיֹּאמֶר נָתָן אֶל־הַמֶּלֶךְ כֹּל אֲשֶׁר בִּלְבָבְךָ לֵךְ עֲשֵׂה כִּי יְהוָה עִמָּךְ׃

said	וַיֹּאמֶר
Nathan	נָתָן
to	אֶל־
the king	הַמֶּלֶךְ
all	כֹּל
which	אֲשֶׁר
in your heart	בִּלְבָבְךָ
go	לֵךְ

do	עֲשֵׂה
because	כִּי
the LORD (read "Adonai")	יְהוָה
with you	עִמָּךְ:

3.2 TUESDAY

1. Distinguish between definite and indefinite nouns in the list below.

הָאָרֶץ definite, the land

הָאִישׁ definite, the man

מֶלֶךְ indefinite, king or a king

אֶרֶץ indefinite, land or a land

גֵּר indefinite, sojourner or a sojourner

הַכְּסִיל definite, the fool

הַנָּבִיא definite, the prophet

נָכְרִי indefinite, foreigner or a foreigner

הַשֹּׁפֵט definite, the judge

הָאֵם definite, the mother

אִשָּׁה indefinite, woman or a woman

הַיָּם definite, the sea

הַכֹּהֵן definite, the priest

עֶבֶד indefinite, servant or a servant

מַלְאָךְ indefinite, messenger/angel or a messenger/angel

הַשָּׂר definite, the captain

2. Translate the words above.

3. Write the translation of these words in Hebrew. If the definite article is needed, it will be spelled as it usually is: hey, patach, and a dagesh for the next letter.

אָב a father

הַיָּם the sea

עֶבֶד a servant

הַנָּבִיא the prophet

הַמֶּלֶךְ the king

אִישׁ a man

מַלְאָךְ an angel

הַשֹּׁפֵט the judge

הוּא he

3.3 WEDNESDAY

Read aloud and translate.

אָב וְאֵם a father and a mother

הַכֹּהֵן וְהַמֶּלֶךְ וְהַשֹּׁפֵט the priest and the king and the judge

דָּוִד וְשָׂרָה David and Sarah

הַשָּׂר the captain

מֶלֶךְ king

הַגֵּר וְהַנָּכְרִי the sojourner and the foreigner

הַנָּבִיא the prophet

אִשָּׁה וְאֵם a woman and a mother

עֶבֶד וָמֶלֶךְ a servant and a king

הַכְּסִיל the fool

הָאָרֶץ וְהַיָּם the land and the sea

הָאִישׁ the man

מַלְאָךְ an angel/messenger

דָּוִד וְהַכֹּהֵן David and the priest

3.4 THURSDAY

1. Translate these noun sentences.

דָּוִד עֶבֶד David is a servant.

הוּא גֵּר He is a sojourner.

הִיא שָׂרָה She is Sarah.

הָאָב הַמֶּלֶךְ The father is the king.

הָאִישׁ הַמֶּלֶךְ The man is the king.

הוּא כֹּהֵן וְנָבִיא He is a priest and a prophet.

הוּא מַלְאָךְ He is an angel. (or, He is a messenger.)

הָאִשָּׁה אֵם The woman is a mother.

הַנָּכְרִי כְּסִיל The foreigner is a fool.

דָּוִד שַׂר David is a captain.

הָאָב נָכְרִי The father is a foreigner.

הַמֶּלֶךְ הַשֹּׁפֵט The king is the judge.

2. Write these sentences in Hebrew.

הוּא אָב He is a father.

הָאִישׁ מֶלֶךְ The man is a king.

הִיא אֵם She is a mother.

הוּא הַכֹּהֵן He is the priest.

הַמֶּלֶךְ נָבִיא The king is a prophet.

הוּא הַיָּם It is the sea.

הִיא הָאָרֶץ It is the land.

3.5 FRIDAY

1. Translate.

הַשֹּׁפֵט וְהַמֶּלֶךְ וְהַנָּבִיא the judge and the king and the prophet

הָאִישׁ אָב The man is a father.

הָאֵם שָׂרָה The mother is Sarah.

הַנָּכְרִי the foreigner

מַלְאָךְ an angel/a messenger

הוּא כְּסִיל He is a fool.

דָּוִד הַשָּׂר David is the captain.

הוּא הַכֹּהֵן He is the priest.

הָאָרֶץ the land

עֶבֶד וְגֵר a servant and a sojourner

יָם a sea

הָאִשָּׁה אֵם The woman is a mother.

2. Number these artifacts in order of age:

2 ‣Mesad Hashavyahu ostracon clay pottery

7 ‣BHS paper

4 ‣Nash Papyrus papyrus

5 ‣Aleppo Codex parchment (leather)

1 ‣Gezer Calendar limestone

6 ‣Leningrad Codex parchment (leather)

3 ‣Ketef Hinnom scrolls silver

8 ‣Biblia Hebraica Quinta paper

3. Identify the material of each of the above, e.g. copper, paper. Underline those that record Scripture.

PLURAL NOUNS

CHAPTER FOUR

4.1 MONDAY

Memorize this week's vocabulary words, all of which are nouns related to geography.

Practice reading Ecclesiastes 1:14 this week. Three words in Ecclesiastes 1:14, in accordance with the rules for syllable stress you have learned, are not accented on their final syllable. One appears here with the definite article. Identify the three.

רָאִיתִי אֶת־כָּל־הַמַּעֲשִׂים שֶׁנַּעֲשׂוּ תַּחַת הַשָּׁמֶשׁ וְהִנֵּה הַכֹּל הֶבֶל וּרְעוּת רוּחַ׃

Did you find these three words: רוּחַ, הֶבֶל, הַשָּׁמֶשׁ? Pronounce them with the stress on the penultimate (next to last) syllable.

The kametz in כָּל־ is pronounced *o* as in *go* since it is followed by a letter without a dagesh and then a makkef. See Appendix B in your textbook for details of kametz pronunciation.

Identify three instances of the definite article and two of the vav prefix in this verse.

I have seen	רָאִיתִי
(untranslatable)	אֶת־
all	כָּל־
the deeds (definite article here)	הַמַּעֲשִׂים

which have been done	שֶׁנַּעֲשׂוּ
under	תַּחַת
the sun (definite article here)	הַשָּׁמֶשׁ
and behold! (vav prefix here)	וְהִנֵּה
everything (definite article here)	הַכֹּל
vapor, unsubstantial	הֶבֶל
and striving (vav prefix here)	וּרְעוּת
wind	רוּחַ׃

4.2 TUESDAY

1. Disregarding vowels, write the plural forms of these singular nouns.

example: שפטים שֹׁפֵט

עֶבֶד עבדים

הַר הרים

אֶרֶץ ארצות

כֹּהֵן כהנים

נָהָר נהרים

מֶלֶךְ מלכים

אֲדָמָה אדמות

2. Translate.

הַשָּׂרִים כֹּהֲנִים The captains are priests.

הַשֶּׁמֶשׁ וְהָרוּחַ the sun and the wind

הַמִּדְבָּר the desert

הַמְּלָכִים נְבִיאִים The kings are prophets.

הֶהָרִים the mountains

שָׂדֶה וְנָהָר a field and a river

הָאָרֶץ וְהַשָּׁמַיִם the land and the sky

רוּחַ wind/spirit

הִיא עִיר It is a city.

הוּא גֵּר He is a sojourner.

אִשָּׁה וְאֵם a woman and a mother

דָּוִד נָכְרִי David is a foreigner.

הַשֹּׁפְטִים כְּסִילִים The judges are fools.

4.3 WEDNESDAY

1. Translate.

הָאֲנָשִׁים מַלְאָכִים The men are kings.

עָרִים cities

הָאֲרָצוֹת the lands

הָרִים וְשָׂדוֹת mountains and fields

הַשֶּׁמֶשׁ the sun

הוּא נָהָר It is a river.

הָאָבוֹת שֹׁפְטִים The fathers are judges.

הָעֲבָדִים גֵּרִים The servants are sojourners.

הַמַּלְאָךְ the angel/messenger

נָשִׁים וַאֲנָשִׁים women and men

הוּא וְדָוִד אָבוֹת וְשָׂרִים He and David are fathers and captains.

הֶעָרִים the cities

הַמִּדְבָּר the desert

אֲדָמוֹת lands

2. Write the plural of these singular nouns.

אִשָּׁה	נָשִׁים
אִישׁ	אֲנָשִׁים
עִיר	עָרִים
אֲדָמָה	אֲדָמוֹת
אֶרֶץ	אֲרָצוֹת
שָׂדֶה	שָׂדוֹת
אָב	אָבוֹת

4.4 THURSDAY

1. Read aloud and translate these nouns. Mark each with *m.* for masculine or *f.* for feminine, and *s.* for singular or *pl.* for plural.
example: הִיא she: *f.*, *s.*

הָרִים mountains: m., pl.

עֲבָדִים servants: m., pl.

אָבוֹת fathers: m., pl.

הַשֶּׁמֶשׁ the sun: m. or f., s.

עִיר city: f., s.

הַשָּׁמַיִם the sky: m., pl.

כֹּהֲנִים priests: m., pl.

אֲנָשִׁים men: m., pl.

גֵּר sojourner: m., s.

אֲדָמָה ground/earth/land: f., s.

הַשָּׂדֹת the fields: m., pl.

שָׂרָה Sarah: f., s.

נָשִׁים women: f., pl.

נָהָר river: m., s.

הַיַּמִּים the seas: m., pl.

2. Write Hebrew translations.

הָאֲנָשִׁים אָבוֹת The men are fathers.

הִיא עִיר It is a city.

הַנָּשִׁים וְשָׂרָה the women and Sarah

מְלָכִים וְהַנְּבִיאִים kings and the prophets

4.5 FRIDAY

1. Explain a few reasons why the survival of the Hebrew Scriptures is surprising.

An ancient people group and their language have remained alive.

The Hebrew Scriptures were kept for centuries by persecuted people without a homeland.

Rather than preserve an ancient, authoritative manuscript or two, old copies were retired and buried.

The Hebrew Scriptures have been repeatedly outlawed and destroyed by powerful civilizations.

The transmission of Scripture has depended upon copying long books by hand.

2. What is a geniza? What is its purpose?

A geniza is a storeroom for retired, holy things. It collects sacred documents and objects that have outlived their practical usefulness until they can be buried with due ceremony in a cemetery.

3. Find and translate the words you can read in these Bible verses.

the seas the land the sky the sky

אַתָּה עָשִׂיתָ אֶת־הַשָּׁמַיִם שְׁמֵי הַשָּׁמַיִם וְכָל־צְבָאָם הָאָרֶץ וְכָל־אֲשֶׁר עָלֶיהָ הַיַּמִּים וְכָל־אֲשֶׁר
בָּהֶם

and and and

excerpted from Nehemiah 9:6

David city

וַיִּקְרָא־לָהּ עִיר דָּוִד

from 2 Samuel 5:9

and land desert rivers

אֶפְתַּח עַל־שְׁפָיִים נְהָרוֹת וּבְתוֹךְ בְּקָעוֹת מַעְיָנוֹת אָשִׂים מִדְבָּר לַאֲגַם־מַיִם וְאֶרֶץ צִיָּה
לְמוֹצָאֵי מָיִם

Isaiah 41:18

ADJECTIVES

CHAPTER FIVE

5.1 MONDAY

By your chosen methods, memorize this week's vocabulary words.

You'll find two of them in Genesis 24:50. Identify three vav prefixes and one definite article. Spell aloud the men's names.

וַיַּעַן לָבָן וּבְתוּאֵל וַיֹּאמְרוּ מֵיְהוָה יָצָא הַדָּבָר לֹא נוּכַל דַּבֵּר אֵלֶיךָ רַע אוֹ־טוֹב׃

answered (vav prefix here)	וַיַּעַן
Laban spelled: "lamed, kametz, vet, kametz, nun sofit"	לָבָן
and Bethuel* (vav prefix here)	וּבְתוּאֵל
and said (vav prefix here)	וַיֹּאמְרוּ
from the LORD (*Adonai*)	מֵיְהוָה
went out	יָצָא
the matter (definite article here)	הַדָּבָר
not	לֹא
we are able	נוּכַל

*spelled: "vet, sheva, tav, shurek, alef, tzeirei, lamed"

to speak	דַּבֵּר
to you	אֵלֶיךָ
bad	רַע
or	אוֹ־
good	טוֹב:

5.2 TUESDAY

1. Translate these adjectives.

חֲדָשָׁה new, f., s.

חַי alive, m., s.

קְטַנָּה little, f., s.

קְדוֹשָׁה holy, f., s.

זְקֵנָה old, f., s.

גָּדוֹל big, m., s.

רָע bad, m., s.

טוֹבָה good, f., s.

חַיָּה alive, f., s.

חָדָשׁ new, m., s.

רָעָה bad, f., s.

טוֹב good, m., s.

Answers for #2 and #3 will vary, but included here with the translations are the gender and number that answers should be in.

For instance, something "old, f., s." might be your student's great-grandmother.

Since English does not have genders for all nouns, accept any suitable English noun for English examples that are objects. For example, "my bike" might answer "new, m., s.," even though in English we don't know if that bike is masculine or feminine.

The Hebrew nouns asked for in #3 need to agree in gender and number with the Hebrew adjectives given. Feminine nouns are noted as such in the textbook chapter vocabulary lists.

זָקֵן old, m., s.

קָטָן little, m., s.

גְּדוֹלָה big, f., s.

חָכָם wise, m., s.

קָדוֹשׁ holy, m., s.

חֲכָמָה wise, f., s.

2. Next to each adjective above, write an English noun that the adjective could describe.
examples: חָכָם Dad, חֲכָמָה Mom

3. Next to each adjective above, write a Hebrew noun that the adjective could describe. Take care to match adjective and noun genders.
example: אָב חָכָם

5.3 WEDNESDAY

1. Match these Hebrew phrases with their English translations.

a. an old prophet
b. a little field
c. holy priests
d. big cities
e. good women
f. good kings
g. evil judges
h. a living king
i. wise men
j. a big desert

c. כֹּהֲנִים קְדוֹשִׁים	f. מְלָכִים טוֹבִים
i. אֲנָשִׁים חֲכָמִים	g. שֹׁפְטִים רָעִים
e. נָשִׁים טוֹבוֹת	h. מֶלֶךְ חַי
j. מִדְבָּר גָּדוֹל	b. שָׂדֶה קָטָן
a. נָבִיא זָקֵן	d. עָרִים גְּדוֹלוֹת

2. More matching.

a. a new king
b. many angels
c. a little mountain
d. wise judges
e. an evil fool
f. a great wind
g. sun and sky
h. a wise captain
i. many servants
j. good fathers

d. שֹׁפְטִים חֲכָמִים	j. אָבוֹת טוֹבִים
h. שַׂר חָכָם	c. הַר קָטָן
g. שֶׁמֶשׁ וְשָׁמַיִם	b. מַלְאָכִים רַבִּים
i. עֲבָדִים רַבִּים	e. כְּסִיל רָע
a. מֶלֶךְ חָדָשׁ	f. רוּחַ גָּדוֹל

5.4 THURSDAY

Translate.

הָרִים גְּדוֹלִים big mountains

נְהָרִים קְטַנִּים small rivers

אִישׁ חָכָם קָדוֹשׁ וְטוֹב a wise, holy, and good man

אֲרָצוֹת רַבּוֹת many lands

הַשָּׁמַיִם the sky/Heaven

עִיר קְטַנָּה a small city

שֹׁפֵט חַי a living judge

נָשִׁים רַבּוֹת many women

מֶלֶךְ רָע וְזָקֵן a bad and old king

עֲבָדִים חֲדָשִׁים new servants

אֲדָמָה טוֹבָה good ground

כֹּהֲנִים קְדוֹשִׁים holy priests

אֶרֶץ גְּדוֹלָה וְטוֹבָה a big and good land

גֵּרִים רַבִּים many sojourners

אָבוֹת זְקֵנִים old fathers

מֶלֶךְ חָכָם a wise king

5.5 FRIDAY

1. What is so special about the Dead Sea Scrolls?

Before their discovery, the oldest, complete Hebrew Bible manuscript was from about A.D. 1000. The oldest known Hebrew manuscript fragment was from about 150 B.C. and contained only a few verses. The Dead Sea Scrolls, on the other hand, comprise almost all of the Hebrew Scriptures and date from around the time of Christ. Since they were hidden for 2000 years and predated the oldest Bible manuscript by 1000 years, they revealed the accuracy of Scripture transmission during that time, which was found to be outstanding.

2. Supply a Hebrew adjective for each noun below. Adjectives must agree in gender and number with the nouns they describe.

Answers will vary. The correct gender and number are given. The adjectives in the Chapter 5 vocabulary list are masculine and singular. Feminine, masculine plural, and feminine plural forms are given in the textbook on pages 44-45 and in the textbook lexicons.

שָׂדוֹת m., pl.

כֹּהֲנִים m., pl.

מֶלֶךְ m., s.

אֵם f., s.

עֲבָדִים m., pl.

עָרִים f., pl.

אָב m., s.

אֲרָצוֹת f., pl.

נָשִׁים f., pl.

3. Find and translate words you know in the Bible verses below.

big sun

כִּי מִמִּזְרַח־שֶׁמֶשׁ וְעַד־מְבוֹאוֹ גָּדוֹל שְׁמִי

Malachi 1:11a

alive

father he alive

חַי חַי הוּא יוֹדֶךָ כָּמוֹנִי הַיּוֹם אָב לְבָנִים יוֹדִיעַ אֶל־אֲמִתֶּךָ׃

Isaiah 38:19

good many

נִבְחָר שֵׁם מֵעֹשֶׁר רָב מִכֶּסֶף וּמִזָּהָב חֵן טוֹב׃

Proverbs 22:1

REVIEW

CHAPTER SIX

6.1 MONDAY

No new vocabulary this week, but keep practicing fluent reading with Psalm 48:1. Besides the chart blanks for you to fill in, notice there are two other words you know here: עִיר has a prefix; קָדוֹשׁ has a suffix.

שִׁיר מִזְמוֹר לִבְנֵי־קֹרַח: גָּדוֹל יְהוָה וּמְהֻלָּל מְאֹד בְּעִיר אֱלֹהֵינוּ הַר־קָדְשׁוֹ:

song	שִׁיר
psalm	מִזְמוֹר
to the sons of	לִבְנֵי־
Korach	קֹרַח:
great	גָּדוֹל
the LORD (*Adonai*)	יְהוָה
and to be praised	וּמְהֻלָּל
very	מְאֹד
in the city (of)	בְּעִיר
our God	אֱלֹהֵינוּ
mountain	הַר־

His holiness	קָדְשׁוֹ:

Translate sentences and phrases:

נָבִיא זָקֵן an old prophet

נָשִׁים רַבּוֹת many women

שָׂדוֹת קְטַנִּים little fields

אֲנָשִׁים חֲכָמִים wise men

דָוִד מֶלֶךְ טוֹב David is a good king.

הַנָּהָר וְהֶהָרִים the river and the mountains

הוּא גֵר He is a sojourner.

הַשֶּׁמֶשׁ וְהַשָּׁמַיִם the sun and the sky

שֹׁפֵט חַי a living judge

כֹּהֵן זָקֵן חָכָם וְקָדוֹשׁ an old, wise, and holy priest

מִדְבָּר גָּדוֹל a big desert

הִיא אֵם She is a mother.

נְבִיאִים רַבִּים many prophets

6.2 TUESDAY

1. Write the alef-bet, including sofit letters, in alphabetical order. Read aloud.

א בּ ב ג ד ה ו ז ח ט י

כּ כ ך ל מ ם נ ן ס ע פּ פ ף צ ץ

ק ר שׁ שׂ ת

2. Write each vowel point next to its transliterated name.

cholem ◌ֹ, וֹ

chataf patach ◌ֲ

segol ◌ֶ

kametz ◌ָ

sheva ◌ְ

patach ◌ַ

shurek וּ

chirek ◌ִ

chataf segol ◌ֱ

tzeirei ◌ֵ

chataf kametz ◌ֳ

kibutz ◌ֻ

3. List the beged kefet letters. What distinguishes them?

בגדכפת

The beged kefet letters are those which once changed pronunciation with the addition of a dagesh (dot) in the middle. In modern pronunciation, only bet, pey, and kaf do.

4. What is a guttural letter? How do the guttural letters affect Hebrew spelling?

Guttural letters are those which are or were pronounced in the throat, like alef. Guttural letters generally do not accept a dagesh.

6.3 WEDNESDAY

1. Briefly define:

a. Masoretes
Medieval, Jewish Hebrew scholars who added vowel points, stress accents, punctuation, and critical annotations to Scripture. There were schools of Masoretes in Tiberias, Jerusalem, and Babylon.

b. Aleppo Codex
For centuries, the oldest complete manuscript of the Hebrew Scriptures. The Aleppo Codex is in book form. It was written by Masorete scholars in Tiberias in the 10th century. It lost one-third of its pages in 1947 rioting.

c. Biblia Hebraica Stuttgartensia
A 1977 edition of the Leningrad Codex with critical apparatus, published by the German Bible Society in Stuttgart.

d. noun sentence
a complete sentence without any word that is a verb; the verb "to be" is implied.

e. codex
an ancient manuscript in book, rather than scroll, form

f. Dead Sea Scrolls
Complete scrolls and thousands of fragments on parchment, papyrus, and bronze which include documents from the Bible, Apocrypha, and other religious literature from before the time of Christ in Hebrew, Aramaic, Greek, and Nabatean. Discovered in caves near the Dead Sea, 1940s–50s.

g. nikkud
the transliterated Hebrew word for vowel points

2. Match the Hebrew with its English translation.

a. holy priests
b. evil men
c. wise women
d. He is a sojourner.
e. a big desert
f. good judges
g. a living king
h. a little mountain
i. wise judges
j. an evil fool
k. David is the king.
l. a great wind
m. a little field
n. little cities
o. great and good kings
p. many angels
q. the sky and the wind
r. a wise captain
s. many foreigners
t. old fathers
u. She is a mother.

e. מִדְבָּר גָּדוֹל	c. נָשִׁים חֲכָמוֹת
h. הַר קָטָן	l. רוּחַ גָּדוֹל
s. נָכְרִים רַבִּים	f. שֹׁפְטִים טוֹבִים
q. הַשָּׁמַיִם וְהָרוּחַ	j. כְּסִיל רָע
a. כֹּהֲנִים קְדוֹשִׁים	r. שַׂר חָכָם
n. עָרִים קְטַנּוֹת	d. הוּא גֵּר
p. מַלְאָכִים רַבִּים	b. אֲנָשִׁים רָעִים
i. שֹׁפְטִים חֲכָמִים	u. הִיא אֵם
k. דָּוִד הַמֶּלֶךְ	m. שָׂדֶה קָטָן
g. מֶלֶךְ חַי	t. אָבוֹת זְקֵנִים
o. מְלָכִים גְּדוֹלִים וְטוֹבִים	

6.4 THURSDAY

1. Mark the stressed syllable in these words:

קֹדֶשׁ	שָׁוְא	שָׂמֵחַ	אָבוֹת
אֹזֶן	יֵשׁוּעַ	אֹהֶל	רוּחַ
לָהֶם	בֶּגֶד	בְּרִית	חֶסֶד

2. Translate noun sentences.

דָּוִד כֹּהֵן David is a priest.

הוּא מֶלֶךְ טוֹב He is a good king.

הָאִשָּׁה אֵם The woman is a mother.

הָאָבוֹת שֹׁפְטִים The fathers are judges.

הוּא הַמִּדְבָּר It is the desert.

הָאֲנָשִׁים עֲבָדִים The men/people are servants.

הוּא מַלְאָךְ He is an angel/a messenger.

הַשָּׂרִים שֹׁפְטִים The captains are judges.

הִיא שָׂרָה She is Sarah.

הוּא הַשֶּׁמֶשׁ It is the sun.

הַכֹּהֲנִים מְלָכִים The priests are kings.

הִיא אִשָּׁה טוֹבָה She is a good woman.

ב + ט"ו = י"ז

6.5 FRIDAY

1. What are the four forms of Hebrew adjectives?

masculine singular, feminine singular, masculine plural, feminine plural

2. Translate adjective phrases.

הָרִים גְּדוֹלִים big mountains

כֹּהֲנִים קְדוֹשִׁים holy priests

שֹׁפְטִים חֲכָמִים wise judges

מְלָכִים גְּדוֹלִים וְטוֹבִים great and good kings

כְּסִיל רָע an evil fool

עָרִים רַבּוֹת many cities

שָׂדוֹת קְטַנִּים small fields

רוּחַ גָּדוֹל a big wind

אִישׁ טוֹב a good man

נָשִׁים חֲכָמוֹת wise women

נְבִיאִים חַיִּים living prophets

עֲבָדִים רַבִּים many servants

ADJECTIVES IN SENTENCES

CHAPTER SEVEN

7.1 MONDAY

Memorize this week's vocabulary words: all nouns, all people. The plurals are given for reference and familiarity. It is not necessary to memorize plural forms, but only to be able to recognize them. Notice the irregular plural form of *daughters*.

You can complete some of the chart for Genesis 29:10. In addition, אָח and אֵם are here with suffixes. Notice that vowels may change when words receive attachments. Identify two definite articles and five vav prefixes.

וַיְהִי כַּאֲשֶׁר רָאָה יַעֲקֹב אֶת־רָחֵל בַּת־לָבָן אֲחִי אִמּוֹ וְאֶת־צֹאן לָבָן אֲחִי אִמּוֹ וַיִּגַּשׁ יַעֲקֹב וַיָּגֶל
אֶת־הָאֶבֶן מֵעַל פִּי הַבְּאֵר וַיַּשְׁקְ אֶת־צֹאן לָבָן אֲחִי אִמּוֹ׃

And so it was that (vav prefix here)	וַיְהִי
when	כַּאֲשֶׁר
saw	רָאָה
Jacob	יַעֲקֹב
(untranslatable)	אֶת־
Rachel	רָחֵל

daughter [of]	בַּת־
Laban	לָבָן
the brother of	אֲחִי
his mother	אִמּוֹ
and (with an untranslatable word) (vav prefix here)	וְאֶת־
the flock of	צֹאן
Laban	לָבָן
the brother of	אֲחִי
his mother	אִמּוֹ
approached (vav prefix here)	וַיִּגַּשׁ
Jacob	יַעֲקֹב
and rolled away (vav prefix here)	וַיָּגֶל
(untranslatable)	אֶת־
the stone (definite article here)	הָאֶבֶן
from on	מֵעַל
the mouth of	פִּי
the well (definite article here)	הַבְּאֵר
and watered (vav prefix here)	וַיַּשְׁקְ
(untranslatable)	אֶת־
the flock of	צֹאן
Laban	לָבָן
the brother of	אֲחִי
his mother	אִמּוֹ:

7.2 TUESDAY

Translate the Hebrew phrases. Identify definite nouns in the list below.

Mars definite noun

הַבֵּן definite noun: the son

שָׂרָה וְרָחֵל definite nouns: Sarah and Rachel

הַר גָּדוֹל a big mountain

my cookie definite noun

a fine summer day

אֶרֶץ טוֹבָה a good land

עֶבֶד חָכָם a wise servant

Richard the Lionheart definite noun

הַשָּׁמַיִם definite noun: the sky/Heaven

נַעַר חָכָם a wise young man

שָׂדֶה טוֹב a good field

יַעֲקֹב definite noun: Jacob

הַכְּסִיל זָקֵן definite noun: the old fool

כֹּהֲנִים קְדוֹשִׁים holy priests

נָשִׁים women

שַׂר וְעִיר גְּדוֹלָה a captain and a big city

Abraham Lincoln's top hat definite noun

הָרוּחַ   definite noun: the wind/spirit

מִדְבָּר גָּדוֹל   a big desert

הָאָרֶץ וְהַיָּם   definite nouns: the land and the sea

נָבִיא חַי   a living prophet

her favorite book   definite noun

גֵּר   a sojourner

הָרוּחַ וְהַשֶּׁמֶשׁ   definite nouns: the wind and the sun

מֶלֶךְ רָע וְדוֹר רָע   a bad king and a bad generation

אֲנָשִׁים רַבִּים   many men/people

הָרֵעַ   definite noun: the neighbor

7.3 WEDNESDAY

Translate these sentences and phrases.

הַמִּדְבָּר גָּדוֹל   The desert is big.

הַמֶּלֶךְ זָקֵן   The king is old.

מֶלֶךְ זָקֵן   an old king, or A king is old.

הַמֶּלֶךְ הַזָּקֵן   the old king

זָקֵן הַמֶּלֶךְ   The king is old.

הַשָּׂרִים רָעִים   The captains are evil.

שָׂרִים רָעִים   evil captains, or Captains are evil.

דָוִד הֶחָכָם wise David, or David the Wise

דָוִד חָכָם David is wise.

הַנְּעָרִים וְהַנַּעֲרָה חֲכָמִים The young men and the young women are wise.

הַנְּעָרִים חֲכָמִים אַחִים The wise young men are brothers.

קְדוֹשִׁים הַנְּעָרִים The young men are holy.

הַנְּעָרִים הקְדוֹשִׁים the holy young men

יַעֲקֹב טוֹב Jacob is good.

בָּנוֹת טוֹבוֹת good daughters

גְּדוֹלוֹת הֶעָרִים וְרָעִים הָאֲנָשִׁים The cities are big and the men/people are bad.

הוּא עֶבֶד טוֹב He is a good servant.

7.4 THURSDAY

Translate.

הַחֲכָמִים מַלְאָכִים The wise ones are kings.

הוּא הַטּוֹב He is the good one.

הַגָּדוֹל אָב The great one is a father.

הַזָּקֵן נָבִיא The old one is a prophet.

הָרָעִים אַחִים The evil ones are brothers.

הַטּוֹבָה אֵם The good one is a mother.

הִיא אֵם She is a mother.

הַנְּעָרִים הַקְּדוֹשִׁים the holy young men

רָעִים כְּסִילִים evil fools, or Fools are evil.

בֵּן טוֹב a good son, or A son is good.

הַמֶּלֶךְ הַגָּדוֹל the great king

הַמֶּלֶךְ גָּדוֹל The king is great.

רָחֵל חַיָּה Rachel is alive.

הַשֹּׁפְטִים חֲכָמִים the wise judges

רַע הַדּוֹר The generation is evil.

רַבּוֹת הַבָּנוֹת The daughters are many.

נָהָר גָּדוֹל a big river, or A river is big.

7.5 FRIDAY

1. Translate these phrases into Hebrew.

אָח רָע an evil brother

הַבֵּן חָדָשׁ the new son

הַקְּדוֹשִׁים the holy ones

בָּנִים וּבָנוֹת sons and daughters

הָאָב הַטּוֹב the good father

2. What is textual criticism?

Textual criticism seeks to ascertain the original wording of a text by identifying obvious transcription errors or editorial additions and deletions.

3. Define ketiv and qere.

Ketiv means in Hebrew, "that which is written," referring to the critical notes made by the Masoretes, indicating Biblical words as received.

Qere, on the other hand, means "that which is read," referring to the critical notes made by the Masoretes, indicating Biblical words as it is believed they should be read and understood.

4. Match Hebrew with its English translation.

a. He is the great king.	c. יַעֲקֹב וְדָוִד הַנְּבִיאִים הַטּוֹבִים
b. many young men	i. שָׂדוֹת קְטַנִּים
c. Jacob and David are the good prophets.	f. הַזְּקֵנִים שֹׁפְטִים
d. The father is wise and the son is a fool.	a. הוּא הַמֶּלֶךְ הַגָּדוֹל
e. He is a good neighbor.	d. הָאָב חָכָם וְהַבֵּן כְּסִיל
f. The elders are judges.	g. הָאָח זָקֵן וְחָכָם
g. The brother is old and wise.	b. נְעָרִים רַבִּים
h. Rachel is a young woman.	h. רָחֵל נַעֲרָה
i. little fields	j. הַדּוֹר הֶחָי רָע
j. The living generation is evil.	e. הוּא רֵעַ טוֹב

VERBS

CHAPTER EIGHT

8.1 MONDAY

Practice vocabulary. Check back to the list of ideas in 2.1 and see if there is a new one you could try this week.

You can fill in some of Psalm 98:3. In addition, you may recognize *steadfast love* with a suffix and *Israel*. Jesus' name in Hebrew is יֵשׁוּעַ and has the same root as *salvation*. Notice the similarity in this verse.

זָכַר חַסְדּוֹ ׀ וֶֽאֱמוּנָתוֹ לְבֵית יִשְׂרָאֵל רָאוּ כָל־אַפְסֵי־אָרֶץ אֵת יְשׁוּעַת אֱלֹהֵינוּ׃

remembered	זָכַר
his steadfast love	חַסְדּוֹ
and his faithfulness	וֶאֱמוּנָתוֹ
to the house of	לְבֵית
Israel	יִשְׂרָאֵל
saw	רָאוּ
all	כָל־
ends of	אַפְסֵי־
land	אָרֶץ

(untranslatable, but shows that *what was seen* is whatever directly follows this word)	אֶת
the salvation of	יְשׁוּעַת
our God	אֱלֹהֵינוּ׃

8.2 TUESDAY

1. Identify the verbs in these sentences.

> If you prick us do we not bleed? If you tickle us do we not laugh? If you poison us do we not die? And if you wrong us shall we not revenge?
> —William Shakespeare, *The Merchant of Venice*

> There is a time for everything,
> and a season for every activity under the heavens:
> a time to be born and a time to die,
> a time to plant and a time to uproot,
> a time to kill and a time to heal,
> a time to tear down and a time to build,
> a time to weep and a time to laugh,
> a time to mourn and a time to dance,
> —Ecclesiastes 3:1-4

> They halted between the river and the eastern spur; but a few held on their way, and crossing the river drew near the camp; and there they laid down their weapons and held up their hands in sign of peace.
> —J.R.R. Tolkien, *The Hobbit*

In the sentences above, "born" and "crossing" are participles (more in Chapter 24). Some would and some would not consider them verbs in these sentences.

2. Translate these sentences as many ways as possible.

example: הוּא הָלַךְ "He walked. He has walked. He did walk. He was walking. He had walked."

יַעֲקֹב זָכַר Jacob remembered. Jacob has remembered. Jacob did remember. Jacob was remembering. Jacob had remembered.

דָוִד מָלַךְ

David ruled. David has ruled. David did rule. David was ruling. David had ruled.

הָאָח טוֹב שָׁמַר

The good brother guarded. The good brother has guarded. The good brother did guard. The good brother was guarding. The good brother had guarded.

נַעַר חָכָם אָמַר

A wise young man said. A wise young man has said. A wise young man did say. A wise young man was saying. A wise young man had said.

8.3 WEDNESDAY

Translate.

יַעֲקֹב אָמַר Jacob said. (In these and future exercises, any of the above ways of translating a perfect tense verb are correct.)

מָלַךְ הַמֶּלֶךְ הַטּוֹב The good king ruled.

זָכַר הַנָּבִיא הֶחָכָם The wise prophet remembered.

נַעַר הָלַךְ A young man walked.

זָכַר הַזָּקֵן The old one (m.) remembered.

הַשָּׂר הַגָּדוֹל שָׁמַר The great captain guarded.

הָאָב הַטּוֹב אָמַר The good father said.

שָׁמַר רֵעַ A neighbor guarded.

הָלַךְ כְּסִיל A fool walked.

דָוִד שֹׁפֵט David is a judge.

הַנָּשִׁים טוֹבוֹת The women are good.

הָעִיר גְּדוֹלָה The city is big.

זָכַר נָכְרִי A foreigner remembered.

כֹּהֲנִים קְדוֹשִׁים holy priests

הַשָּׂדֶה קָטָן The field is little.

שָׂרָה אֵם טוֹבָה Sarah is a good mother.

8.4 THURSDAY

1. Which stem accounts for most verbs in Scripture and for all verbs taught in this book?

qal

2. The Hebrew perfect tense describes actions that are completed.

3. Using the verb *break*, give examples of simple, intensive, and causative action.

   a. simple He broke it.

   b. intensive He destroyed it.

   c. causative He caused it to be broken.

4. Using the verb *praise*, give examples of the active voice, passive voice, and middle voice.

   a. active voice I praised.

   b. passive voice I was praised.

   c. middle voice I praised myself.

5. Label the number, gender, and person of each noun.

הַכֹּהֲנִים pl., m., third

רָחֵל s., f., third

we pl., m. or f., first

הָאָרֶץ s., f., third

עֲבָדִים pl., m., third

nurses pl., unknown in English, third

עָרִים pl., f., third

נָשִׁים pl., f., third

you s. or pl., m. or f., second

הַשָּׂר s., m., third

אֲדָמָה s., f., third

I s., m. or f., first

נָכְרִים pl., m., third

The King of Kings s., m., third

הִיא s., f., third

y'all pl., m. or f., second

שָׂדוֹת רַבִּים pl., m., third

8.5 FRIDAY

1. Briefly define:

a. Mishnaic Hebrew

Mishnaic Hebrew is the Hebrew dialect of the 1st to 4th centuries and the Talmud. A few syntax and verb tense changes and the influence of Aramaic distinguish Mishnaic Hebrew from Biblical Hebrew.

b. Yiddish

a language based on Hebrew and medieval German, written with Hebrew characters, developed by Ashkenazic Jews and spoken to this day

c. Ladino, or Judeo-Spanish

a language based on Hebrew and Old Spanish, written with Hebrew characters, developed by Sephardic Jews and spoken to this day

d. illuminated manuscript

a handwritten text with decorations and illustrations

2. Would you rather have a latke or a jelly doughnut? If you don't know, find out.

Answers will vary and may require extensive research. See page 62 for help.

3. Translate these English sentences and phrases into Hebrew.

A man walked. אִישׁ הָלַךְ or הָלַךְ אִישׁ

David is the king. דָּוִד הַמֶּלֶךְ

She is good. הִיא טוֹבָה or טוֹבָה הִיא

The prophet remembered. הַנָּבִיא זָכַר or זָכַר הַנָּבִיא

a big mountain הַר גָּדוֹל

many sons בָּנִים רַבִּים

The brother guarded. הָאָח שָׁמַר

A great latke recipe for the undecided:

1 peeled potato (about 10 ounces worth)
1 peeled sweet potato (also about 10 ounces)
1/4 of an onion, finely chopped
1 egg
2 Tbsp white flour
1 tsp salt (or so)
1/4 tsp freshly ground black pepper

Directions: Grate potatoes. Combine ingredients in a mixing bowl. Heat oil in a cast iron skillet. Drop batter in by heaping tablespoonfuls. Cook for a few minutes until nicely golden brown. Turn, press lightly, and let the other side cook a few minutes until done. Good with plain yogurt, sour cream, or applesauce.

Variation: Use Yukon Gold potatoes instead of white and sweet potatoes. Add 2 Tbsp horseradish, pressed dry.

ROOTS & CONJUGATIONS

CHAPTER NINE

9.1 MONDAY

This week's vocabulary words are verbs, but they are listed with only their basic root letters and meanings, rather than being conjugated. This week you will learn how to conjugate perfect tense qal verbs for all of the numbers, genders, and persons. In the meantime, memorize the meanings of these three-letter roots.

Read aloud Genesis 19:27.

וַיַּשְׁכֵּם אַבְרָהָם בַּבֹּקֶר אֶל־הַמָּקוֹם אֲשֶׁר־עָמַד שָׁם אֶת־פְּנֵי יְהוָה׃

rose early	וַיַּשְׁכֵּם
Abraham	אַבְרָהָם
in the morning	בַּבֹּקֶר
to	אֶל־
the place	הַמָּקוֹם
which	אֲשֶׁר־
stood	עָמַד

there	שָׁם
(untranslatable)	אֶת־
in the presence of	פְּנֵי
the LORD (*Adonai*)	יְהוָה׃

9.2 TUESDAY

1. Here are various conjugations of one Hebrew verb and nouns formed from the same root. Identify the root letters in each word.

הֶחֱזִיק	חֶזְקָה	אֲחַזְּקֶנּוּ	חָזֵק
תְּחַזֵּקְנָה	אֲחַזֵּק	הִתְחַזַּקְתִּי	וּמְחֻזָּקָה
חִזְקוּ	הַמִּתְחַזְּקִים	חָזַק	חֹזֶק

2. Translate.

הַמֶּלֶךְ הַזָּקֵן חַי The old king is alive.

הַשֶּׁמֶשׁ גָּדוֹל The sun is big.

זָכַר הָאִישׁ The man remembered.

אַחִים רָעִים evil brothers

רָחֵל נַעֲרָה Rachel is a young woman.

שָׂדוֹת רַבִּים many fields

הַיָּם הַגָּדוֹל the big sea

הוּא שֹׁפֵט He is a judge.

מָלַךְ הַשָּׂר The captain rules.

דָּוִד שָׁמַר David guarded.

הֶחָכָם אָב טוֹב The wise one is a good father.

כֹּהֵן קָדוֹשׁ הָלַךְ A holy priest walked.

9.3 WEDNESDAY

1. Read aloud and translate these verbs, supplying the appropriate pronoun in your translation. For example, הָלַךְ "he walked." Next to each verb, write its three root letters.

הָלַכְתְּ You (f., s.) walked. הלך

עָמַדְנוּ We stood. עמד

שָׁמַעְתִּי I heard. שׁמע

שָׁמַרְתָּ You (m., s.) guarded. שׁמר

מָלְכָה She ruled. מלך

אֲמַרְתֶּם You (m., pl.) said. אמר

זָכְרָה She remembered. זכר

עָמַדְתִּי I stood. עמד

עֲבַרְתֶּן You (f., pl.) crossed over. עבר

יָשַׁבְתָּ You (m., s.) sat. ישׁב

עָשָׂה He did/made. עשׂה

אָמְרוּ They said. אמר

2. Read aloud and match the Hebrew with its English translation.

a. The women stood.

b. The wise sons remembered.

c. Jacob heard.

d. A priest crossed over.

e. Many men guarded.

f. Good kings ruled.

g. The wise one walked.

h. Sarah crossed over.

i. The young women sat.

j. A judge said.

a. הַנָּשִׁים עָמְדוּ

g. הֶחָכָם הָלַךְ

e. שָׁמְרוּ אֲנָשִׁים רַבִּים

h. עָבְרָה שָׂרָה

j. אָמַר שֹׁפֵט

b. זָכְרוּ הַבָּנִים הַחֲכָמִים

d. כֹּהֵן עָבַר

i. יָשְׁבוּ הַנְּעָרוֹת

c. שָׁמַע יַעֲקֹב

f. מָלְכוּ מְלָכִים טוֹבִים

9.4 THURSDAY

Translate.

לֹא שָׁמַע הוּא He did not hear.

לֹא זָכַר הַדּוֹר The generation did not remember.

שָׁמְרוּ הָאָבוֹת הַחֲכָמִים The wise fathers guarded.

לֹא עָבְרָה נַעֲרָה A young woman did not cross over.

לֹא מָלַךְ הַמֶּלֶךְ הָרָע The evil king did not rule.

לֹא יָשְׁבָה הַחֲכָמָה The wise one (f.) did not sit.

לֹא זָכְרוּ הַשֹּׁפְטִים The judges did not remember.

דָּוִד לֹא אָמַר David did not say.

הַנָּשִׁים לֹא עָמְדוּ The women did not stand.

לֹא הָלַךְ כֹּהֵן The priest did not walk.

לֹא עָשָׂה רָע הַמַּלְאָךְ The angel/messenger did not do evil.

לֹא עָבְרוּ אֲנָשִׁים רַבִּים Many men/people did not cross over.

9.5 FRIDAY

1. How did Eliezer Ben-Yehuda work to revive Hebrew as an everyday language?

He spoke only Hebrew in his family, moved to the land of Israel and spoke Hebrew for daily business with people there, taught Hebrew, wrote and published a Hebrew newspaper and magazine, invented Hebrew words for modern items and ideas for which there were none, wrote a seventeen volume Hebrew dictionary, endured jail and discouragement.

2. Choose the correct verb to complete each sentence.

א. הוּא יָשַׁב / יָשְׁבוּ He sat.

ב. הַנָּשִׁים יָשְׁבוּ / יְשַׁבְתֶּן The women sat.

ג. דָּוִד הָלַכְתִּי / הָלַךְ David walked.

ד. נַעֲרָה אָמַר / אָמְרָה A young woman said.

ה. הַדּוֹר זָכַרְנוּ / זָכַר The generation remembered.

ו. הָאָח שָׁמַעְתָּ / שָׁמַע The brother heard.

ז. אָחוֹת אָמַרְתָּ / אָמְרָה A sister said.

ח. הַבָּנִים עָבְרוּ / עֲבַרְתֶּם The sons/children crossed over.

ט. בָּנוֹת זָכְרוּ / זָכְרָה Daughters remembered.

י. יַעֲקֹב עָשׂוּ / עָשָׂה Jacob did/made.

כ. הַקָּטָן הָלַכְתִּי / הָלַךְ The little one walked.

3. Translate the sentences in #2.

SUBJECT PRONOUNS

CHAPTER TEN

10.1 MONDAY

You have already learned the singular, third person subject pronouns, **הוּא** and **הִיא**. This week memorize the subject pronouns for the rest of the number/person/gender possibilities.

Read and fill in the blanks for Genesis 29:4.

וַיֹּאמֶר לָהֶם יַעֲקֹב אַחַי מֵאַיִן אַתֶּם וַיֹּאמְרוּ מֵחָרָן אֲנָחְנוּ׃

said	וַיֹּאמֶר
to them	לָהֶם
Jacob	יַעֲקֹב
my brothers (see *brother* in there?)	אַחַי
from where	מֵאַיִן
you (m., pl.)	אַתֶּם
and they said	וַיֹּאמְרוּ
from Haran	מֵחָרָן

we	אֲנַחְנוּ:

10.2 TUESDAY

1. Translate and read aloud.

אַתָּה הַמֶּלֶךְ הַגָּדוֹל You are the great king.

אֲנַחְנוּ נְבִיאִים We are prophets.

אֲנִי אֵם I am a mother.

הֵם אַחִים They are brothers.

הוּא הַשֶּׁמֶשׁ It is the sun.

הֵנָּה נְעָרוֹת They are young women.

אַתֶּם הַחֲכָמִים You are the wise ones.

הֵם זָכְרוּ They remembered.

אֲנַחְנוּ זָכַרְנוּ We remembered.

לֹא עָבַרְתָּ אַתָּה You (m., s.) did not cross over.

שְׁמַעְתֶּם אַתֶּם You (m., pl.) heard.

אֲנִי מָלַכְתִּי I ruled.

אֲנַחְנוּ יָשַׁבְנוּ We sat/dwelt.

הֵמָּה עָשׂוּ They did/made.

הֵנָּה לֹא שָׁמְרוּ They (f.) did not guard.

2. Choose the right verb for the sentence and translate.

אָנֹכִי שָׁמַרְנוּ / שָׁמַרְתִּי I guarded.

אַתָּה עָבַרְתָּ / עָבַרְתְּ You crossed over.

אַתְּ עָשִׂית / עָשְׂתָה You did/made.

אַתֶּם הָלְכוּ / הֲלַכְתֶּם You walked.

הֵם זָכַר / זָכְרוּ They remembered.

10.3 WEDNESDAY

1. Write the Hebrew subject pronouns suitable to replace these English nouns.

הוּא Abraham

הֵם, הֵמָּה John, his wife, and four daughters

הֵנָּה Mrs. Wiggins, Mrs. Wogus, and Mrs. Wurzburger

הוּא the desert

הִיא Queen Esther

הֵם, הֵמָּה the French

הִיא the land

2. Translate and read aloud.

אֲנִי עָמַדְתִּי I stood.

הָלַךְ דָּוִד David walked.

זָכַר הַנַּעַר הֶחָכָם The wise young man remembered.

לֹא עָשְׂתָה רָחֵל Rachel did not do/make.

יָשַׁבְנוּ אֲנַחְנוּ We sat/dwelt.

שָׁמַעְתָּ אַתָּה You (m., s.) heard.

הֵמָּה עָבְרוּ They crossed over.

הֲלַכְתֶּם אַתֶּם You (m., pl.) walked.

אֲנַחְנוּ אָמַרְנוּ We said.

אֲנִי זָכַרְתִּי I remembered.

לֹא שָׁמְעָה הִיא She did not hear.

הֵנָּה יָשְׁבוּ They (f.) sat/dwelt.

לֹא מָלַכְנוּ אֲנַחְנוּ We did not rule.

אַתְּ עָבַרְתְּ You (f., s.) crossed over.

שְׁמַרְתֶּן אַתֶּן You (f., pl.) guarded.

הֵם שָׁמְרוּ They guarded.

אָנֹכִי עָשִׂיתִי I did/made.

10.4 THURSDAY

Translate and read aloud.

אֲנַחְנוּ הַמְּלָכִים We are the kings.

דָוִד הוּא הֶחָכָם David is the wise one.

רָחֵל הִיא לֹא הָלְכָה Rachel did not walk.

הָאָחִים הַחֲכָמִים הֵם הַטּוֹבִים The wise brothers are the good ones.

הַנָּבִיא הוּא הָלַךְ The prophet walked.

לֹא עָמַדְתָּ אַתָּה You (m., s.) did not stand.

אֲנִי זָכַרְתִּי I remembered.

הַכֹּהֵן הַזָּקֵן הֶחָכָם יָשַׁב The old, wise priest sat/dwelt.

אַתֶּם עֲבַרְתֶּם You (m., pl.) crossed over.

יַעֲקֹב הוּא שָׁמַע Jacob heard.

עָשִׂינוּ אֲנַחְנוּ We did/made.

הָאָבוֹת הַטּוֹבִים שָׁמְרוּ The good fathers guarded.

10.5 FRIDAY

1. Translate.

הַמֶּלֶךְ הָרָע מָלַךְ הוּא The bad king ruled.

עָבְרוּ הַנָּשִׁים The women crossed over.

לֹא זָכְרוּ יַעֲקֹב וְשָׂרָה Jacob and Sarah did not remember.

הָלַכְתָּ אַתָּה You (m., s.) walked.

הָעֶבֶד הוּא הָרָע The servant is the evil one.

עָשׂוּ הָאָחִים הַטּוֹבִים The good brothers did/made.

הַכֹּהֵן הַטּוֹב הוּא זָכַר The good priest remembered.

לֹא עָשִׂיתָ אַתָּה You (m., s.) did not do/make.

עָמְדוּ הֵם They stood.

לֹא זָכַר הַדּוֹר הָרָע The evil generation did not remember.

2. Name some sources of colloquial expressions in modern Israeli Hebrew with an example of each.

- Bible references and terms: Go to Azazel; We overcame Pharaoh, we'll get through this; Thank you
- Arabic: sababa, achla
- German: shtrudel
- Body imagery: beten gav, la panim, al ha panim

3. Write the Hebrew subject pronouns suitable to replace these English nouns.

אֲנַחְנוּ you and I

אַתֶּם, אַתֶּן y'all

הֵם, הֵמָּה the mountains

הֵם, הֵמָּה Grandma and Grandpa

אֲנִי, אָנֹכִי me, myself, and I

הֵנָּה Naomi and Ruth

הוּא the wind

REVIEW

CHAPTER ELEVEN

11.1 MONDAY

Review week. No new vocabulary.

Practice fluent reading with Isaiah 45:18.

כִּי כֹה אָמַר־יְהוָה בּוֹרֵא הַשָּׁמַיִם הוּא הָאֱלֹהִים יֹצֵר הָאָרֶץ וְעֹשָׂהּ הוּא כוֹנְנָהּ לֹא־תֹהוּ בְרָאָהּ
לָשֶׁבֶת יְצָרָהּ אֲנִי יְהוָה וְאֵין עוֹד׃

because	כִּי
thus	כֹּה
said	אָמַר־
the LORD (*Adonai*)	יְהוָה
Creator of	בּוֹרֵא
the sky/Heaven	הַשָּׁמַיִם
he	הוּא
the God	הָאֱלֹהִים
formed	יֹצֵר
the land	הָאָרֶץ

and made it	וְעָשָׂהּ
He	הוּא
established it	כוֹנְנָהּ
not	לֹא־
chaos, emptiness	תֹהוּ
created it	בְרָאָהּ
to be inhabited	לָשֶׁבֶת
formed	יְצָרָהּ
I	אֲנִי
the LORD (*Adonai*)	יְהוָה
and there is not	וְאֵין
anyone beside	עוֹד׃

11.2 TUESDAY

Translate.

הַכֹּהֵן הֶחָכָם הַזָּקֵן זָכַר The wise, old priest remembered.

אַתָּה הָלַכְתָּ You (m., s.) walked.

יָשְׁבוּ הֵנָּה They (f.) sat/dwelt.

הַנָּבִיא הוּא הַחַי The prophet is the living one (or, the one who is alive).

עָבַר הַנַּעַר הוּא The young man crossed over.

לֹא שָׁמַרְנוּ אֲנַחְנוּ We did not guard.

הִיא עָשְׂתָה She did/made.

שָׂדוֹת קְטַנִּים little fields, or Fields are little.

מֶלֶךְ לֹא עָמַד A king did not stand.

שָׁמְעוּ הַחֲכָמִים The wise ones heard.

יַעֲקֹב וְדָוִד יָשְׁבוּ Jacob and David sat/dwelt.

דָוִד הוּא הַמֶּלֶךְ הַטּוֹב David is the good king.

אֲנִי הָלַכְתִּי I walked.

הָאָרֶץ וְהַשָּׁמַיִם וְהַשֶּׁמֶשׁ The land/earth and the sky/Heaven and the sun

הָאָבוֹת שָׂרִים The fathers are captains.

לֹא עָבְרוּ רֵעִים The neighbors did not cross over.

לֹא זָכַרְתִּי אָנֹכִי I did not remember.

הוּא הַנָּהָר It is the river.

הַיָּם הַגָּדוֹל the big sea

11.3 WEDNESDAY

1. Name the man credited with the revival of Hebrew as a spoken, national language.

Eliezer Ben-Yehuda

2. Here is the verb *to guard* conjugated in each gender, number, and person. Identify the gender, number, and person of each word. Use the abbreviations *f.*, *m.*, *s.*, *pl.*, 1st, 2nd, 3rd.

שָׁמַר m., s., 3rd

שָׁמְרוּ m. or f., pl., 3rd

שְׁמַרְתֶּן	f., pl., 2nd
שָׁמְרָה	f., s., 3rd
שָׁמַרְתָּ	m., s., 2nd
שְׁמַרְתֶּם	m., pl., 2nd
שָׁמַרְתִּי	m. or f., s., 1st
שָׁמַרְנוּ	m. or f., pl., 1st
שָׁמַרְתְּ	f., s., 2nd

3. Next to each verb below, write the suitable Hebrew pronoun.

הָלַכְנוּ	אֲנַחְנוּ
שְׁמַרְתָּ	אַתָּה
זָכַרְתִּי	אֲנִי, אָנֹכִי
אֲמַרְתֶּם	אַתֶּם
מָלַכְנוּ	אֲנַחְנוּ
עָמַד	הוּא
עָשׂוּ	הֵם, הֵמָּה, הֵנָּה
שָׁמְעָה	הִיא
עָבְרוּ	הֵם, הֵמָּה, הֵנָּה
יָשַׁבְתָּ	אַתָּה

11.4 THURSDAY

1. Define ketiv and qere.

Ketiv means in Hebrew, "that which is written," referring to the critical notes made by the Masoretes, indicating Biblical words as received.

Qere, on the other hand, means "that which is read," referring to the critical notes made by the Masoretes, indicating Biblical words as it is believed they should be read and understood.

2. Choose the right word to complete the sentence.

הֵנָּה בָּנִים / בָּנוֹת	They are daughters.
אֲנִי זָכַרְתִּי / זָכַרְנוּ	I remembered.
אֲנַחְנוּ עָמְדוּ / עָמַדְנוּ	We stood.
הַכֹּהֲנִים הַטּוֹבִים שְׁמַעְתֶּם / שָׁמְעוּ	The good priests heard.
לֹא הָלַךְ הַבֵּן הֶחָכָם / הַחֲכָמִים	The wise son did not walk.
אָחוֹת אָמַרְתָּ / אָמְרָה	A sister said.
עָבַר מֶלֶךְ / אֵם	A king crossed over.
הֶעָרִים הַגָּדוֹלוֹת / הַגְּדֹלִים	the big cities
אַתָּה יָשַׁבְתָּ / יָשַׁבְתְּ	You sat/dwelt.
הַנַּעַר הָלְכָה / הָלַךְ	The young man walked.
אַתֶּן שְׁמַרְתֶּן / שָׁמַרְתִּי	You guarded.
לֹא מָלַכְתִּי אֲנִי / אֲנַחְנוּ	I did not rule.
הִיא הַר / עִיר	It is a city.

לֹא עָשִׂינוּ אֲנַחְנוּ / הֵם We did not do/make.

דָוִד הוּא הָאָח / הָאָחוֹת הַטּוֹב David is the good brother.

3. Translate the sentences in #2.

11.5 FRIDAY

1. At the time of the Apostles, was the Oral Torah oral? yes

2. Under what pressures was the Oral Torah committed to parchment?

the destruction of the Temple; the destruction of Israel as an independent, Jewish state; severe Roman persecution; scattering of communities

3. Distinguish between Mishnah, Gemara, and Talmud.

The Mishnah was the first recording of the Oral Torah: the customs, commentary, legal precedent, exposition, and interpretation that were handed down orally with the written Word.

The Gemara is subsequent analysis of and commentary on the Mishnah.

The Mishnah plus the Gemara is the Talmud. The Talmud was compiled in the 4th and 5th centuries.

4. Translate.

אֲנַחְנוּ הַמְּלָכִים We are the kings.

שָׂרָה וְרָחֵל יָשְׁבוּ Sarah and Rachel sat/dwelt.

שָׁמְרוּ הֵם They guarded.

עָבְרָה אֵם A mother crossed over.

אֲנַחְנוּ יָשַׁבְנוּ We sat/dwelt.

לֹא שְׁמַעְתֶּם אַתֶּם You did not hear.

הַדּוֹר הָרָע לֹא זָכַר The evil generation did not remember.

מָלַכְתָּ אַתָּה You ruled.

אַתְּ אָחוֹת You are a sister.

יַעֲקֹב וְדָוִד הֵם הָלְכוּ Jacob and David walked.

הַבֵּן הַטּוֹב קָטָן The good son is little.

DEMONSTRATIVES

CHAPTER TWELVE

12.1 MONDAY

Practice vocabulary today. מַיִם is accented on its first syllable and, though plural in form in Hebrew, may be translated as *water*.

Write out the conjugations of eat and drink in the charts below, following the pattern you have learned.

plural	singular	EAT
אָכַלְנוּ	אָכַלְתִּי	first person
אֲכַלְתֶּם	אָכַלְתָּ	second person, m.
אֲכַלְתֶּן	אָכַלְתְּ	second person, f.
אָכְלוּ	אָכַל	third person, m.
אָכְלוּ	אָכְלָה	third person, f.

plural	singular	DRINK
שָׁתִינוּ	שָׁתִיתִי	first person
שְׁתִיתֶם	שָׁתִיתָ	second person, m.
שְׁתִיתֶן	שָׁתִית	second person, f.
שָׁתוּ	שָׁתָה	third person, m.
שָׁתוּ	שָׁתְתָה	third person, f.

Read Deuteronomy 29:6 this week.

לֶחֶם לֹא אֲכַלְתֶּם וְיַיִן וְשֵׁכָר לֹא שְׁתִיתֶם לְמַעַן תֵּדְעוּ כִּי אֲנִי יְהוָה אֱלֹהֵיכֶם׃

bread	לֶחֶם
not	לֹא
you ate	אֲכַלְתֶּם
and wine	וְיַיִן
and strong drink	וְשֵׁכָר
not	לֹא
you drank	שְׁתִיתֶם
for the sake of	לְמַעַן
you will know	תֵּדְעוּ
that	כִּי
I	אֲנִי

the LORD (*Adonai*)	יְהוָה
your God	אֱלֹהֵיכֶם׃

12.2 TUESDAY
Translate.

זֶה כֹּהֵן   This is a priest.

זֹאת אָחוֹת   This is a sister.

אֵלֶּה נְבִיאִים   These are prophets.

זֶה הָעֶבֶד   This is the servant.

זֹאת הָאָרֶץ   This is a the land/earth.

זֶה לֶחֶם   This is bread/food.

אֵלֶּה הַנָּשִׁים הַחֲכָמוֹת   These are the wise women.

הָאִישׁ הַזֶּה קָדוֹשׁ   This man is holy.

הָאַחִים הָאֵלֶּה נְבִיאִים   These brothers are prophets.

לֹא זָכַר הַדּוֹר הַזֶּה   This generation did not remember.

זָכַר הַבֵּן הַזֶּה   This son remembered.

עָבְרוּ הַמְּלָכִים הָאֵלֶּה   These kings crossed over.

שָׁמְרוּ הַנְּעָרִים   The young men guarded.

לֹא הָלַךְ הָרֵעַ הַזֶּה   This neighbor did not walk.

הַמַּיִם הַזֶּה וְהַיַּיִן הַזֶּה   this water and this wine

12.3 WEDNESDAY

1. Translate.

יֵשׁ לֶחֶם וְיַיִן There is bread and wine.

יֵשׁ מֶלֶךְ טוֹב There is a good king.

יֵשׁ שָׂדוֹת רַבִּים There are many fields.

יֵשׁ בָּנוֹת There are daughters.

יֵשׁ נָהָר There is a river.

2. Find and translate words you know in these verses. Read the verses aloud.

you heard — this land — not — and you

וְאַתֶּם לֹא־תִכְרְתוּ בְרִית לְיוֹשְׁבֵי הָאָרֶץ הַזֹּאת מִזְבְּחוֹתֵיהֶם תִּתֹּצוּן וְלֹא־שְׁמַעְתֶּם בְּקֹלִי מַה־
זֹּאת עֲשִׂיתֶם׃

and not — you did this

Judges 2:2

I — this — they heard

שִׁמְעוּ אֶת־הַדָּבָר הַזֶּה אֲשֶׁר אָנֹכִי נֹשֵׂא עֲלֵיכֶם קִינָה בֵּית יִשְׂרָאֵל׃

Amos 5:1

women — bread

בְּשִׁבְרִי לָכֶם מַטֵּה־לֶחֶם וְאָפוּ עֶשֶׂר נָשִׁים לַחְמְכֶם בְּתַנּוּר אֶחָד וְהֵשִׁיבוּ לַחְמְכֶם בַּמִּשְׁקָל
וַאֲכַלְתֶּם וְלֹא תִשְׂבָּעוּ׃

and not

Leviticus 26:26

12.4 THURSDAY

Translate.

אֵין הוּא אִישׁ טוֹב He is not a good man.

אֵין הִיא אָחוֹת She is not a sister.

אֵין בָּנִים There are not sons/children.

אֵין יַיִן There is not wine.

אֵין הֵם גֵּרִים They are not sojourners.

אֵין שֹׁפֵט There is not a judge.

אֵין הוּא שַׂר He is not a captain.

אֵין הִיא בַּת She is not a daughter.

אֵין נְבִיאִים There are not prophets.

אֵין נָהָר There is not a river.

אֵין כְּסִילִים הֵם They are not fools.

אֵין הָרִים גְּדוֹלִים There are not big mountains.

אֵין נַעַר There is not a young man.

12.5 FRIDAY

To parse a sentence is to identify the role each word plays. Parse the sentences below. Identify each word's part(s) of speech: noun, pronoun, verb, demonstrative, definite article, conjunction, or adjective. Further note the gender and number of nouns and adjectives, and the gender, number, person of each pronoun and verb.

example: אַתָּה הַמֶּלֶךְ "**You**: pronoun, *m.*, *s.*, 2nd; **the king**: definite article with *m.*, *s.* noun"

אֲנִי אֵם

I: pronoun, m. or f. (clearly feminine in this sentence, though), s., 1st
a mother: noun, f., s.

אֲנַחְנוּ הָלַכְנוּ

we: pronoun, m. or f., pl., 1st
walked: verb, m. or f., pl., 1st

הוּא אָכַל הַלֶּחֶם הַטּוֹב

he: pronoun, m., s., 3rd
ate: verb, m., s., 3rd
the bread: definite article with m., s. noun
the good: definite article with m., s. adjective

כֹּהֵן קָדוֹשׁ

a priest: noun, m., s.
holy: adjective, m., s.

הֵם עָבְרוּ

they: pronoun, m., pl., 3rd
crossed over: verb, m., pl., 3rd

הָאִישׁ הַזֶּה שָׁתָה מַיִם

the man: noun, m., s.
the this: definite article plus m., s. demonstrative
drank: verb, m., s., 3rd
water: noun, m., pl.

הֶהָרִים הָאֵלֶּה גְּדוֹלִים

the mountains: noun, m., pl.
the these: definite article plus pl. demonstrative
big: adjective, m., pl.

אַתָּה שָׁמַעְתָּ

you: pronoun, m., s., 2nd
heard: verb, m., s., 2nd

הַבָּנִים וְהַבָּנוֹת אָכְלוּ לֶחֶם

the sons: definite article plus m., pl. noun
and the daughters: conjunction plus definite article plus f., pl. noun
ate: verb, m., pl. 3rd
bread: noun, m., s.

DIRECT OBJECTS

CHAPTER THIRTEEN

13.1 MONDAY

Practice vocabulary words today. בֶּ֫גֶד is accented on the first syllable.

Read aloud Genesis 1:1.

בְּרֵאשִׁית בָּרָא אֱלֹהִים אֵת הַשָּׁמַיִם וְאֵת הָאָרֶץ׃

in the beginning	בְּרֵאשִׁית
created	בָּרָא
God	אֱלֹהִים
(untranslatable)	אֵת
the sky/Heaven	הַשָּׁמַיִם
and (with same untranslatable word)	וְאֵת
the land	הָאָרֶץ׃

Yud drops out entirely when שׂים is conjugated. As a root letter, it feels awkward in middle position. Chapters 30 and 31 will explain why and when. In the meantime, become familiar with these conjugations:

plural	singular	PUT
שַׂמְנוּ	שַׂמְתִּי	first person
שַׂמְתֶּם	שַׂמְתָּ	second person, m.
שַׂמְתֶּן	שַׂמְתְּ	second person, f.
שָׂמוּ	שָׂם	third person, m.
שָׂמוּ	שָׂמָה	third person, f.

13.2 TUESDAY

1. In each sentence below, underline the verbs, and identify them as transitive or intransitive. Circle direct objects. Identify direct objects as definite or indefinite.

example: Rebecca milked cows. "transitive v., indefinite d.o."

יַעֲקֹב הָלַךְ intransitive verb

אָכַל לֶחֶם הוּא transitive verb, indefinite direct object

A woman uses her intelligence to find reasons to support her intuition.
—G.K. Chesterton

transitive verbs; "her intelligence" and "her intuition" are definite direct objects, "reasons" is an indefinite direct object

A man can no more diminish God's glory by refusing to worship Him than a lunatic can put out the sun by scribbling the word, "darkness" on the walls of his cell. —C.S. Lewis

Each of these are transitive verbs (and it would be possible to argue that some are not actually verbs in this sentence) because they have direct objects. Each of the direct objects is definite.

As soon go kindle fire with snow, as seek to quench the fire of love with words. —William Shakespeare

"Go" and "seek" do not have direct objects as "kindle" and "quench" do. The object of kindle is "fire," an indefinite noun. The object of "quench" is "the fire of love," a definite noun.

And they were both righteous before God, walking blamelessly in all the commandments and statutes of the Lord. Luke 1:6

intransitive verbs

נָשָׂאנוּ מַיִם אֲנַחְנוּ

transitive verb, indefinite direct object

I have eaten my honeycomb and my honey; I have drunk my wine and my milk. Song of Solomon 5:1

transitive verbs with definite direct objects

As it is written, "Jacob I loved, but Esau I hated." Romans 9:13

transitive verbs with definite direct objects

In the days of Abiathar the high priest, he entered the house of God and ate the consecrated bread... Mark 2:26

transitive verbs with definite direct objects

עָמְדוּ הָאֲנָשִׁים

intransitive verb

2. Now write a sentence with a transitive verb and a definite direct object. English is fine, but try Hebrew if you like.

Answers will vary. Here are examples: I ate Mom's pie. The Germans invaded Paris. We sang our favorite songs together. David plowed his fields today.

3. Write a sentence with a transitive verb and indefinite direct object.

Answers will vary. Here are examples: I drank lemonade. The Assyrians conquered cities. We played music all afternoon. David fixed machinery today.

4. Write one with an intransitive verb.

Answers will vary. Here are examples: I laughed. We went to town. Bees buzzed around the buckwheat. He slept in the hammock under the stars.

13.3 WEDNESDAY

Add the direct object marker before any definite direct objects. Translate.

He carried wine.	הוּא נָשָׂא ______ יַיִן
We feared the men/people.	יָרֵאנוּ אֲנַחְנוּ __אֵת__ הָאֲנָשִׁים
They guarded the house.	הֵם שָׁמְרוּ __אֵת__ הַבַּיִת
He remembered a young woman.	זָכַר הוּא ______ נַעֲרָה
He ate this food.	הוּא אָכַל __אֵת__ הַלֶּחֶם הַזֶּה
David put a garment there.	דָּוִד שָׂם ______ בֶּגֶד שָׁם
You drank the wine.	אַתֶּם שְׁתִיתֶם __אֵת__ הַיַּיִן
These men are priests.	הָאֲנָשִׁים הָאֵלֶּה ______ כֹּהֲנִים

יֵשׁ ______ בֶּגֶד — There is a garment.

הַנְּבִיאִים הַחֲכָמִים ______ עָבְרוּ — The wise prophets crossed over.

אֲנִי עָבַדְתִּי __אֵת__ הַמֶּלֶךְ הַטּוֹב — I served the good king.

אַתָּה יָרֵאתָ ______ כְּסִיל — You feared a fool.

דָוִד שָׁמַר ______ נַעַר ______ וְנַעֲרָה — David guarded a young man and a young woman.

הָאִשָּׁה זָכְרָה __אֵת__ הָאָרֶץ — The woman remembered the land.

אָנֹכִי נָשָׂאתִי __אֵת__ הַמַּיִם הַזֶּה — I carried this water.

אֵין ______ בַּיִת פֹּה — There is not a house here.

לֹא עָבַדְנוּ ______ נָכְרִי ______ אֲנַחְנוּ — We did not serve a foreigner.

הֵם ______ יָשְׁבוּ — They sat/dwelt.

אֲנַחְנוּ שָׁתִינוּ ______ מַיִם ______ וְיַיִן — We drank water and wine.

13.4 THURSDAY

Translate.

אֲנִי שָׁתִיתִי אֵת הַמַּיִם וְהַיָּיִן — I drank the water and the wine.

דָוִד זָכַר אֵת הַנַּעַר וְאֵת הַנַּעֲרָה — David remembered the young man and the young woman.

אֵין מֶלֶךְ — There is not a king.

יַעֲקֹב קָרָא — Jacob called.

לֹא אָמְרוּ הֵם — They did not say.

יֵשׁ בַּיִת שָׁם There is a house there.

לֹא עָבַד אֶת־הַנָּבִיא יַעֲקֹב Jacob did not serve the prophet.

הוּא שָׂם אֵת הַבֶּגֶד פֹּה He put the garment here.

הָאֲנָשִׁים הָאֵלֶּה חֲכָמִים These men are wise.

יֵשׁ מְלָכִים רָעִים פֹּה There are bad kings here.

הַלֶּחֶם הַזֶּה טוֹב This bread/food is good.

לֹא שָׁמַרְתָּ You did not hear.

הֵמָּה יָרְאוּ הַנְּבִיאִים They feared the prophets.

אֲנַחְנוּ שָׁתִינוּ יַיִן We drank wine.

הַבְּגָדִים הָאֵלֶּה חֲדָשִׁים These garments are new.

אֵין לֶחֶם פֹּה There is not bread/food here.

אַתָּה יָרֵאתָ אֵת רָחֵל You feared Rachel.

הַבֵּן וְהַבַּת עָבְרוּ The son and the daughter crossed over.

אֲנִי נָשָׂאתִי אֶת־הַבֵּן I carried the son.

הָעִיר הַזֹּאת גְּדוֹלָה This city is big.

יָרֵא הַשֶּׁמֶשׁ הוּא He feared the sun.

13.5 FRIDAY

Let's parse. Identify each word's part(s) of speech: noun, pronoun, verb, demonstrative, definite article, direct object marker, conjunction, or adjective. Mark the subject (subj.) of each sentence and any direct objects (d.o.). Note the gender and number of demonstratives and nouns, and the gender, number, person of each pronoun and verb. Then translate.

example: הַמֶּלֶךְ הַזָּקֵן אָכַל אֵת הַלֶּחֶם

d.o. subj.

the king: definite article, noun: *m.*, *s.*
the old: definite article, adjective: *m.*, *s.*
ate: verb: *m.*, *s.*, 3rd
direct object marker
the bread: definite article, noun: *m.*, *s.*
translation: The old king ate the bread.

d.o. subj.
הֵם עָבְדוּ מֶלֶךְ רָע

they: pronoun, m., pl., 3rd
served: verb, m. or f., pl., 3rd
king: noun, m., s.
bad: adjective, m., s.

They served a bad king.

subj.
אֲנַחְנוּ קָרָאנוּ

we: pronoun, m. or f., pl., 1st
called: verb, m. or f., pl., 1st

We called.

הִיא שָׁתְתָה אֵת הַמַּיִם
d.o. subj.

she: pronoun, f., s., 3rd
drank: verb, f., s., 3rd
direct object marker
the water: definite article plus m., pl. noun

She drank the water.

d.o. subj.
אַתָּה אָכַלְתָּ אֶת־הַלֶּחֶם

you: pronoun, m., s., 2nd
ate: verb, m., s., 2nd
direct object marker
the bread/food: definite article with noun, m., s.

You ate the bread/food.

subj.
הָאָרֶץ טוֹבָה

the land: definite article plus f., s. noun
good: adjective, f., s.

The land is good.

יַעֲקֹב וְדָוִד עָבְרוּ
subj.

Jacob: noun, m., s.
and David: conjunction and m., s. noun
crossed over: verb, m., pl., 3rd

Jacob and David crossed over.

DIRECT OBJECT PRONOUNS

CHAPTER FOURTEEN

14.1 MONDAY

This week's vocabulary words are pronoun suffixes that never stand alone. The X's in the textbook list represent the last letter of any word to which an ending is affixed. Memorize these endings. You will see them attached to the direct object marker, nouns, verbs, and prepositions.

Genesis 1:22 this week:

וַיְבָרֶךְ אֹתָם אֱלֹהִים לֵאמֹר פְּרוּ וּרְבוּ וּמִלְאוּ אֶת־הַמַּיִם בַּיַּמִּים וְהָעוֹף יִרֶב בָּאָרֶץ׃

blessed	וַיְבָרֶךְ
them	אֹתָם
God	אֱלֹהִים
saying	לֵאמֹר
bear fruit	פְּרוּ
and multiply	וּרְבוּ
and fill	וּמִלְאוּ

direct object marker	אֶת־
the water	הַמַּיִם
in the seas	בַּיַּמִּים
and the birds	וְהָעוֹף
will multiply	יִרֶב
on the land	בָּאָרֶץ׃

14.2 TUESDAY

Fill in these subject and object pronoun charts in English and Hebrew.

ENGLISH SUBJECTS	singular	plural
first person	I	we
second person	you	you
third person	he/she/it	they

ENGLISH OBJECTS	singular	plural
first person	me	us
second person	you	you
third person	him/her/it	them

plural	singular	HEBREW SUBJECTS
אֲנַחְנוּ	אֲנִי, אָנֹכִי	first person
אַתֶּם	אַתָּה	second person masculine
אַתֶּן	אַתְּ	second person feminine
הֵם, הֵמָּה	הוּא	third person masculine
הֵנָּה	הִיא	third person feminine

plural	singular	HEBREW OBJECTS
Xנוּ	Xִי	first person
כֶם	Xְךָ	second person masculine
כֶן	Xָךְ	second person feminine
הֶם	וֹ	third person masculine
הֶן	Xָהּ	third person feminine

14.3 WEDNESDAY

Translate.

אוֹתִי me (a direct object)

אֶתְכֶן you, f., pl. (a direct object)

אֹתְךָ you, m., s. (a direct object)

אֹתָן them, f., pl. (a direct object)

אוֹתָם them, m., pl. (a direct object)

אוֹתָךְ you, f., s. (a direct object)

אֹתָנוּ us (a direct object)

אוֹתוֹ him, m., s. (a direct object)

אֹתָהּ her, f., s. (a direct object)

אֹתוֹ him, m., s. (a direct object)

אֶתְכֶם you, m., pl. (a direct object)

אוֹתְךָ you, m., s. (a direct object)

הַמֶּלֶךְ הַטּוֹב נָשָׂא אֹתוֹ The good king carried him/it.

לֹא יָרֵאנוּ אֲנַחְנוּ אוֹתוֹ We did not fear him/it.

רֵעִים שָׁמְרוּ אֶתְכֶם Neighbors guarded you (m., pl.).

14.4 THURSDAY

Translate and read aloud.

הִיא שָׁמְעָה אֹתָנוּ She heard us.

הַנְּבִיאִים זָכְרוּ אוֹתָהּ The prophets remembered her.

הַנְּעָרִים הַחֲכָמִים שָׁמְעוּ אוֹתִי The wise young men heard me.

נָשְׂאוּ אוֹתְךָ הֵנָּה They (f.) carried you (m., s.).

הָאַחִים שָׁמְרוּ אֹתְךָ The brothers guarded you (m., s.).

לֹא שָׁמְעוּ אוֹתָן הָאֲנָשִׁים הָרָעִים The evil men did not hear them (f.).

זְכַרְתֶּם אֹתָם אַתֶּם You (m., pl.) remembered them (m.).

לֹא נָשָׂא אוֹתוֹ הוּא He did not carry him/it.

הֵם שָׁתוּ אֹתוֹ They drank it.

שָׁמַעְתִּי אֹתוֹ אֲנִי I heard him/it.

יַעֲקֹב שָׁמַר אוֹתָהּ Jacob guarded her.

זָכַרְתָּ אֶת הָעִיר הַזֹּאת אַתָּה: זָכַרְתָּ אֹתָהּ You remembered this city. You remembered it.

הַכֹּהֲנִים שָׁמְעוּ אֹתָנוּ The priests heard us.

14.5 FRIDAY

1. Name the language in which each was written:

- Septuagint Greek
- Vulgate Latin
- Syriac Peshitta Aramaic
- Targums Aramaic
- Masoretic text Hebrew

2. Parsing time. Identify each word's part(s) of speech: noun, pronoun, verb, demonstrative, definite article, direct object marker, conjunction, or adjective. Mark the subject (subj.) of each sentence and any direct objects (d.o.). Note the gender and number of demonstratives and nouns, and the gender, number, person of each pronoun and verb. Then translate.

example: הַכֹּהֲנִים שָׁמְעוּ אֹתָנוּ

d.o. subj.

the priests: definite article, noun: *m.*, *pl.*
heard: verb: *m.*, *pl.*, 3rd
us: direct object marker with pronoun: *f.* or *m.*, *pl.*, 1st
translation: The priests heard us.

subj. d.o.
שָׁמְרוּ אוֹתְךָ הַבָּנִים הַטּוֹבִים

guarded: verb, m., pl., 3rd
you: direct object marker with object pronoun: m., s., 2nd
the sons: definite article plus m., pl. noun
good: definite article plus m., pl. adjective

The good sons guarded you.

subj.
הָרֵעַ הַזֶּה הָלַךְ

the neighbor: definite article plus m., s. noun
this this: definite article plus m., s. demonstrative
walked: verb, m., s., 3rd

This neighbor walked.

d.o. subj.
הִיא זָכְרָה אוֹתָהּ

she: pronoun, f., s., 3rd
remembered: verb, f., s., 3rd
her: direct object marker plus f., s. pronoun

She remembered her.

הֶעָרִים הָאֵלֶּה גְּדוֹלוֹת
subj.

the cities: definite article plus f., pl. noun
the these: definite article plus m. or f., pl. demonstrative
big: adjective, f., pl.

These cities are big.

subj. d.o.
נָשָׂאתָ אֵת הַבֶּגֶד אַתָּה

carried: verb, m., s., 2nd
direct object marker
the garment: definite article plus m., s. noun
you: pronoun, m., s., 2nd

You carried the garment.

d.o. subj.
אָנֹכִי יָרֵאתִי אֶתְכֶם

I: pronoun, m. or f., s., 1st
feared: verb, m. or f., s., 1st
you: direct object marker with object pronoun: m., pl., 2nd

I feared you.

INDEPENDENT PREPOSITIONS

CHAPTER FIFTEEN

15.1 MONDAY

Memorize this week's vocabulary words, all of which are prepositions.

Work on fluently reading Malachi 3:18.

וְשַׁבְתֶּם וּרְאִיתֶם בֵּין צַדִּיק לְרָשָׁע בֵּין עֹבֵד אֱלֹהִים לַאֲשֶׁר לֹא עֲבָדוֹ׃

and you will return	וְשַׁבְתֶּם
and you will see	וּרְאִיתֶם
between	בֵּין
a righteous man	צַדִּיק
to an evil man	לְרָשָׁע
between	בֵּין
one who serves	עֹבֵד
God	אֱלֹהִים

to who	לַאֲשֶׁר
does not	לֹא
serve him	עֲבָדוֹ:

15.2 TUESDAY

Translate.

לִפְנֵי הַבֵּן before the son

אַחַר הַנְּבִיאִים after the prophets

תַּחַת הַשֶּׁמֶשׁ under the sun

בְּתוֹךְ נְעָרִים in the midst of young men

מִן בַּיִת from a house

כְּמוֹ נָבִיא like a prophet

עִם רָחֵל with Rachel

לִפְנֵי הַנָּשִׁים before the women

אֶל הַמִּדְבָּר to the desert

תַּחַת הַשָּׁמַיִם under Heaven/the sky

כְּמוֹ כְּסִיל like a fool

עִם הַשֹּׁפְטִים with the judges

עַל הָהָר on the mountain

אֶל אֵם to a mother

מִן הָעִיר from the city

סָבִיב הַשָּׂדֶה around the field

עַל הָאָרֶץ on the land/earth

אַחַר יַיִן after wine

בְּתוֹךְ כֹּהֲנִים in the midst of priests

סָבִיב הָעִיר around the city

15.3 WEDNESDAY

1. Write the adverbs out of these sentences by substituting prepositional phrases. This will not necessarily produce better English, but it will give you a feel for how Hebrew is likely to express ideas.

Answers will vary. Here are examples:

He walked quickly and resolutely.

He walked with speed and resolution.

Sadly he packed his bags.

In sadness, he packed his bags.

Joyfully we sang while working happily.

We sang with joy while we worked with happiness.

Loudly he answered my call.

He answered my call in a loud voice.

2. Translate.

אֲנִי הָלַכְתִּי עִם דָּוִד I walked with David.

אֲנַחְנוּ אָכְלוּ בְּתוֹךְ הָאֲנָשִׁים We ate in the midst of the men/people.

עָמַדְתָּ אַתָּה כְּמוֹ כְּסִיל You stood like a fool.

עָמַד הוּא עַל הָהָר הַגָּדוֹל He stood on the big mountain.

הִיא שָׂמָה בֶּגֶד עַל יַעֲקֹב She put a garment on Jacob.

הַמֶּלֶךְ עָבַר מִן הַשָּׂדֶה The king crossed over from the field.

יָשַׁב הוּא תַּחַת הַשָּׁמַיִם He dwelt/sat under the sky/Heaven.

הַבֵּן קָרָא בְּתוֹךְ הַנָּשִׁים The son called in the midst of the women.

הַקְּדוֹשִׁים הָלְכוּ סָבִיב הָעִיר The holy ones walked around the city.

עָמַד הוּא לִפְנֵי הַשֹּׁפְטִים He stood before the judges.

אֵין יַיִן כְּמוֹ הַיַּיִן הַזֶּה There is not wine like this wine.

15.4 THURSDAY

Translate.

עָמַדְתִּי אֲנִי בֵּין הָאִישׁ וּבֵין הָאִשָּׁה I stood between the man and the woman.

הָאָחוֹת הַזֹּאת רָעָה מִן רָחֵל This sister is worse/more evil than Rachel.

הָאִישׁ הָלַךְ בֵּין הַחֲכָמִים The man walked among the wise ones.

הַשֶּׁמֶשׁ גָּדוֹל מִן הָהָר The sun is bigger than the mountain.

הַשֹּׁפְטִים חֲכָמִים מִן הַמֶּלֶךְ The judges are wiser than the king.

הֵם יָשְׁבוּ בֵּן הָאַחִים וּבֵין הָאָחוֹת They sat between the brothers and the sister.

הָלְכוּ אֲנַחְנוּ בֵּין הַנָּהָר וּבֵין הֶהָרִים We walked between the river and the mountains.

הַנְּבִיאִים טוֹבִים מִן הַשָּׂרִים The prophets are better than the captains.

15.5 FRIDAY

1. Assyrian relics kicked unicorns out of the Bible. Explain how unicorns got *into* the Bible.

At the time that the King James Bible was written, no one knew exactly what animal a certain Biblical Hebrew word represented. The Septuagint translation into Greek used "monoceros," meaning "one horn." The Latin Vulgate used "unicorn," meaning "one horn." With nothing better to go on, the KJV translators used the word unicorn, too. Today, based on nineteenth century archaeological discoveries of Assyrian artifacts, it is believed that animal was the auroch or perhaps the water buffalo. The "one horn" names probably came from the ancient Near Eastern convention of drawing the wild bull in profile, seemingly with one horn.

2. Let's parse again. Identify each word's part(s) of speech: noun, pronoun, verb, demonstrative, definite article, direct object marker, conjunction, adjective, or preposition. Mark the subject (subj.) of each sentence and any direct objects (d.o.). Note the gender, number, and person of each noun, pronoun suffix, and verb. Note the gender and number of demonstratives and nouns. Identify the gender, number, and person of each pronoun, pronoun suffix, and verb. Translate the sentences.

subj.

עָמַדְתִּי אֲנִי בֵּין הָאִישׁ הַזָּקֵן וּבֵין הָאִשָּׁה הַזְּקֵנָה

stood: verb, m. or f., s., 1st

I: pronoun, m. or f., s., 1st

between: preposition

the man: definite article plus m., s. noun

the old: definite article plus m., s. adjective

and between: conjunction plus preposition

the woman: definite article plus f., s. noun

the old: definite article plus f., s. adjective

I stood between the old man and the old woman.

הַקְּדוֹשִׁים יָשְׁבוּ עַל הָהָר
subj.

the holy ones: definite article plus m., pl. adjective working as noun
sat/dwelt: verb, m., pl., 3rd
on: preposition
the mountain: definite article plus m., s. noun

The holy ones sat/dwelt on the mountain.

d.o. subj.
אָכַלְנוּ אֲנַחְנוּ אֶת־הַלֶּחֶם הַזֶּה

ate: verb, m. or f., pl., 1st
we: pronoun, m. or f., pl., 1st
direct object marker
the bread/food: definite article plus m., s. noun
the this: definite article plus m., s. demonstrative

We ate this bread/food.

PREFIX PREPOSITIONS

CHAPTER SIXTEEN

16.1 MONDAY

This week's vocabulary words include four prepositions that do not stand alone, but are attached as prefixes. The nouns speak of troublous times.

Micah 4:3 speaks of the end of troublous times and includes several words you know. The last phrase has become lyrics of a folk song. If you don't know it, find it online and have a listen by searching for *Lo Yisa Goy*.

וְשָׁפַט בֵּין עַמִּים רַבִּים וְהוֹכִיחַ לְגוֹיִם עֲצֻמִים עַד־רָחוֹק וְכִתְּתוּ חַרְבֹתֵיהֶם לְאִתִּים
וַחֲנִיתֹתֵיהֶם לְמַזְמֵרוֹת לֹא־יִשְׂאוּ גּוֹי אֶל־גּוֹי חֶרֶב וְלֹא־יִלְמְדוּן עוֹד מִלְחָמָה׃

will judge	וְשָׁפַט
between	בֵּין
peoples	עַמִּים
many	רַבִּים
and will adjudicate	וְהוֹכִיחַ
to nations	לְגוֹיִם

mighty	עֲצֻמִים
even to	עַד־
far away	רָחוֹק
and they will beat	וְכִתְּתוּ
their swords	חַרְבֹתֵיהֶם
to plowshares	לְאִתִּים
and their spears	וַחֲנִיתֹתֵיהֶם
to pruning hooks	לְמַזְמֵרוֹת
not	לֹא־
will lift (familiar verb root, different tense)	יִשְׂאוּ
a nation	גוֹי
against	אֶל־
a nation	גוֹי
sword	חֶרֶב
and not	וְלֹא־
they will learn	יִלְמְדוּן
again	עוֹד
war	מִלְחָמָה:

16.2 TUESDAY

Match Hebrew phrases with English translations.

a. in a good land	לְרֵעַ c.
b. from a big city	בְּצָבָא f.
c. to a neighbor	עִם רָעָב m.
d. like a king	סָבִיב הַבַּיִת i.
e. to Sheol	כְּמֶלֶךְ d.
f. in an army	תַּחַת מָגֵן o.
g. with a sword	מִן שָׂדוֹת k.
h. on a shield	לִפְנֵי רָעָב p.
i. around the house	בְּאֶרֶץ טוֹבָה a.
j. like elders	לְבַיִת r.
k. from fields	כִּזְקֵנִים j.
l. in the midst of an army	מִן עִיר גְּדוֹלָה b.
m. with famine	לְדָוִד t.
n. after a war	עִם חֶרֶב g.
o. under a shield	כְּבֵן s.
p. before a famine	בְּתוֹךְ צָבָא l.
q. from a house	מִן בַּיִת q.
r. to a house	עַל מָגֵן h.
s. like a son	לִשְׁאוֹל e.
t. to David	אַחַר מִלְחָמָה n.

16.3 WEDNESDAY

Match Hebrew phrases with English translations.

a. to the men	מִן הַבַּיִת t.
b. from the cities	תַּחַת הַשָּׁמַיִם d.
c. in the big mountains	לְנָשִׁים i.
d. under the sky	כְּשֹׁפְטִים k.
e. like the prophet	בַּבַּיִת h.
f. from the war	כְּרָעָב p.
g. to the daughter	בְּשָׂדוֹת l.
h. in the house	מִן שְׁאוֹל n.
i. to women	כַּמָּגֵן r.
j. from a house	מִן הַמִּלְחָמָה f.
k. like judges	מִן הֶעָרִים b.
l. in fields	בְּתוֹךְ הַצָּבָא m.
m. in the midst of the army	לְאַחִים o.
n. from Sheol	בַּחֶרֶב q.
o. to brothers	לָאָחוֹת g.
p. like a famine	בֵּין אָב וּבֵין אֵם s.
q. with the sword	כַּנָּבִיא e.
r. like the shield	מִן בַּיִת j.
s. between a father and a mother	בֶּהָרִים הַגְּדוֹלִים c.
t. from the house	לָאֲנָשִׁים a.

16.4 THURSDAY

Translate phrases and sentences.

הָלַכְנוּ אֲנַחְנוּ אֶל־עִיר We walked to a city.

בֵּין מִלְחָמָה וּבֵין רָעָב between a war and a famine

הָאִישׁ הֶחָכָם יָשַׁב בַּבַּיִת The wise man sat/dwelt in the house.

נָשָׂאתָ אוֹתָם אַתָּה You carried them.

יַעֲקֹב הוּא כְּאָח Jacob is like a brother.

בִּשְׁאוֹל in Sheol

מִן הָאָרֶץ from the land

הוּא כְּמָגֵן גָּדוֹל He/it is like a big shield.

הַשֹּׁפְטִים אָכְלוּ עִם הַמְּלָכִים The judges ate with the kings.

כֹּהֵן נָשָׂא מַיִם לַמִּדְבָּר A priest carried water to the desert.

עָמְדוּ הֵם בַּמִּדְבָּר They stood in the desert.

שָׁתָה הוּא יַיִן עִם הַשָּׂר He drank wine with the captain.

הָעֶבֶד שָׂם לֶחֶם בַּבַּיִת The servant put bread/food in the house.

אֵין מִלְחָמָה כַּמִּלְחָמָה הַזֹּאת There is no war like this war.

אִישׁ נָשָׂא אֵת הַמָּגֵן לַבַּיִת A man carried the shield to the house.

כְּמִלְחָמָה כְּרָעָב as a war, so also a famine

הִיא שָׂמָה בֶּגֶד פֹּה She put a garment here.

16.5 FRIDAY

1. Ugarit: what? who? when?

Ugarit was a Canaanite city whose ruins from about 1200 B.C. were discovered in Syria in 1928.

2. Explain three ways that finding Ugarit has affected Bible acceptance and scholarship.

Because the oldest Bible manuscripts were from about A.D. 1000, some people doubted they were genuine and accurate copies of very ancient writings. In fact, some people doubted the ancient Israelites were even literate since so few artifacts with writing on them were known. Since the Bible claims to have been written by men from way back when, like Moses and David, its credibility was on the line when the Ugarit documents were discovered.

The Ugarit language and style were very like some Scripture and established the plausibility of ancient Israelites like David having written books. Linguistically, the Ugarit writings and Scripture were similar and similarly different than compositions written at about the time of Christ discovered among the Dead Sea Scrolls, which dated Bible books to the earlier time period.

Ugarit writings shed light on the practices and beliefs of the Canaanites that help us understand Scriptural context.

Since Ugarit is a cognate language of Biblical Hebrew, it can illuminate usage and rare words in Scripture.

3. Sing *Lo Yisa Goy* a few times today!

4. Parse. Identify each word's part(s) of speech: noun, pronoun, verb, demonstrative, definite article, direct object marker, conjunction, adjective, or preposition. Mark the subject (subj.) of each sentence and any direct objects (d.o.). Note the gender and number of demonstratives and nouns. Identify the gender, number, and person of each pronoun, pronoun suffix, and verb. Then translate.

הָלַךְ הוּא כְּמֶלֶךְ לָעִיר
subj.

walked: verb, m., s., 3rd
he: pronoun, m., s., 3rd
like a king: preposition plus m., s. noun
to the city: preposition plus definite article (apparent only in the vowel) plus f., s. noun

He walked like a king to the city.

d.o. d.o. subj.
הַנָּשִׁים הָאֵלֶּה נָשְׂאוּ אֵת הַלֶּחֶם וְאֵת הַמַּיִם לַצָּבָא הַגָּדוֹל

the women: definite article plus f., pl. noun
the these: definite article plus pl. demonstrative
carried: verb, m. or f. (f. in this sentence), pl., 3rd
direct object marker
the food/bread: definite article plus m., s. noun
and: conjunction plus direct object marker
the water: definite article plus m., pl. noun
to the army: preposition plus definite article plus m., s. noun
the big: definite article plus m., s. adjective

These women carried the bread/food and the water to the big army.

REVIEW

CHAPTER SEVENTEEN

17.1 MONDAY

Use this week's exercises for review and testing.

Work on examining and fluently reading 2 Kings 23:25, which is full of prepositions. Many of them have pronoun suffixes: see if you can recognize the familiar prepositions with pronoun endings.

וְכָמֹהוּ לֹא־הָיָה לְפָנָיו מֶלֶךְ אֲשֶׁר־שָׁב אֶל־יְהוָה בְּכָל־לְבָבוֹ וּבְכָל־נַפְשׁוֹ וּבְכָל־מְאֹדוֹ כְּכֹל
תּוֹרַת מֹשֶׁה וְאַחֲרָיו לֹא־קָם כָּמֹהוּ׃

and like him	וְכָמֹהוּ
not	לֹא־
there was	הָיָה
before him	לְפָנָיו
a king	מֶלֶךְ
which	אֲשֶׁר־
returned	שָׁב
to	אֶל־

the LORD (*Adonai*)	יְהוָה
in all	בְּכָל־
his heart	לְבָבוֹ
and in all	וּבְכָל־
his soul	נַפְשׁוֹ
and in all	וּבְכָל־
his might	מְאֹדוֹ
according to all	כְּכֹל
the teaching of	תּוֹרַת
Moses	מֹשֶׁה
and after him	וְאַחֲרָיו
not	לֹא־
arose	קָם
any like him	כָּמֹהוּ׃

17.2 TUESDAY

Choose the right word to complete the sentence, then translate and read aloud.

בַּמִּדְבָּר אֲנַחְנוּ הָלְכוּ / הָלַכְנוּ עִם הַצָּבָא

In the desert, we walked with the army.

אֵין עֶבֶד / אֶרֶץ טוֹב תַּחַת הַשֶּׁמֶשׁ

There is not a good servant under the sun.

הָרָעָב רָע / רַבָּה

The famine is bad.

אֲנַחְנוּ עָמַדְנוּ/ עָמְדוּ עַל הָהָר

We stood on the mountain.

אֵין לֶחֶם כַּלֶּחֶם הַזֶּה/ מִן הַלֶּחֶם הַזֶּה

There is no bread/food like this bread/food.

יָרְאוּ הֵם אֵת חֶרֶב/ הַחֶרֶב

They fear the sword.

אַתָּה/ אַתֶּם שָׁתִיתָ יַיִן בַּבַּיִת

You drank wine in the house.

הוּא עָבַד/ יָשַׁב כֹּהֲנִים

He served priests.

אֲנִי/ הוּא עָמַדְתִּי בֵּין אָחוֹת וּבֵין אָח

I stood between a sister and a brother.

הַנָּבִיא זָכַר/ זָכְרוּ נָהָר בָּאָרֶץ

The prophet remembered a river in the land.

17.3 WEDNESDAY

Translate phrases and sentences.

יֵשׁ בַּיִת פֹּה There is a house here.

אֵין אָח כְּמוֹ הָאח הַזֶּה There is not a brother like this brother.

אָנֹכִי מָגֵן לַנָּשִׁים I was/am/will be a shield to the women.

עָבַד יַעֲקֹב אֵת הַחֲכָמִים Jacob served the wise ones.

כְּאָח כְּאָחוֹת as a brother, so also a sister

בָּהָר הַזֶּה הַמֶּלֶךְ הוּא עָמַד The king stood on this mountain.

הוּא עָשָׂה He did/made.

הִיא יָשְׁבָה בְּתוֹךְ הָעִיר She sat/dwelt in the midst of the city.

תַּחַת הַשָּׁמַיִם אֵין אִישׁ כְּדָוִד Under the sky/Heaven, there is not a man like David.

אֲמַרְתֶּם אַתֶּם You said.

קָרְאוּ הֵמָּה They called.

אַתָּה שָׁמַעְתָּ אֵת הָאֲנָשִׁים בַּבַּיִת You heard the men/people in the house.

הַצָּבָא מָלַךְ אֵת הָאָרֶץ The army ruled the land.

עָבַרְנוּ אֲנַחְנוּ לִפְנֵי הַנָּכְרִים We crossed over before the foreigners.

יַעֲקֹב הוּא אָכַל וְשָׁתָה עִם הַשָּׂרִים הָאֵלֶּה Jacob ate and drank with these captains.

לֹא הָלַךְ הוּא מִן שְׁאוֹל He did not walk from Sheol.

יָרְאוּ הֵם אֵת הַחֶרֶב They feared the sword.

17.4 THURSDAY

1. Define/describe:

   a. Septuagint

      ancient translation of the Hebrew Scriptures; translation from Hebrew into Greek before the time of Christ; called the LXX; has been the authoritative base text for some Christians at some times

   b. Vulgate

      Latin translation of the Bible by Jerome in the 4th century

c. Targums

Aramaic paraphrases and explanations of the Hebrew Scriptures used for teaching and interpretation purposes by Jews

d. Samaritan Pentateuch

Samaritan version of the Books of Moses written in the Samaritan alphabet

e. Syriac Peshitta

an ancient translation from Hebrew, the Septuagint, and the Greek New Testament Scriptures used by Eastern, Aramaic-speaking Christians from at least the fifth century

f. Talmud

the compilation of the Mishnah (a record of the Oral Torah) with the Gemara (subsequent analysis and commentary from Jewish scholars in the early centuries): a vast collection of Jewish Bible interpretation and application

2. Name three major archaeological discoveries of the last 200 years that have affirmed Bible accuracy and influenced Bible translation.

discovery of Assyrian ruins and texts, Ugarit ruins and texts, and the Dead Sea Scrolls

3. Hebrew generally uses ___prepositional phrases___ rather than adverbs.

4. Name a part of speech that Hebrew has, but English does not. How is it translated?

English does not have a direct object marker. That Hebrew word is not translated as any English word, but does guide the word order a translation would use to differentiate a sentence's subject and direct object.

5. Which is easier to define, a Hebrew preposition or noun? Why?

Generally a noun is easier to define because Hebrew prepositions are quite versatile. A Hebrew preposition might get translated by 25 or so different English words.

17.5 FRIDAY

Parse these sentences, identifying each word's part(s) of speech and if applicable, its number, gender, and person. Translate.

יַעֲקֹב הוּא אָכַל וְשָׁתָה עִם הַשָּׂרִים הָאֵלֶּה

Jacob: proper noun, m., s.
he: pronoun, m., s., 3rd
ate: verb, m., s., 3rd
and drank: conjunction plus verb: m., s., 3rd
with: preposition
the captains: definite article plus m., pl. noun
the these: definite article plus pl. demonstrative

Jacob ate and drank with these captains.

אַתָּה שָׁמַעְתָּ אֵת הָאֲנָשִׁים בַּבַּיִת

you: pronoun, m., s., 2nd
heard: verb, m., s., 2nd
direct object marker
the men/people: definite article plus m., pl. noun
in the house: preposition plus definite article plus m., s. noun

You heard the men/people in the house.

אָנֹכִי מָגֵן לַנַּעֲרָה

I: pronoun, m. or f., s., 1st
shield: noun, m., s.
to the young woman: preposition plus definite article plus f., s. noun

I am/was/will be a shield to the young woman.

PREPOSITIONS WITH PRONOUNS

CHAPTER EIGHTEEN

18.1 MONDAY

A bunch of useful little words this week. Some are conjunctions; they connect words or phrases: *but*, *or*, *if*, *lest*, *because*.

Others are words that in English would take a whole prepositional phrase to say: *for the sake of*, *from among*, *from the midst of*. Perhaps you recognize now that תּוֹךְ means *midst*. בְּתוֹךְ and מִתּוֹךְ are formed by prefixing prepositions. Similarly, קֶרֶב means *inward part* or *midst* and בְּקֶרֶב was formed by adding a preposition. You will also see מִקֶּרֶב in Scripture which means *from within*, or *from among*.

And one adverb: *then*.

Exodus 1:10 features a few of this week's words and others you know.

הָבָה נִתְחַכְּמָה לוֹ פֶּן־יִרְבֶּה וְהָיָה כִּי־תִקְרֶאנָה מִלְחָמָה וְנוֹסַף גַּם־הוּא עַל־שֹׂנְאֵינוּ וְנִלְחַם־בָּנוּ
וְעָלָה מִן־הָאָרֶץ׃

come on	הָבָה
let us act wisely	נִתְחַכְּמָה

to it (*it* refers to the nation of Israel)	לוֹ
lest	פֶּן־
will multiply	יִרְבֶּה
and it will be	וְהָיָה
because	כִּי־
will befall	תִקְרֶאנָה
war	מִלְחָמָה
and will be joined	וְנוֹסַף
also	גַּם־
it (the nation)	הוּא
to	עַל־
those who hate us	שֹׂנְאֵינוּ
and will fight	וְנִלְחַם־
with us	בָּנוּ
and will go up	וְעָלָה
from	מִן־
the land	הָאָרֶץ:

18.2 TUESDAY Prepositions have multiple meanings. A student need supply only one of the options given below.

1. Translate.

בִּי in/with/on me

בָּהֶם in/with/on them

לוֹ to/for him/it

בָּךְ in/with/on you

לָהּ to/for her/it

בָּכֶם in/with/on you (m., pl.)

לָהֶם to/for them (m.)

לָנוּ to/for us

בּוֹ in/with/on him/it

לְךָ to/for you

בָּהּ in/with/on her/it

לָהֶן to/for them (f.)

לִי to/for me

בָּךְ in/with/on you (f.)

בָּנוּ in/with/on us

לָכֶם to/for you (m., pl.)

2. Write a noun, in English, to which these prepositional phrases could refer.
example: לוֹ "William Wilberforce"

Answers will vary. The appropriate number, gender, and person for answers are given below with one example in quotation marks.

בּוֹ m., s., 3rd: "Dad"

לִי m. or f., s., 1st: "me"

בָּהֶם m., pl., 3rd: "U.S. Presidents"

לָנוּ m. or f., pl., 1st: "our family"

בָּהּ f., s., 3rd: "Queen Elizabeth"

בָּהֶן f., pl., 3rd: "Ruth and Naomi"

לָכֶן f., pl., 2nd: "my sisters (being spoken to and addressed as 'you')"

18.3 WEDNESDAY

Translate.

עֲלֵיהֶם on them

אֵלֶיהָ to her/it

לְפָנַי before me

אַחֲרֵינוּ after us

לָךְ to/for you (f.)

עִמּוֹ with him/it

בָּכֶם in/with/on you (m., pl.)

עָלַי on me

אֲלֵיהֶן to them (f.)

אַחֲרֵיהֶן after them (f.)

לְפָנֶיךָ before you (m., s.)

עִמְּךָ with you (m., s.)

בָּךְ in/with/on you (f., s.)

לָכֶם to/for you (m., pl.)

עָלָיו on him/it

עִמָּהּ with her/it

לְךָ to/for you (m., s.)

בָּנוּ in/with/on us

לְפָנָיו before him

אַחֲרֵיכֶם after you (m., pl.)

18.4 THURSDAY

Translate phrases and sentences.

קָרָא הוּא מִתּוֹךְ הַמִּלְחָמָה He called from the midst of the war.

יֵשׁ בָּכֶם אִישׁ טוֹב There is a good man with you.

אִם יֵשׁ הֶחָכָם פֹּה אָז הַמֶּלֶךְ הוּא If there is a wise one here, then he is/was/will be the king.

הָלַכְתָּ אַתָּה אַךְ אֲנִי יָשַׁבְתִּי You walked but I sat. (or, You went, but I stayed.)

דָּוִד אוֹ יַעֲקֹב שָׁתָה אֵת הַיַּיִן הַזֶּה David or Jacob drank this wine.

לְמַעַן הַבָּנִים הוּא נָשָׂא לֶחֶם לָעִיר For the sake of the sons/children, he carried bread/food to the city.

פֶּן יֵשׁ בָּכֶם אִישׁ רָע lest there be in you an evil man

הוּא הַמֶּלֶךְ כִּי הוּא טוֹב He is the king because he is good.

אֵין רָעָב בָּאָרֶץ אַךְ יֵשׁ מִלְחָמָה There is not a famine in the land, but there is a war.

יֵשׁ מִלְחָמָה כִּי הַמְּלָכִים אֲנָשִׁים רָעִים There is a war because the kings are evil men.

אֲנִי שָׁמַרְתִּי אוֹתוֹ לְמַעַן הַנַּעֲרָה I guarded it/him for the sake of the young woman.

אָז יַעֲקֹב הוּא זָכַר וְהוּא יָרֵא Then Jacob remembered and he feared.

בְּקֶרֶב רָעָב הִיא אָכְלָה לֶחֶם In the midst of famine she ate bread/food.

18.5 FRIDAY

1. Some Scripture phrases you can read and translate:

It would be very worthwhile to have students look up these verses in their Bibles after completing this and all other Scripture translation exercises. It will prove immensely valuable to compare with their own translation and to compare various translations.

It might be handy to use a website that presents several translations of any verse side-by-side. At the time of this writing, you can find such a service, for free, at http://biblehub.com/genesis/1-1.htm. Type in any verse reference in the search bar to see the verse displayed in over a dozen translations. If you are working in a different section of the website (reading a verse in Hebrew, for example) the "Parallel" tab will allow you to view various English translations at once.

עָרִים גְּדֹלֹת וְטֹבֹת

Deuteronomy 6:10

great and good cities

הָרָעָב בְּקֶרֶב הָאָרֶץ

Genesis 45:6

the famine in the midst of the land

אֵין מִלְחָמָה בֵּין אֲרָם וּבֵין יִשְׂרָאֵל

1 Kings 22:1

(proper nouns אֲרָם and יִשְׂרָאֵל are Aram and Israel)

there is not war between Aram and Israel

אָנֹכִי מָגֵן לָךְ

Genesis 15:1

I am your shield

הָלְכוּ עִם־דָּוִד

1 Samuel 30:22

[they] walked with David

לֹא־הָלְכוּ עִמִּי

1 Samuel 30:22

[they] did not walk with me

בְעִיר־דָּוִיד עִם־הַמְּלָכִים כִּי־עָשָׂה טוֹבָה בְּיִשְׂרָאֵל

2 Chronicles 24:16

(you know טוֹב as an adjective, here it appears as a feminine noun)

in the city of David with the kings that did good in Israel

הַמַּיִם מִתַּחַת הַשָּׁמַיִם

Genesis 1:9

the water from under the sky/Heaven

2. Name as many ways as you can think of that a message from God could be garbled *en route* to being acted upon properly by someone who speaks a different language.

Possible difficulties include, but are not limited to:

person to whom God gives message is unwilling to believe it or to share it, does not understand or remember it properly, adds to or subtracts from the message purposefully

writing does not necessarily capture an event or an idea fully

listener fails to grasp cultural context and misunderstands the message

listener listens to only what he wishes to hear and disregards the rest

wicked folks seek to destroy God's Word and His prophets

copying errors in a written record

listener does not learn original language, but no translation fully conveys the original

listener chooses to disobey even when he understands perfectly

words in the original and target language do not exactly correspond

some of the context is lost over time; for instance, modern urban people may not comprehend draft animal metaphors, or once-attractive false gods are forgotten

listener uses a translator rather than learn original language, but translator ignorantly or purposefully mistranslates, unbeknownst to listener

POSSESSIVE ENDINGS: SINGULAR NOUNS

CHAPTER NINETEEN

19.1 MONDAY

Memorize the three-letter roots of this week's verbs and conjugate *to judge* and *to go down* in the charts below, according to the pattern you have learned.

plural	singular	JUDGE
שָׁפַטְנוּ	שָׁפַטְתִּי	first person
שְׁפַטְתֶּם	שָׁפַטְתָּ	second person, m.
שְׁפַטְתֶּן	שָׁפַטְתְּ	second person, f.
שָׁפְטוּ	שָׁפַט	third person, m.
שָׁפְטוּ	שָׁפְטָה	third person, f.

GO DOWN

	plural	singular
first person	יָרַדְנוּ	יָרַדְתִּי
second person, m.	יְרַדְתֶּם	יָרַדְתָּ
second person, f.	יְרַדְתֶּן	יָרַדְתְּ
third person, m.	יָרְדוּ	יָרַד
third person, f.	יָרְדוּ	יָרְדָה

Turn aside's conjugation is irregular because of its vav in middle position. Like yud, a vav in middle position drops out of conjugations. More on this phenomenon coming up in Chapters 30 and 31. Verb conjugations are listed for reference in Appendix D of your textbook.

TURN ASIDE

	plural	singular
first person	סַרְנוּ	סַרְתִּי
second person, m.	סַרְתֶּם	סַרְתָּ
second person, f.	סַרְתֶּן	סַרְתְּ
third person, m.	סָרוּ	סָר
third person, f.	סָרוּ	סָרָה

Work on reading 1 Kings 12:4 fluently, aloud.

אָבִיךָ הִקְשָׁה אֶת־עֻלֵּנוּ וְאַתָּה עַתָּה הָקֵל מֵעֲבֹדַת אָבִיךָ הַקָּשָׁה וּמֵעֻלּוֹ הַכָּבֵד אֲשֶׁר־נָתַן עָלֵינוּ
וְנַעַבְדֶךָּ׃

your father	(noun with possessive pronoun suffix)	אָבִיךָ
made difficult		הִקְשָׁה
(direct object marker)		אֶת־
our yoke	(noun with possessive pronoun suffix)	עֻלֵּנוּ
and you		וְאַתָּה
now		עַתָּה
lighten		הָקֵל
the service of		מֵעֲבֹדַת
your father	(noun with possessive pronoun suffix)	אָבִיךָ
difficult		הַקָּשָׁה
and his yoke	(noun with possessive pronoun suffix)	וּמֵעֻלּוֹ
heavy		הַכָּבֵד
which		אֲשֶׁר־
gave		נָתַן
on us	(preposition with pronoun suffix)	עָלֵינוּ
and we will serve you	(verb with object pronoun suffix)	וְנַעַבְדֶךָּ׃

19.2 TUESDAY

1. Identify the nouns with possessive pronoun suffixes in 1 Kings 12:4. Find also a pronoun ending on a preposition in this verse, and one attached to a verb as its direct object.

2. Translate.

צְבָאוֹ his army

מָגִנִּי my shield

בְּנָהּ her son

נְבִיאֵיכֶם your prophets

עַבְדְּךָ your servant

אִמִּי my mother

לַחְמְךָ your bread/food

לַחְמֵנוּ our bread/food

מַלְכֵּנוּ our king

אַרְצוֹ his land

מַלְכְּכֶן your king

דּוֹרִי my generation

עִירְךָ your city

בֵּיתִי my house

בְּנֵנוּ our son

רֵעֲךָ your neighbor

שַׂרְכֶם your captain

בֵּיתָם their house

19.3 WEDNESDAY

1. Translate.

בִּתּוֹ his daughter

אַדְמָתֵנוּ our ground

בִּתְּךָ your daughter

אַדְמָתִי my ground

2. Translate these English phrases into Hebrew by adding the appropriate suffix to the Hebrew noun provided. The Hebrew nouns are presented with any vowel and sofit letter changes already made so that they are ready to accept a suffix.

your (*m.*, *s.*) king	מַלְכְּךָ
my son	בְּנִי
their (*m.*) food	לַחְמָם
our land	אַרְצֵנוּ
your (*m.*, *s.*) mother	אִמְּךָ
your (*m.*, *pl.*) servant	עַבְדְּכֶם
their (*m.*) shield	מָגִנָּם
his son	בְּנוֹ
my servant	עַבְדִּי
your (*m.*, *pl.*) king	מַלְכְּכֶם
your (*f.*, *pl.*) house	בֵּיתְכֶן

19.4 THURSDAY

Translate.

הָלַךְ אָבִיו בֵּין הָאֲנָשִׁים וּבֵין הַנָּשִׁים His father walked between the men and the women.

שָׁמַר אֲבִיהֶם אֵת הָעִיר Their father guarded the city.

הִיא נָשְׂאָה אֶת־לַחְמָהּ לְאָבִיהָ She carried her food to her father.

עָבַד אָבִינוּ אֵת הַכֹּהֲנִים Our father served the priests.

בְּתוֹךְ הַשָּׂדֶה עָמַד אָבִיךָ Your father stood in the midst of the field.

אָבִיו לָקַח חֶרֶב His father took a sword.

סָר אֲבִיהֶם Their father turned aside.

אָבִינוּ שָׁפַט אֵת הָעֲבָדִים Our father judged the servants.

יָרַד מִן הָהָר אֲבִיכֶם Your father went down from the mountain.

אָבִיו אָכַל לֶחֶם וְשָׁתָה יַיִן בַּבַּיִת עִמִּי His father are bread/food and drank wine in the house with me.

19.5 FRIDAY

1. Translate.

פָּתַחְתִּי אֲנִי לְאָבִי I opened to my father.

לָקַח הוּא אֶת־אִשְׁתּוֹ וְאֶת־בָּנָיו He took his wife and his sons.

הַמֶּלֶךְ שָׁפַט בֵּינִי וּבֵינֶךָ The king judged between you and me. (In Hebrew, it is not impolite to name yourself first in a list of people like this one; in proper English we name ourselves last.)

Scripture phrases you can read and translate:

Here again is a Scripture translation exercise. Have your students find these verses in their English Bible and in various translations to compare with their own answers. By doing this, students will powerfully build not only their Hebrew skills, but their understanding of the art of translation and how that affects Bible interpretation and study.

It would be good, too, to look up the verses in a Hebrew Bible for practice finding things in a Hebrew Bible (the books are in a different order) and for practice visually scanning through Hebrew text.

רָעָב בָּאָרֶץ

Genesis 12:10

famine in the land

וְלֹא יָרַד אֶל־בֵּיתוֹ

2 Samuel 11:9

and did not go down to his house

לְמַעַן דָּוִד עַבְדִּי

1 Kings 11:13

for the sake of my servant David

כִּי לֹא פָּתַח

2 Kings 15:16

because did not open

עֲבַדְתִּי אֹתְךָ

Genesis 30:26

I served you.

לָקַח מִן־הָאָדָם לְאִשָּׁה

Genesis 2:22

(Ha-adam means "the man." Does that ring any bells? Especially in Genesis 2? Can you guess what was taken?)

[He] took from the man for the woman

מִשְׁפָּטֶיךָ לְיַעֲקֹב

Deuteronomy 33:10

your judgements to Jacob

2. Name some of the most difficult facets of a text to translate.

Possible answers include, but are not limited to:

poetry; wordplay in general, but especially that based on the sound of words; register; tone; style; rhyme; words that are specific to a culture; idioms, like "long noses" meaning "patience"

3. To study a word in your Bible, why is an English dictionary of little use?

Hebrew and English words do not fully correspond. An English translation word may indeed translate a Hebrew word well in one of its usages, but have other legitimate meanings that the Hebrew word does not have. The reader may not know which meaning is intended and get the entirely wrong idea.

POSSESSIVE ENDINGS: PLURAL NOUNS

CHAPTER TWENTY

20.1 MONDAY

Work on memorizing vocabulary today.

Exodus 34:6 contains several of this week's words. The root letters of *grace* are here in the adjective *gracious*: חַנּוּן; and the root letters of *compassion* appear here in the adjective *compassionate*: רַחוּם.

וַיַּעֲבֹר יְהוָה עַל־פָּנָיו וַיִּקְרָא יְהוָה יְהוָה אֵל רַחוּם וְחַנּוּן אֶרֶךְ אַפַּיִם וְרַב־חֶסֶד וֶאֱמֶת׃

crossed over (familiar verb root, but unfamiliar conjugation)	וַיַּעֲבֹר
the LORD	יְהוָה
on	עַל־
his face (we might say, "in front of him")	פָּנָיו
and proclaimed (familiar verb root, unfamiliar conjugation)	וַיִּקְרָא

the LORD	יְהוָה
the LORD	יְהוָה
God	אֵל
compassionate (notice similarity to *compassion*)	רַחוּם
and gracious (notice similarity to *grace*)	וְחַנּוּן
long	אֶרֶךְ
noses ("long noses" = slow to anger)	אַפַּיִם
and abundant	וְרַב־
steadfast love	חֶסֶד
and faithfulness	וֶאֱמֶת׃

20.2 TUESDAY

Translate these English phrases into Hebrew by adding the appropriate suffix to אָבוֹת, provided here in its ready-for-a-suffix form, אֲבוֹת.

my fathers	אֲבוֹתַי
our fathers	אֲבוֹתֵינוּ
your (*m., s.*) fathers	אֲבוֹתֶיךָ
your (*m., pl.*) fathers	אֲבוֹתֵיכֶם
your (*f., pl.*) fathers	אֲבוֹתֵיכֶן
their (*m.*) fathers	אֲבוֹתֵיהֶם

20.3 WEDNESDAY

Translate.

תּוֹרֹתָיו his laws/instructions/teachings

מִשְׁפָּטֶיךָ your judgements

בָּנֶיהָ her sons

אַחְוֹתֵיכֶם your sisters

אֲחֵיהֶם their brothers

שְׂדוֹתֵינוּ our fields

כֹּהֲנָיו his priests

מְלָכֵינוּ our kings

עֲבָדַי my servants

בְּנוֹתֶיהָ her daughters

בָּתֵּינוּ our houses

צִבְאוֹתֵיכֶם your armies

בְּגָדֶיךָ your garments

נַעֲרֵיהֶם their young men

דֹּרֹתֵיכֶם your generations

תּוֹרֹתַי my laws/instructions/teachings

אֲבוֹתֶיךָ your fathers

בְּנוֹתֵיכֶן your sons

20.4 THURSDAY

Translate.

יָרֵאנוּ אֲנַחְנוּ אֵת מַלְכֵיהֶם We feared their kings.

יָרֵאנוּ אֲנַחְנוּ מַלְכָּם הַגָּדוֹל We feared their great king.

עִירָם קְטַנָּה Their city is little.

עִירָם הַקְּטַנָּה their little city

לַחְמֵנוּ רַב Our bread/food is abundant.

לַחְמֵנוּ הָרַב our abundant bread/food

מַלְכּוֹ הַטּוֹב הֶחָכָם his good, wise king

אָבִיו זָקֵן His father is old.

מַלְכֵּנוּ קָדוֹשׁ Our king is holy.

שָׁתוּ הֵם אֶת־יֵינָהּ They drank her wine.

נָשָׂא הוּא אֵת מָגִנִּי He carried my shield.

מִשְׁפָּטָיו אֱמֶת His judgements are truth.

תּוֹרֹתָיו שָׁלוֹם His laws/instructions/teachings are peace.

עָבַדְתִּי אֲנִי אֵת אָבִיו I served his father.

20.5 FRIDAY

1. Another term for essentially literal: word-for-word/formal equivalence.

2. Another term for dynamic equivalence: thought-for-thought.

3. Distinguish between essentially literal, dynamic equivalence, and paraphrase translations.

Essentially literal translations seek to preserve original words and syntax as much as possible in order to respect the text, facilitate Bible study by consistently translating words, and minimize the translator's interpretations.

A dynamic equivalence translation intends to communicate the ideas of the original without strict adherence to the author's particular words.

A paraphrase is freest of all in translating the ideas of the original and might update idioms and metaphors in an attempt to convey the original meaning, or the author's interpretation.

4. Explain an advantage of an essentially literal translation.

Translators' interpretations should be minimized with this method.

5. Explain an advantage of a paraphrase.

A paraphrase can help bridge historical and cultural distance by substituting expressions, idioms, and metaphors that are more meaningful to the intended reader. A paraphrase can jolt someone familiar with the Bible out of boredom or complacency by delivering ideas in unfamiliar words. A paraphrase might be easier to read and understand for someone new to the Bible.

6. From which sort of translation do you most often read?

Answers will, of course, vary. The translation philosophy behind a modern translation may be printed in a Bible preface or available from the publisher's website. This would be a good time for your student to research the translation philosophy and style of the Bible he reads most and the one used in his congregation. Perhaps a pastor could be interviewed to explain his choice of translation for various purposes, if he uses more than one. This would also be a good opportunity to read passages in an unfamiliar version, especially one very different in style from the one with which a student is most familiar.

7. Translate from Scripture.

Have students compare their answers with Bible translations.

כִּי־אֵין מִשְׁפָּט

Isaiah 59:15

because there is not/was not justice

אַשְׁרֵי אֲנָשֶׁיךָ וְאַשְׁרֵי עֲבָדֶיךָ אֵלֶּה הָעֹמְדִים לְפָנֶיךָ תָּמִיד וְשֹׁמְעִים אֶת־חָכְמָתֶךָ

2 Chronicles 9:7

You can read the underlined words. Find the root letters of *stand* and *hear* in the circled words. Look up the verse in your Bible to figure out the others.

Happy are your men/people and happy are these servants of yours, the ones who stand before you continually/regularly and are the ones who hear your wisdom.

וְאִם־אָב אָנִי אַיֵּה (where) כְבוֹדִי

Malachi 1:6

and if I am a father, where is my honor?

אִם־יַעַזְבוּ (forsake) בָנָיו תּוֹרָתִי וּבְמִשְׁפָּטַי לֹא יֵלֵכוּן (will walk)

Psalm 89:30

if his sons forsake my law and they will not walk in my judgements

חֶסֶד וֶאֱמֶת יִצְּרוּ (preserve) מֶלֶךְ

Proverbs 20:28

steadfast love and truth/faithfulness preserve a king

וַיֹּאמֶר (said) שְׁלֹמֹה (Solomon) אַתָּה עָשִׂיתָ עִם־עַבְדְּךָ דָוִד אָבִי חֶסֶד גָּדוֹל

כַּאֲשֶׁר (when) הָלַךְ לְפָנֶיךָ בֶּאֱמֶת וּבִצְדָקָה

1 Kings 3:6

Solomon said, "You showed great, steadfast love to my father, your servant David, when he walked before You in truth/faithfulness and in righteousness."

כִּי שֶׁמֶשׁ וּמָגֵן יְהוָה (the LORD) אֱלֹהִים (God) חֵן וְכָבוֹד יִתֵּן (will give)

יְהוָה (the LORD) לֹא יִמְנַע (withhold) טוֹב

Psalm 84: 11

...because the LORD God is a sun and a shield. The LORD will give grace and honor. He will not withhold goodness.

חָכְמָתִי עָמְדָה

Ecclesiastes 2:9

my wisdom stood

וַיְהִי (it would have been) כַנָּהָר שְׁלוֹמֶךָ וְצִדְקָתְךָ כְּגַלֵּי (like the waves of) הַיָּם

Isaiah 48:18

Your peace/wholeness would have been like a river and your righteousness like the waves of the sea.

יִתֵּן (May He give) לָכֶם רַחֲמִים לִפְנֵי הָאִישׁ וְשִׁלַּח (he will release) לָכֶם אֶת־אֲחִיכֶם

Genesis 43:14

May He give to you compassion before the man and he will release to you your brother.

CONSTRUCT CHAINS: SINGULAR

CHAPTER TWENTY-ONE

21.1 MONDAY

This week's words are related to the Temple. Check back to 2.1 and see if there is a new method of practicing vocabulary that you could try this week.

Genesis 8:20

וַיִּבֶן נֹחַ מִזְבֵּחַ לַיהוָה וַיִּקַּח מִכֹּל הַבְּהֵמָה הַטְּהוֹרָה וּמִכֹּל הָעוֹף הַטָּהֹר וַיַּעַל עֹלֹת בַּמִּזְבֵּחַ׃

built	וַיִּבֶן
Noah	נֹחַ
an altar	מִזְבֵּחַ
to the LORD	לַיהוָה
and took (familiar verb, but unfamiliar conjugation)	וַיִּקַּח
from every	מִכֹּל

animal	הַבְּהֵמָה
clean	הַטְּהוֹרָה
and from every	וּמִכֹּל
bird	הָעוֹף
clean	הַטָּהֹר
and he sent up	וַיַּעַל
a burnt offering	עֹלֹת
on the altar	בַּמִּזְבֵּחַ׃

21.2 TUESDAY

Match construct chains with their English translations (continued on next page).

a. true instruction	o. עֶבֶד מֶלֶךְ
b. a warrior	d. בֶּן מֶלֶךְ
c. Bethlehem	b. אִישׁ מִלְחָמָה
d. a king's son	r. מֶלֶךְ עִיר
e. teaching of steadfast love	f. שְׂדֵה מִלְחָמָה
f. a battlefield	t. מֶלֶךְ צְדָקָה
g. a woman of peace	s. עִיר שָׁלוֹם
h. a man's wife	m. אִישׁ הַר
i. true judgement	e. תּוֹרַת חֶסֶד
j. a priest's daughter	k. בֵּית נְבִיאִים
k. a house of prophets	h. אֵשֶׁת אִישׁ
l. a garment of honor	g. אֵשֶׁת שָׁלוֹם
m. a mountain man	l. בֶּגֶד כָּבוֹד

n. a servant's tent	j. בַּת כֹּהֵן
o. a servant of a king	n. אֹהֶל עֶבֶד
p. a judgement of a father	q. אֶרֶץ צְדָקָה
q. a land of righteousness	c. בֵּית לֶחֶם
r. a king of a city	p. מִשְׁפַּט אָב
s. a city of peace	i. מִשְׁפָּט אֱמֶת
t. a king of righteousness	a. תּוֹרַת אֱמֶת

21.3 WEDNESDAY

Translate.

אֵשֶׁת דָּוִד David's wife

עֶבֶד הַכֹּהֲנִים the servant of the priests

עֶבֶד כֹּהֲנִים a servant of priests

בֶּן הַכְּסִיל the son of the fool

בֶּן כְּסִיל a son of a fool

אֶרֶץ הָאַחִים the land of the brothers

אִישׁ הַמִּדְבָּר the man of the desert

חַכְמַת הַמֶּלֶךְ the wisdom of the king

אֲחוֹת יַעֲקוֹב Jacob's sister

בַּת הַשֹּׁפֵט the sister of the judge

בַּת מֶ֫לֶךְ a daughter of a king

מַלְאַךְ הַמֶּ֫לֶךְ the messenger of the king

בֵּית גֵּר a house of sojourner

בֵּית הַגֵּר the house of the sojourner

אֵם הַנַּ֫עַר the mother of the young man

יֵ֫יִן הַמֶּ֫לֶךְ the wine of the king

אֶ֫רֶץ הָרָעָב the land of the famine

מִלְחֶ֫מֶת מְלָכִים a war of kings

מִלְחֶ֫מֶת הַמְּלָכִים the war of the kings

מָגֵן דָּוִד the shield of David

שֶׁ֫מֶן הַמֶּ֫לֶךְ the king's oil

עֹלַת הַכֹּהֵן the whole burnt offering of the priest

21.4 THURSDAY

1. Translate.

אִישׁ שָׁלוֹם עָלָה עִמּוֹ A man of peace went up with him.

עָבַד הוּא אֵת מֶ֫לֶךְ הַמִּדְבָּר He served the king of the desert.

אֵ֫שֶׁת עֶ֫בֶד הַמֶּ֫לֶךְ שָׁמְעָה אֵת יַעֲקֹב The wife of the servant of the king heard Jacob.

מַלְאַךְ הַנְּבִיאִים אָכַל לֶחֶם עִמִּי The messenger of the prophets ate bread/food with me.

בֶּן הָאִישׁ זָכַר עִיר The son of the man remembered a city.

זָכַר הוּא אֵת אִישׁ הַמִּלְחָמָה He remembered the man of war/the warrior.

2. Choose the correct verb to complete the sentence. Translate and read aloud.

אַב בָּנִים שָׁתָה / שָׁתוּ יַיִן
A father of sons drank wine.

בַּת כֹּהֲנִים עָמְדוּ / עָמְדָה בַּשָּׂדֶה הַגָּדוֹל
A daughter of priests stood in the big field.

עֶבֶד הַמְּלָכִים זָכַר / זָכְרָה אֵת הַמִּלְחָמָה
The servant of the kings remembered the war.

אֵם הָאַחִים לָקְחוּ / לָקְחָה לֶחֶם וָמַיִם אֶל־הָאֹהֶל
The mother of the brothers took bread/food and water to the tent.

אִישׁ מִלְחָמָה יָרַד / יָרַדְנוּ עִמָּנוּ
A man of war went down with us.

בֶּן שַׂר הָאָרֶץ עָשָׂה / עָלָה חֶסֶד
The son of the captain of the land showed steadfast love.

21.5 FRIDAY

Translate from Scripture.

וְחֶרֶב לֹא־תַעֲבֹר (*cross over* in another tense, notice the root letters) בְּאַרְצְכֶם

Leviticus 26:6

The sword will not cross over in your land.

שֶׁמֶשׁ צְדָקָה

Malachi 4:2

sun of righteousness

Quite literal, basic translations are given here. Students will learn much by comparing their answers with at least one Bible translation.

כִּי־נַעַר אַתָּה וְהוּא אִישׁ מִלְחָמָה

1 Samuel 17:33

because you are a young man and he is a man of war

נַעַר הַכֹּהֵן

1 Samuel 2:15

the young man of the priest

וַיֵּלֶךְ (and went) אֲבִימֶלֶךְ (a name, the basic meaning of which you can discern)
בֶּן־יְרֻבַּעַל (name after makkef) שְׁכֶמָה (to Shechem) אֶל־אֲחֵי אִמּוֹ

Judges 9:1

And Abimelech, the son of Jerubbaal, went to Shechem to the brothers of his mother

פִּיהָ (her mouth) פָּתְחָה בְחָכְמָה וְתוֹרַת־חֶסֶד עַל־לְשׁוֹנָהּ (her tongue)

Proverbs 31:26

Her mouth opened in wisdom and the instruction of steadfast love was on her tongue.

וּמָשַׁחְתָּ (and shall anoint) אֶת־מִזְבַּח הָעֹלָה... וְהָיָה (and it will be) הַמִּזְבֵּחַ קֹדֶשׁ קָדָשִׁים

Exodus 40:10

And you shall anoint the altar of the burnt offering...and it will be the holiest altar.

זֶה קֹדֶשׁ הַקֳּדָשִׁים

Ezekiel 41:4

This is the holiest (the "Holy of Holies," the Temple's inner sanctuary).

אֲרוֹן הָעֵדֻת (the testimony) בְּקֹדֶשׁ הַקֳּדָשִׁים

Exodus 26:34

the ark of the testimony in the Holy of Holies

CONSTRUCT CHAINS: PLURAL

CHAPTER TWENTY-TWO

22.1 MONDAY

Work on memorizing vocabulary today.

Finish the translation of Numbers 36:7. Practice reading this verse today and each day this week.

וְלֹא־תִסֹּב נַחֲלָה לִבְנֵי יִשְׂרָאֵל מִמַּטֶּה אֶל־מַטֶּה כִּי אִישׁ בְּנַחֲלַת מַטֵּה אֲבֹתָיו יִדְבְּקוּ בְּנֵי
יִשְׂרָאֵל׃

and not	וְלֹא־
will transfer	תִסֹּב
inheritance	נַחֲלָה
before	לִבְנֵי
Israel	יִשְׂרָאֵל
from a tribe	מִמַּטֶּה

to	אֶל־
a tribe	מַטֶּה
because	כִּי
a man	אִישׁ
in the inheritance of	בְּנַחֲלַת
the tribe of	מַטֵּה
his fathers	אֲבֹתָיו
will hold fast	יִדְבְּקוּ
the sons of	בְּנֵי
Israel	יִשְׂרָאֵל׃

The final hey in the root that means *answer* results in some unusual conjugations. Complete the chart below by referring to Appendix D in your textbook, then read the conjugations aloud to familiarize yourself with this verb.

plural	singular	ANSWER
עָנִינוּ	עָנִיתִי	first person
עֲנִיתֶם	עָנִיתָ	second person, m.
עֲנִיתֶן	עָנִית	second person, f.
עָנוּ	עָנָה	third person, m.
עָנוּ	עָנְתָה	third person, f.

22.2 TUESDAY

Match Hebrew phrases with English translations.

a. sons of a family	f. אַנְשֵׁי קָהָל
b. daughters of a mother	l. נְבִיאֵי עַם
c. kings of a nation	n. שֹׁפְטֵי יִשְׂרָאֵל
d. princes of tribes	c. מַלְכֵי עַם
e. the voice of the father	i. אַרְצוֹת הַמֶּלֶךְ
f. men of a congregation	k. נַעֲרוֹת דּוֹר
g. brothers of a sister	r. נְשֵׁי הָעָם
h. encampments of a nation	o. מַלְאֲכֵי מֶלֶךְ
i. the king's lands	d. שָׂרֵי מַטּוֹת
j. an army's shields	p. אָהֳלֵי הַמַּחֲנֶה
k. young women of a generation	t. מִנְחָה אִישׁ
l. prophets of a nation	a. בְּנֵי מִשְׁפָּחָה
m. a woman's servants	m. עַבְדֵי אִשָּׁה
n. judges of Israel	g. אֲחֵי אָחוֹת
o. messengers of a king	s. אֲבוֹת הַמַּטֶּה
p. the tents of the camp	q. קוֹל הַקָּהָל
q. the congregation's voice	b. בְּנוֹת אֵם
r. the women of the nation	j. מָגִנֵּי צָבָא
s. the fathers of the tribe	e. קוֹל הָאָב
t. a man's offering	h. מַחֲנוֹת עַם

22.3 WEDNESDAY

1. Translate.

נְשֵׁי דָוִד David's wives

בְּנֵי אִישׁ sons of a man

מַטּוֹת הָעָם the tribes of the nation

אַרְצוֹת הַמֶּלֶךְ the lands of the king

אַנְשֵׁי עַם men of a nation

כְּאַנְשֵׁי יִשְׂרָאֵל like the men of Israel

בְּאָהֳלֵי הַמַּחֲנֶה in the tents of the camp

כְּאִישׁ מִלְחָמָה like a man of war

חַרְבוֹת יִשְׂרָאֵל the swords of Israel

כְּקוֹל הַשֹּׁפֵט like the voice of the judge

לְאַרְצוֹת הָעָם to the lands of the people/nation

בִּקְהַל הַמְּלָכִים in the assembly of the kings

בְּנוֹת הָאָרֶץ the daughters of the land

לְהָרֵי הַמִּדְבָּר to the mountains of the desert

כִּשְׂדֵי דָוִד like the fields of David

בְּמַחֲנֵה יִשְׂרָאֵל in the camp of Israel

2. Translate into Hebrew.

כְּאָב מִשְׁפָּחָה like a father of a family

בְּאֹהֶל יַעֲקֹב in the tent of Jacob

22.4 THURSDAY

Translate.

אַנְשֵׁי הָעָם הַטּוֹבִים the good men of the nation

חָכְמָה הַנָּשִׁים the wisdom of the women

כְּחֶסֶד אִמִּי like my mother's steadfast love

כֹּהֲנִים הַקָּהָל הַקְּדוֹשִׁים the holy priests of the assembly

כְּאַנְשֵׁי הַמִּשְׁפָּחָה הַזְּקֵנִים like the old men of the family

שְׂדֵי דָוִד הָרַבִּים the abundant fields of David

בְּעָרֵי הָאָרֶץ הָרָעוֹת in the evil cities of the land

אָהֳלֵי הַמַּחֲנֶה הָרַבִּים the many tents of the camp

אֲחֵי מִשְׁפָּחָה רָעִים bad brothers of a family

לִפְנֵי שֹׁפְתִים יִשְׂרָאֵל הַחֲכָמִים before the wise judges of Israel

עַמִּים הַמִּדְבָּר הַגְּדוֹלִים the great nations of the desert

עִם אַנְשֵׁי הָעִיר הָרָעִים with the bad man of the city

מִשְׁפָּחָה כֹּהֲנִים קְדוֹשִׁים a family of holy priests

לְמַחֲנֵה הָעָם to the camp of the nation

כְּקוֹל הָאָחוֹת הַטֹּבָה like the voice of the good daughter

תּוֹרַת יִשְׂרָאֵל הַקְּדוֹשָׁה the holy Torah/teaching/law/instruction of Israel

שְׁלוֹם הֶהָרִים הָרַב the abundant peace of the mountains

22.5 FRIDAY

Translate from Scripture.

Students should compare their answers with one or more Bible translations.

וַיִּשְׂמְחוּ (rejoiced) כָּל (all) קְהַל יְהוּדָה (Judah) וְהַכֹּהֲנִים וְהַלְוִיִּם (and the Levites)
וְכָל (and all) הַקָּהָל הַבָּאִים (the ones who came) מִיִּשְׂרָאֵל וְהַגֵּרִים
הַבָּאִים (the ones who came) מֵאֶרֶץ יִשְׂרָאֵל

2 Chronicles 30:25

all the assembly of Judah rejoiced, and the priests and the Levites, and all the assembly of those who came from Israel, and the sojourners who came from the land of Israel

אֵלֶּה מִשְׁפְּחֹת לֵוִי (Levi)

Numbers 26:58

These are the families of Levi

וַיַּכֵּר (recognized) שָׁאוּל (proper name: figure it out) אֶת־קוֹל דָּוִד וַיֹּאמֶר (and said)
הֲקוֹלְךָ (Is your voice?) זֶה בְּנִי דָוִד וַיֹּאמֶר (and said) דָּוִד קוֹלִי אֲדֹנִי (my lord) הַמֶּלֶךְ

1 Samuel 26:17

Saul recognized the voice of David and said, "Is this your voice, David, my son?" And David said, "It is my voice, my lord the king."

וַיִּשְׁתַּחוּ (bowed) אַבְרָהָם (proper name: figure it out) לִפְנֵי עַם הָאָרֶץ

Genesis 23:12

Abraham bowed before the people of the land.

וַיֹּאמֶר (and said) אֶל־עַמּוֹ הִנֵּה (behold) עַם בְּנֵי יִשְׂרָאֵל רַב וְעָצוּם (mighty) מִמֶּנּוּ

Exodus 1:9

And said to his people, "Behold! The people of the sons of Israel are much mightier than we."

כִּי יְהוָה (the LORD) אֱלֹהֶיךָ (your God) מִתְהַלֵּךְ (walks: notice the root letters) בְּקֶרֶב
מַחֲנֶךָ... וְהָיָה (will be) מַחֲנֶיךָ קָדוֹשׁ

Deuteronomy 23:14

Because the LORD your God walks in the midst of your camp...your camp will be holy.

וְהָאָדָם (and the man) יָדַע אֶת־חַוָּה (proper name: figure it out) אִשְׁתּוֹ

Genesis 4:1

And the man knew Eve his wife.

כִּי אִם־יִהְיֶה (will be) עַמְּךָ יִשְׂרָאֵל כְּחוֹל (like the sand of) הַיָּם

Isaiah 10:22

because if your people Israel will be like the sand of the sea

וְעוֹד (furthermore) רָאִיתִי (I have seen) תַּחַת הַשָּׁמֶשׁ מְקוֹם (place) הַמִּשְׁפָּט
שָׁמָּה (ignore the final letter for now) הָרֶשַׁע (the evil) וּמְקוֹם הַצֶּדֶק (figure it out?)
שָׁמָּה (again, ignore the final letter for now) הָרָשַׁע (the evil)

Ecclesiastes 3:16

Furthermore, I have seen under the sun that in the place of justice there was evil, and in the place of righteousness there was evil.

REVIEW

CHAPTER TWENTY-THREE

23.1 MONDAY

Use this week's exercises for review and testing. Pick up one or two of the resources suggested in the textbook at your library.

Examine and read fluently 1 Samuel 16:13.

וַיִּקַּח שְׁמוּאֵל אֶת־קֶרֶן הַשֶּׁמֶן וַיִּמְשַׁח אֹתוֹ בְּקֶרֶב אֶחָיו וַתִּצְלַח רוּחַ־יְהוָה אֶל־דָּוִד מֵהַיּוֹם הַהוּא וָמָעְלָה וַיָּקָם שְׁמוּאֵל וַיֵּלֶךְ הָרָמָתָה׃

took (familiar root in unfamiliar conjugation)	וַיִּקַּח
proper name: figure it out Samuel	שְׁמוּאֵל
(direct object marker)	אֶת־
horn	קֶרֶן
the oil	הַשֶּׁמֶן
and anointed	וַיִּמְשַׁח
him	אֹתוֹ
in the midst of	בְּקֶרֶב
his brothers	אֶחָיו

and brought success	וַתִּצְלַח
the Spirit of	רוּחַ־
the LORD	יְהוָה
to	אֶל־
David	דָּוִד
day = יוֹם from the day	מֵהַיּוֹם
that ("from that day")	הַהוּא
and going forward	וָמָעְלָה
and arose	וַיָּקָם
same proper name as before	שְׁמוּאֵל
and went	וַיֵּלֶךְ
to Ramah	הָרָמָתָה׃

23.2 TUESDAY

Translate.

אָז then

סָרוּ הֵם They turned aside.

בְּרַחֲמִים in compassion

אָהֳלֵי יִשְׂרָאֵל the tents of Israel

יָדַע הוּא He knew.

אִם if

שָׁפַטְתָּ אַתָּה You judged.

כְבוֹדִי my honor

עָלִיתִי אֲנִי I went up.

מַטּוֹת הָעָם the tribes of the people/nation

אוֹ or

הוּא לָקַח He took.

כְּחָכְמַת דָוִד like the wisdom of David

בַּמִּזְבֵּחַ on the altar

מִשְׁפְּחוֹת הָאָרֶץ הַטּוֹבוֹת the good families of the land

בָּתֵּי מֶלֶךְ גְּדוֹלִים great houses of a king

כִּי יָרַדְתָּ אַתָּה because you went down

בֶּאֱמֶת in truth

עָנָה הוּא He answered.

23.3 WEDNESDAY

Translate.

תּוֹרָתִי my teaching/law/instruction

לְמַעַן בָּנָיו for the sake of his sons

יָרַד אָבִיו His father went down.

לָקַחְתָּ אַתָּה אֵת הַלֶּחֶם You took the bread/food.

בְּחֵן בְּחֶסֶד וּבְרַחֲמִים in grace, in steadfast love, and in compassion

עָבַד בֶּאֱמֶת הוּא He worshipped/served/worked in truth/faithfulness.

בְּאָהֳלֵי הַמֶּלֶךְ הַגְּדוֹלִים in the big tents of the king

עַם קָדוֹשׁ a holy nation/people

בְּתוֹךְ אֲנָשִׁים יִשְׂרָאֵל הַחֲכָמִים in the midst of the wise men of Israel

לֹא פָּתַח הוּא he/it did not open

תּוֹרָתוֹ אֱמֶת His Torah/law/teaching/instruction is true.

מִנְחָה קְדוֹשָׁה בַּמִּזְבֵּחַ a holy offering on the altar

מַטּוֹת יִשְׂרָאֵל the tribes of Israel

אֲנָשִׁים שָׁלוֹם men of peace

צִדְקָתוֹ his righteousness

אַךְ but

אֲחֹתִי יָרְדָה אֶל הָעִיר My sister went down to the city.

מִשְׁפָּטָיו his judgements/justice

עָנָה הוּא קוֹלִי He answered my voice.

הוּא עָשָׂה צְדָקָה He did righteousness/justice.

23.4 THURSDAY

1. What do you suppose *field of fields* would mean?

the best field

2. List and describe three Bible translation methods.

1. essentially literal/word-for-word/formal equivalence: a translation style that aims to express meaning in words and syntax as consistent and close to the original as possible

2. thought-for-thought/dynamic equivalence: a translation style that aims to express original meaning without adherence to original words and syntax

3. paraphrase: a translation style that aims to express original meaning without adherence to original words and syntax, perhaps very freely and with deliberate adaptations of idiom and metaphor, especially to convey ideas into a very different time and culture or to express a certain style

3. Why is Bible translation so difficult?

Possible answers include, but are not limited to: Vocabularies of different languages do not correspond. There is not always a good English word for a Hebrew word. Translation words might carry multiple meanings that the original did not have. Literary devices like rhyme and wordplay are usually untranslatable. No translation can convey everything, so translators must choose words based on priorities. Literal does not necessarily mean accurate. A translation that tries to remain faithful to original words and syntax may lose the style and impact of the original. The Bible is even more difficult to translate than other books because of the reverence due the words of God and the life-and-death import of the words. That importance also means that translators have more invested in their own interpretation than translators of other documents; there can be bias transmitted with a translation and there is quite an incentive to do so when it comes to the Bible. Most of us are quite removed from the culture and time of the authors, making some context, metaphors, idioms, and words difficult to convey.

4. Define each and give examples as directed:

a. absolute state
   a noun's normal, stand-alone form

b. construct state

the form a noun takes when serving in a construct chain as any but the final noun

c. construct chain (give one Hebrew example)

two or more nouns in a row with only the last in the absolute state which together express possession of the latter by the former

Hebrew examples will vary. Anything that makes sense and is spelled correctly is fine (absolute and construct state spellings are listed together in this text's lexicons).

d. prepositional phrase (give one English and one Hebrew example)

a preposition plus the noun phrase to which it refers

Answers will vary. Here are a few examples:
English: in the woods, with my friend, against the enemy
Hebrew: כְּחָכְמַת דָּוִד, כְּאִישׁ מִלְחָמָה, בִּי

e. possessive pronoun (give two English examples and two Hebrew examples)

a pronoun that shows ownership

Answers will vary. Here are the possibilities:
English: my, mine, your, yours, his, her, hers, its, our, ours, their, theirs
Hebrew: possessive pronoun suffixes are shown in the chart on p. 132 of the textbook

f. makkef

the high "hyphen" in Hebrew

g. definite noun (give two English examples and two Hebrew examples)

a proper noun, one that is identified as belonging to someone, or one with the definite article

Answers will vary. Here are a few examples:
English: George Washington, John's binoculars, the chestnut mare
Hebrew: הַמֶּלֶךְ הַטּוֹב, מַטּוֹת יִשְׂרָאֵל, דָּוִד, צִדְקָתוֹ

5. Translate orally into Hebrew.

- The honor of the sons of Israel כְּבוֹד בְּנֵי יִשְׂרָאֵל
- We stood in the great house of the king. עָמַדְנוּ אֲנַחְנוּ בְּבֵית הַמֶּלֶךְ הַגָּדוֹל
- He worshipped in truth. עָבַד הוּא בֶּאֱמֶת
- There is not a father like his father. אֵין אָב כְּאָבִיו

23.5 FRIDAY

1. Open your Bible and find your own examples of these forms of poetry.

metaphor personification simile	These literary devices are described in 23.5, beginning on page 163 of the textbook. There are myriad suitable answers.

2. Define these literary devices:

a. metonymy

substitution of the name of something for something else to which it is related

b. merism

a standard phrase that expresses completeness by mentioning constituent parts, contrasting components, or listing several synonyms

c. idiom

a phrase that means something besides what the words actually say that everyone understands anyway

d. allusion

an indirect reference

3. Parse this sentence, identifying each word's part(s) of speech and if applicable, its number, gender, and person. Then translate and read aloud.

אָז יָרַדְנוּ אֲנַחְנוּ לַנָּהָר

then: adverb
went down: verb, m. or f., pl., 1st
we: pronoun, m. or f., pl., 1st
to the river: preposition plus definite article plus m., s. noun

Then we went down to the river.

PARTICIPLES I

CHAPTER TWENTY-FOUR

24.1 MONDAY

Question words from this week's vocabulary list (and question words not included in this week's words) appear in Jonah 1:8. The syntax is very unlike English, though. Fill in the word translations and see if you can unravel the meaning.

וַיֹּאמְרוּ אֵלָיו הַגִּידָה־נָּא לָנוּ בַּאֲשֶׁר לְמִי־הָרָעָה הַזֹּאת לָנוּ מַה־מְּלַאכְתְּךָ וּמֵאַיִן תָּבוֹא מָה אַרְצֶךָ וְאֵי־מִזֶּה עַם אָתָּה׃

and they said	וַיֹּאמְרוּ
to him	אֵלָיו
tell	הַגִּידָה־
please	נָּא
to us	לָנוּ
in which	בַּאֲשֶׁר
from who	לְמִי־
(this noun is a feminine version of רָע: same meaning) the evil	הָרָעָה

the this ("this evil")	הַזֹּאת
on us	לָנוּ
what	מַה־
your work	מְלַאכְתְּךָ
and whence	וּמֵאַיִן
you come	תָּבוֹא
what	מָה
your land	אַרְצֶךָ
and where	וְאֵי־
from this	מִזֶּה
people	עַם
you	אָתָּה:

24.2 TUESDAY

1. Identify the participles.

שׁוֹמֵר ✔

יָדַע

עוֹבְדִים ✔

אָמְרוּ

עוֹמֵד ✔

יוֹרֶדֶת ✔

שַׁמְנוּ

הוֹלֵךְ ✔

שָׁפְטוּ

סַרְתָּ

לָקַח

עוֹבֶדֶת ✔

נָשָׂאתִי

עוֹנֶה ✔

אוֹכֵל ✔

מוֹלֵךְ ✔

שׁוֹתִים ✔

יָשַׁב

שׁוֹמְעִים ✔

עָלוּ

עֹשֶׂה ✔

עָבְרָה

פָּתַח

זָכְרוּ

2. Translate.

מִי דָוִד Who is David?

מִי הָאֲנָשִׁים הָאֵלֶּה עִמָּךְ Who are these men with you?

מֶה עָשִׂיתָ What did you do/make?

מַדּוּעַ לֹא־אֲכַלְתֶּם לֶחֶם Why did you not eat bread/food?

לָמָּה עוֹמֵד הוּא Why is he standing?

אַן הֲלַכְתֶּם Where did you walk?

אַיֵּה שָׂרָה אִשְׁתֶּךָ Where is your wife Sarah?

אֵיךְ אָמַרְתָּ אָחִי הוּא How did you say, "He is my brother"?
How could you have said that is he is your brother?

וַאֲשֶׁר בַּמַּיִם מִתַּחַת לָאָרֶץ and which is in the waters from under the earth

24.3 WEDNESDAY

1. Translate this sentence five different and equally legitimate ways: הוּא הוֹלֵךְ

He is walking. He was walking. He soon will be walking. He walks. He continues to walk.

2. Translate. Only one translation per sentence necessary.

Any of the participle translation forms listed in #1 are legitimate.

בּוֹנָה הִיא אֵת בֵּיתָהּ She is building her house.

עוֹמְדִים אַתֶּם בִּשְׂדֵה דָוִד You are standing in David's field.

שׁוֹמְעִים אֲנַחְנוּ קוֹל We are listening to a voice.

הֵם סָרִים They are turning aside.

שׁוֹפֵט אֵת הָעָם הוּא He is judging the people.

הוּא עוֹשֶׂה חֶסֶד עִם אָבִינוּ He is showing steadfast love to our father. (Literally, "He is doing steadfast love with our father.")

הֵנָּה נוֹשְׂאוֹת מַיִם They are carrying water.

אֲנַחְנוּ קוֹרְאִים We are calling.

אוֹכֵל וְשׁוֹתֶה עִם הַמִּשְׁפָּחָה He is eating and drinking with the family.

אַתֶּם עוֹבְרִים You are crossing over.

יוֹשְׁבִים עִם הַגֵּרִים הֵם They are dwelling with the sojourners.

הִיא זוֹכֶרֶת עִיר She is remembering a a city.

דָּוִד שׁוֹמֵר אֵת הָעִיר David is guarding the city.

מוֹלְכִים הַמְּלָכִים הַגְּדוֹלִים The great kings are ruling.

24.4 THURSDAY

1. Translate this phrase six different and equally legitimate ways: אִשָּׁה עוֹמֶדֶת
   Possibilities include:
   A woman/wife is standing.
   A woman/wife was standing.
   A woman/wife soon will be standing.
   A woman/wife stands.
   A woman/wife continues to stand.
   a standing woman/wife
   a woman/wife who stands
   a woman/wife who was standing
   a woman/wife who is standing
   a woman/wife who will be standing
3. Translate.

הַבֵּן הַזּוֹכֵר the remembering son, the son who remembers, the son who was remembering, the son who is remembering, the son who will be remembering

הַנָּשִׁים הַזּוֹכְרוֹת the remembering women, the women who remember, the women who were remembering, the women who are remembering, the women who will be remembering

הַבַּת זֹכֶרֶת the remembering daughter, the daughter who remembers, the daughter who was remembering, the daughter who is remembering, the daughter who will be remembering

הַמְּלָכִים הַזּוֹכְרִים the remembering kings, the kings who remember, the kings who were remembering, the kings who are remembering, the kings who will be remembering

הָעִיר עֹשָׂה עִמְּךָ מִלְחָמָה The city is making war with you. (plus possible variations as in 24.3 exercise #1).

הוּא שׁוֹפֵט בֵּן בְּנֵי יַעֲקֹב וּבֵין בְּנֵי הַמֶּלֶךְ He is judging between the sons of Jacob and the sons of the king.

2. Match the Hebrew phrase to its English translation.

a. the priests who serve	a. הַכֹּהֲנִים הָעוֹבְדִים
b. a walking family	h. נַעַר יוֹשֵׁב
c. the standing son	e. הַנָּשִׁים הָעוֹבְרוֹת
d. listening men	b. מִשְׁפָּחָה הוֹלְכִים
e. the women who are crossing over	g. הַמֶּלֶךְ הַשּׁוֹפֵט
f. the servants who are eating.	c. הַבֵּן הָעוֹמֵד
g. the king who judges	d. אֲנָשִׁים שׁוֹמְעִים
h. a seated young man	f. הָעֲבָדִים הָאֹכְלִים

24.5 FRIDAY

1. Define and give an English example of each.

a. consonance

poetic repetition of consonant sounds

Answers will vary; here are some examples: "lily-livered poltroon" (Shakespeare), "Do not go gentle into that good night" (Dylan Thomas), "buzzing bees"

b. alliteration

poetic repetition of beginning sounds in adjacent or related words

Answers will vary; here are some examples: "Peter Piper picked a peck of pickled peppers," "world wide web"

c. onomatopoeia

formation of a word from a sound associated with what is named

Answers will vary; here are some examples: crash, whir, jingle, clank, pop

d. assonance

poetic repetition of vowel sounds

Answers will vary; here are some examples: "light a fire," "ill winds of winter," "blue moon"

2. Translate from Scripture.

Quite literal, basic translations are given here. Students should compare their answers with at least one Bible translation.

מִי־יֹאמַר (will say: familiar root, different tense) אֵלָיו
מַה־תַּעֲשֶׂה (will you do: familiar root, different tense)

Job 9:12

Who will say to Him, "What will you do?"

אַיֵּה הָאֲנָשִׁים אֲשֶׁר־בָּאוּ (came) אֵלֶיךָ

Genesis 19:5

Where are the men who came to you?

עֹשֶׂה שָׁלוֹם

Isaiah 45:7[1]

making peace

---

[1] Remember Song #6 on the *Traditional Hebrew Songs* CD?

אֲנִי יְהוָה (the LORD) עֹשֶׂה חֶסֶד מִשְׁפָּט וּצְדָקָה בָּאָרֶץ

Jeremiah 9:24

I am the LORD, doing steadfast love, justice, and righteousness in the land.

כִּי עָשִׂיתָ זֹּאת אָרוּר (cursed) אַתָּה

Genesis 3:14

because you did this, you are cursed

פֶּן־יֵשׁ בָּכֶם אִישׁ אוֹ־אִשָּׁה אוֹ מִשְׁפָּחָה אוֹ־שֵׁבֶט (tribe) אֲשֶׁר לְבָבוֹ (his heart)
פֹנֶה (is turning: you can recognize a participle without knowing the root) הַיּוֹם (today)
מֵעִם יְהוָה (the LORD)

Deuteronomy 29:18

lest there be in you a man or a woman or a family or a tribe which in his heart is turning today from being with the LORD

מֶה קוֹל הַתְּרוּעָה (shout) הַגְּדוֹלָה הַזֹּאת בְּמַחֲנֵה הָעִבְרִים (the Hebrews)
וַיֵּדְעוּ (knew: familiar root, different tense) כִּי אֲרוֹן יְהוָה (the LORD) בָּא (had come) אֶל־הַמַּחֲנֶה

1 Samuel 4:6

What is this big voice of a shout in the Hebrew camp? And they knew that the Ark of the LORD had come to the camp

PARTICIPLES II

CHAPTER TWENTY-FIVE

25.1 MONDAY

Neither of the verbs in this week's vocabulary words are perfectly regular because pronouncing their root letters according to the pattern would not work well. The alef at the end of *sin* cannot take a sheva. A nun at a root's end, as in *give*, often drops out. Nevertheless, notice that the conjugation endings remain recognizable. Read through the conjugations of *give* and *sin*.

plural	singular	GIVE
נָתַנּוּ	נָתַתִּי	first person
נְתַתֶּם	נָתַתָּ	second person, m.
נְתַתֶּן	נָתַתְּ	second person, f.
נָתְנוּ	נָתַן	third person, m.
נָתְנוּ	נָתְנָה	third person, f.

plural	singular	SIN
חָטָאנוּ	חָטָאתִי	**first person**
חֲטָאתֶם	חָטָאתָ	**second person, m.**
חֲטָאתֶן	not used in Scripture	**second person, f.**
חָטְאוּ	חָטָא	**third person, m.**
חָטְאוּ	חָטְאָה	**third person, f.**

The וֹ in *commandments* and in *guilt* is pronounced *vo* as in *vogue*.

This week, work on reading 2 Chronicles 6:15. You can translate most of it. Notice there is a verb that means to speak with the same root letters as "word." As with חֵטְא and חטא, learning one Hebrew word allows you to figure out many.

אֲשֶׁר שָׁמַרְתָּ לְעַבְדְּךָ דָּוִיד אָבִי אֵת אֲשֶׁר־דִּבַּרְתָּ לוֹ וַתְּדַבֵּר בְּפִיךָ וּבְיָדְךָ מִלֵּאתָ כַּיּוֹם הַזֶּה׃

which	אֲשֶׁר
you guarded	שָׁמַרְתָּ
to your servant	לְעַבְדְּךָ
David	דָּוִיד
my father	אָבִי
(direct object marker)	אֵת
which	אֲשֶׁר־
your word	דִּבַּרְתָּ

to him	לוֹ
you spoke	וַתְּדַבֵּר
with your mouth	בְּפִיךָ
and with your hand	וּבְיָדְךָ
you filled	מִלֵּאתָ
like the day	כַּיּוֹם
the this ("this day")	הַזֶּה׃

25.2 TUESDAY

1. Match Hebrew phrases with English translations.

a. the ones who know	c. מוֹלֵךְ עָם
b. a knowing one	i. עוֹנֶה
c. one who rules a nation	d. שֹׁמְרֶךָ
d. your guardian	f. הַנֹּתֵן מַיִם
e. one who loves steadfastly	a. הַיֹּדְעִים
f. the one who gives water	h. הַשּׁוֹמֵעַ
g. peacemakers	m. עֹשֵׂנִי
h. the one who listens	j. שֹׁפְטֵי יִשְׂרָאֵל
i. one who answers	g. עֹשִׂים שָׁלוֹם
j. the judges of Israel	b. יוֹדֵעַ
k. givers of bread	n. הַחֹטֵאת
l. the guardians of the place	e. עֹשֶׂה חֶסֶד
m. my maker	k. נוֹתְנוֹת לֶחֶם
n. the sinner	l. שׁוֹמְרֵי הַמָּקוֹם

2. Translate.

הוֹלְכִים בַּדֶּרֶךְ   the ones who are walking on the way/road

שׁוֹמֵר הַמִּצְוָה   the one who guards the commandment

הָעֹמֵד לְפָנֶיךָ   the one who is standing before you

הַמַּטֶּה הַמּוֹלֵךְ   the ruling tribe

יֹשְׁבֵי הָעִיר   residents of the city

25.3 WEDNESDAY

1. Translate.

הַתּוֹרָה נָתוּן לְיִשְׂרָאֵל   The Torah/law/teaching/instruction was given to Israel.

עָשׂוּי שֶׁמֶן   It is made of oil.

הָאֹהֶל פָּתוּחַ   The tent is/was/will be opened.

הָאָרֶץ הַזֹּאת נָתוּן לָנוּ   This land was given to us.

הָאָרֶץ אֲשֶׁר נָתוּנ טוֹבָה   The land that was given is good.

הַמִּצְוָה נָתוּן לָנוּ וְלִבְנֵינוּ   The commandment was given to us and to our sons/ children.

הַדָּבָר הֶעָשׂוּי   the thing that was made

2. To decline a noun, pronoun, or adjective is to list its various forms according to person, gender, and number. Decline the following in Hebrew.

example: holy: קָדוֹשׁ קְדוֹשָׁה קְדוֹשִׁים קְדוֹשׁוֹת

house   בַּיִת, בָּתִּים

place   מָקוֹם, מְקוֹמוֹת

good טוֹב, טוֹבָה, טוֹבִים, טוֹבוֹת

little קָטָן, קְטַנָּה, קְטַנִּים, קְטַנּוֹת

3. Translate.

הַמֶּלֶךְ הַמּוֹלֵךְ חָכָם מְאֹד The ruling king is very wise.

חָכָם הַמֶּלֶךְ הַמּוֹלֵךְ מְאֹד The ruling king is very wise.

הַדָּבָר הַזֶּה קָדוֹשׁ מְאֹד This thing/word is very holy.

טוֹבָה הָאֲדָמָה הַזֹּאת מְאֹד This ground is very good.

25.4 THURSDAY

Translate.

הָאֲנָשִׁים עֹשִׂים שָׁלוֹם The men/people are making peace.

הָאֲנָשִׁים הָעֹשִׂים שָׁלוֹם זָכְרוּ אֵת בְּנֵיהֶם The peacemaking men/people remembered their sons/children.

הָעֹשִׂים שָׁלוֹם זָכְרוּ The peacemakers remembered.

הָעֹשִׂים שָׁלוֹם יָשְׁבוּ בַּמִּדְבָּר The peacemakers dwelt in the desert.

עָשׂוּי שָׁלוֹם Peace was made.

הַמַּטֶּה הַמּוֹלֵךְ הָלַךְ בַּדֶּרֶךְ The ruling tribe walked on the road.

שֹׁפְטֵי יִשְׂרָאֵל חֲכָמִים מְאֹד The judges of Israel are very wise.

הַחֹטֵאת כְּסִיל The one who is sinning is a fool.

אַן הַנֹּתֵן Where is the giving one?

מִי הַזּוֹכֵר Who is the one who remembers?

נַעַר נוֹתֵן נָשָׂא לֶחֶם לָעָם A giving young man carried bread/food to the people.

אֵין עוֹנֶה There is no one who answers.

הִיא עֹשָׂה חֶסֶד She is showing steadfast love.

אֲנַחְנוּ עוֹלִים לְמַחֲנֵה יִשְׂרָאֵל We are going up to the camp of Israel.

דָּוִד יוֹדֵעַ כִּי אַתָּה חָטָאתָ David knows that you sinned.

הַנָּשִׁים עוֹבְרוֹת אֶל הָאָרֶץ The women are crossing over to the land.

יֵשׁ שׁוֹמֵעַ There is one who hears.

הוּא נֹתֵן לֶחֶם לִבְנֵי שָׂרָה He is giving bread/food to Sarah's sons/children.

לוֹקֵחַ הוּא שֶׁמֶן וְיַיִן He is taking oil and wine.

25.5 FRIDAY

Translate from Scripture:

Have students compare their answers with Bible translations. These answers are sometimes excessively literal to make understanding and checking answers easier.

It would be instructive to vary translation goals: for instance, to translate as literally as possible one week, but for the next week's exercises to write paraphrases with excellent English vocabulary and style.

הָאָרֶץ אֲשֶׁר־נָתַן לָהֶם יְהוָה (the LORD)

Numbers 32:7

the land which the LORD gave to them

וְאַתָּה נָשָׂאתָ עֲוֹן חַטָּאתִי

Psalm 32:5

And you carried the guilt of my sin.

וְרוּחַ הַקָּדִים (east) נָשָׂא אֶת־הָאַרְבֶּה (the locusts)

Exodus 10:13

And the east wind carried the locusts.

וַיָּבִאוּ (and they brought) הַכֹּהֲנִים אֶת־אֲרוֹן בְּרִית־יְהוָה (of the covenant of the LORD)
אֶל־מְקוֹמוֹ אֶל־דְּבִיר (the inner sanctuary) הַבַּיִת אֶל־קֹדֶשׁ הַקֳּדָשִׁים

1 Kings 8:6

And the priests brought the ark of the covenant of the LORD to his sanctuary, to the inner sanctuary of the house, to the Holy of Holies.

שִׁמְרוּ מְאֹד לַעֲשׂוֹת (to do: preposition plus infinitive form of do/make) אֶת־הַמִּצְוָה וְאֶת־
הַתּוֹרָה אֲשֶׁר צִוָּה (commanded) אֶתְכֶם מֹשֶׁה עֶבֶד־יְהוָה... (the LORD)

Joshua 22:5

Guard very [well] to do the commandment and the teaching/law which Moses, the servant of the LORD, commanded you.

הָאָרֶץ אֲשֶׁר־אֲנִי נֹתֵן לִבְנֵי יִשְׂרָאֵל

Deuteronomy 32:52

the land which I gave to the sons/children of Israel

וַיֹּאמֶר (said) מֹשֶׁה אֶל־הָעָם אַתֶּם חֲטָאתֶם חֲטָאָה (a feminine noun version of this root)
גְדֹלָה וְעַתָּה (and now) אֶעֱלֶה (I will go up: different tense, same root) אֶל־יְהוָה (the LORD)

Exodus 32:30

Moses said to the people, "You sinned a great sin, and now I will go up to the LORD."

עֹשֶׂה שָׁלוֹם וּבוֹרֵא (creating) רָע אֲנִי יְהוָה (the LORD) עֹשֶׂה כָל־ (all) אֵלֶּה

Isaiah 45:7

Making peace and creating bad/evil/calamity, I am the LORD, making all these.

וְהַמַּיִם גָּבְרוּ (prevailed) מְאֹד מְאֹד עַל־הָאָרֶץ וַיְכֻסּוּ (and were covered) כָּל־ (all) הֶהָרִים
הַגְּבֹהִים (high) אֲשֶׁר־תַּחַת כָּל־הַשָּׁמָיִם

Genesis 7:19

And the water prevailed very, very [much] on the land. And all the high mountains which were under the sky were covered.

וְלֹא־נָשָׂא אֹתָם הָאָרֶץ

Genesis 13:6

the land did not carry them

וְהוּא חֵטְא־רַבִּים נָשָׂא

Isaiah 53:12

and he carried the sin of many

פֹּקֵד (visiting: you may not know the root, but you can recognize a participle) עֲוֺן אָבוֹת עַל־בָּנִים וְעַל־בְּנֵי בָנִים

Exodus 34:7

visiting the guilt of fathers on sons/children and on sons' sons/children's children

וְאַרְבֶּה (I will multiply) אוֹתְךָ בִּמְאֹד מְאֹד

Genesis 17:2

I will multiply you very, very [much].

IDIOMS

CHAPTER TWENTY-SIX

26.1 MONDAY

Memorize new vocabulary and practice old vocabulary words today.

All is spelled with cholem or kametz. When it is spelled with a kametz and directly followed by a makkef, it is pronounced *coal*. See Appendix B in the textbook for more on the pronunciation of kametz.

Many of this week's vocabulary words appear in Genesis 13:15.

כִּי אֶת־כָּל־הָאָרֶץ אֲשֶׁר־אַתָּה רֹאֶה לְךָ אֶתְּנֶנָּה וּלְזַרְעֲךָ עַד־עוֹלָם׃

because	כִּי
(direct object marker)	אֶת־
all	כָּל־
the land	הָאָרֶץ
which	אֲשֶׁר־
you	אַתָּה
are seeing	רֹאֶה
to you	לְךָ

I will give it	אֶתְּנֶנָּה
and to your seed	וּלְזַרְעֲךָ
until	עַד־
eternity	עוֹלָם׃

26.2 TUESDAY

Translate from Scripture.

וְלֹא שָׁמָעְנוּ עַל־כֵּן בָּאָה (came) אֵלֵינוּ הַצָּרָה (distress) הַזֹּאת

Genesis 42:21

We did not listen. Therefore this distress came upon us.

וַיַּרְא (and saw) אֱלֹהִים (God) אֶת־כָּל־אֲשֶׁר עָשָׂה וְהִנֵּה־טוֹב מְאֹד

Genesis 1:31

And God saw all which He made, and wow!, it was very good.

כִּי־הִנְנִי בוֹרֵא (creating) שָׁמַיִם חֲדָשִׁים וָאָרֶץ חֲדָשָׁה

Isaiah 65:17

because here I am creating new heavens and a new earth

הִנֵּה אִשְׁתְּךָ

Genesis 12:19

Literal style: Behold, your wife/Here is your woman.
Paraphrase style: Tah-dah! I present to you your wife.

וְשָׁבוּ דְמֵיהֶם בְּרֹאשׁ יוֹאָב וּבְרֹאשׁ

(shall return their blood on the head of Joab and on the head of)

זַרְעוֹ לְעֹלָם וּלְדָוִד וּלְזַרְעוֹ וּלְבֵיתוֹ וּלְכִסְאוֹ (and to his throne) יִהְיֶה (will be) שָׁלוֹם עַד־
עוֹלָם מֵעִם יְהוָה

1 Kings 2:33

Their blood shall return on the head of Joab and on the head of his descendants forever. And to David and to his descendants and to his house and to his throne will be peace until eternity from the LORD.

עַל־כֵּן עַמִּים יְהוֹדֻךָ (will praise you) לְעֹלָם וָעֶד

Psalm 45:17

Therefore the people of Judah will praise you forever and ever.

עָמְדוּ כָל־הָעָם

Nehemiah 8:5

All the people/nation stood.

וְהִקְרִיב (shall offer) הַכֹּהֵן אֶת־הַכֹּל

Leviticus 1:13

the priests shall offer everything/the whole thing

26.3 WEDNESDAY

Translate.

הַדֶּרֶךְ הַהוּא דֶּרֶךְ טוֹב That way/road is a good way/road.

שָׁמַר הוּא הַבַּיִת הַהוּא He guarded that house.

שׁוֹפְטִים הֵם אֵת הָאֲנָשִׁים הָהֵם They are judging those men.

אַתָּה נָשָׂאתָ אֵת הַמָּגֵן הַהוּא You carried that shield.

הַיַּיִן הַהוּא יֵינִי That wine is my wine.

שׁוֹפֵט הוּא בֵּין הָאִישׁ הַזֶּה וּבֵין הָאִישׁ הַהוּא He is judging between this man and that man.

עָבַדְתִּי אֲנִי הַמִּשְׁפָּחָה הַהִיא I served that family.

בָּעִיר הַהִיא יֵשׁ לֶחֶם In that city there is bread/food.

אֵין רָעָב בָּאָרֶץ הַהִיא There is not a famine in that land.

לֹא יוֹדְעִים אֱמֶת הַכְּסִילִים הָרָעִים הָהֵם Those wicked fools do not know truth.

בַּמַּחֲנֶה הַהוּא יֵשׁ מַיִם רַב In that camp there is abundant water.

אַיֵּה הָעֶבֶד הַהוּא Where is that servant?

26.4 THURSDAY

Translate.

הִנָּם פֹּה Behold, they are here!

אֵינֶנָּה אִמָּם She is not their mother.

הוּא אֵינֶנּוּ נוֹתֵן לֶחֶם He is not giving bread/food.

אֵינֶנּוּ עַבְדֵיכֶם We are not your servants.

כֻּלָּנוּ עֹשִׂים שָׁלוֹם All of us are making peace.

נָתַתִּי אֶת־כֻּלָּם לַכֹּהֵן I gave all of them to the priest.

כֻּלָּנוּ אֲנָשִׁים טוֹבִים All of us are good men.

הִנֵּנוּ Here we are.

נוֹתֵן הוּא הַשָּׂדֶה הַזֶּה כֻּלּוֹ He is giving all of this field.

אֵינֶנִּי אָב I am not a father.

הִנְנִי עוֹמֵד עִמְּךָ Here I am standing with you.

יָשַׁב הוּא בַּמָּקוֹם הַזֶּה He is dwelling in this place.

בַּמַּחֲנֶה כֻּלָּם All of them are in the camp.

רָחֵל אֵינֶנָּה אִשְׁתְּךָ Rachel is not your wife.

שָׁמַר אֵת הָאָרֶץ כֻּלָּהּ He guarded all of the land.

26.5 FRIDAY

1. Define acrostic.

In an acrostic poem, the first letter of a recurring feature, such as a line or paragraph, comes in alphabetical order or spells out a word.

2. Translate into Hebrew.

Here is my son. הִנֵּה בְּנִי

He gave us that good bread. הוּא נָתַן לָנוּ הַלֶּחֶם הַטּוֹב הַהוּא

The king is the one who makes peace. הַמֶּלֶךְ הָעֹשֶׂה שָׁלוֹם

There is no people like Israel. אֵין עָם כְּיִשְׂרָאֵל

3. Translate from Scripture. Then compare with a Bible translation or two.

וְהִנֵּה אָנֹכִי הוֹלֵךְ הַיּוֹם (today) בְּדֶרֶךְ כָּל־הָאָרֶץ

Joshua 23:14

And behold, I am walking today in the way of all the earth.

וַיְכֻלּוּ (And were completed) הַשָּׁמַיִם וְהָאָרֶץ וְכָל־צְבָאָם

Genesis 2:1

And the heavens and the earth were completed and all their armies.

וַיַּעֲבֹר (crossed over: familiar root letters*) אַבְרָם (proper name) בָּאָרֶץ עַד מְקוֹם
שְׁכֶם (proper name) עַד אֵלוֹן (oak) מוֹרֶה (proper name) וְהַכְּנַעֲנִי (and the Canaanite)
אָז בָּאָרֶץ

Genesis 12:6

Abram crossed over in the land until the place of Shechem, until the oak of Moreh, and the Canaanite was then in the land.

* If you are very observant and curious, you may have noticed this is not the perfect tense and yet the translation is "crossed over." If you want, I will let you in early on an amazing feature of Biblical Hebrew: the vav prefix can change verb tense. יַעֲבֹר by itself could be translated "will cross over," but the vav prefix knocks it into the perfect tense, and so this word is translated "crossed over." Now if you are especially curious and clever, you might ask, "Why not just use the perfect tense?" That is because the vav prefix also works simultaneously as a conjunction, connecting related phrases of a narrative. We will get back to this in Chapter 40.

IMPERFECT TENSE

CHAPTER TWENTY-SEVEN

27.1 MONDAY

This week's words concern time. Work on them and Genesis 1:5 today. Because of the segol in the final syllable, stress is on the first syllable in *morning*, *evening*, and *month*.

וַיִּקְרָא אֱלֹהִים לָאוֹר יוֹם וְלַחֹשֶׁךְ קָרָא לָיְלָה וַיְהִי־עֶרֶב וַיְהִי־בֹקֶר יוֹם אֶחָד׃

and called	וַיִּקְרָא
God	אֱלֹהִים
the light	לָאוֹר
day	יוֹם
and the darkness	וְלַחֹשֶׁךְ
he called	קָרָא
night	לָיְלָה
and it was	וַיְהִי־
evening	עֶרֶב
and it was	וַיְהִי־
morning	בֹקֶר

day	יוֹם
one	אֶחָד׃

27.2 TUESDAY

Translate.

Remember that answer key translations may be literal to the point of poor English for the sake of understanding and checking work. Students should feel free to craft better English sentences and should compare their work with Bible translations.

עַד־הַיּוֹם הַזֶּה

1 Samuel 29:3

until this day

וְהָעֹלָה אֲשֶׁר־יַקְרִב (shall offer) הַנָּשִׂיא (the prince) לַיהוָה (to the LORD) בְּיוֹם הַשַּׁבָּת

Ezekiel 46:4

and the burnt offering which the prince shall offer to the LORD on the Sabbath day

כֵּן יִהְיֶה (it was) תָמִיד

Numbers 9:16

thus it was continually

זֶה־הַיּוֹם עָשָׂה יְהוָה (the LORD)

Psalm 118:24

this is the day the LORD made

וַיֹּאמֶר (said) שָׁאוּל (proper name) לֹא־יוּמַת (will die) אִישׁ בַּיּוֹם הַזֶּה כִּי הַיּוֹם עָשָׂה יְהוָה (the LORD) תְּשׁוּעָה (salvation) בְּיִשְׂרָאֵל

1 Samuel 11:13

Saul said, "Not a man will die on this day because today the LORD did salvation in Israel."

עֵת מִלְחָמָה וְעֵת שָׁלוֹם

Ecclesiastes 3:8

a time of war and a time of peace

וַתֹּאמֶר (said) הָאִשָּׁה אֶל־אֵלִיָּהוּ (proper name) עַתָּה זֶה יָדַעְתִּי כִּי אִישׁ אֱלֹהִים (God) אָתָּה וּדְבַר־יְהוָה (the LORD) בְּפִיךָ (in your mouth) אֱמֶת

1 Kings 17:24
The woman said to Elijah, "Now this I knew: that you are a man of God and the word of the LORD in your mouth is true."

וַיְהִי (and it was) בַבֹּקֶר וְהִנֵּה־הִיא לֵאָה וַיֹּאמֶר (and said) אֶל־לָבָן (proper name) מַה־זֹּאת עָשִׂיתָ לִּי

Genesis 29:25
And it was in the morning and behold, she was Leah! And [he] said to Laban, "What is this you have done to me?"

לֹא־יוֹם וְלֹא־לָיְלָה

Zechariah 14:7
not a day and not a night

מֵעֶרֶב עַד־עֶרֶב

Leviticus 23:32
from evening until evening

27.3 WEDNESDAY

Read aloud and translate verbs.

אֶעֱלֶה I will go up.

נַעֲבֹד We will serve/worship/work.

תִּפְתַּחְנָה You (f., pl.) will open.

יִקְרָא He will call.

יָסוּרוּ They will turn aside.

שָׁפַט He judged.

יָרְאָה She feared.

עָבַדְתָּ You (m., s.) served.

נְשָׂאתֶם You (m., pl.) carried.

קָרָאתִי I called.

אָכַלְנוּ We ate.

שָׁתְתָה You (f., s.) drank.

יְשַׁבְתֶּם You (m., pl.) sat/dwelt.

שָׁמַע He heard.

עָשׂוּ They did/made.

עָמַד He stood.

עָבְרָה She crossed over.

יִשְׁפְּטוּ They will judge.

תִּשְׁמֹר She (or You, m., s.) will guard.

יִזְכְּרוּ They (m., pl.) will remember.

תֹּאמַר She (or You, m., s.) will say.

תִּמְלְכוּ You (m., pl.) will rule.

יִשְׁפֹּט He will judge.

תִּשְׁתֶּה She (or You, m., s.) will drink.

יַעֲמֹד He will stand.

תֵּשֵׁב She (or You, m., s.) will sit/dwell.

נַעֲשֶׂה We will do/make.

אֶעֱבֹר I will cross over.

יֹאכְלוּ They will eat.

תַּעַבְדִי You (f., s.) will serve.

תִּשְׁפֹּט She (or You, m., s.) will judge.

תִּשְׁמַע She (or You, m., s.) will hear.

27.4 THURSDAY

Translate into Hebrew. Verb conjugations are listed in the textbook's Appendix D.

אֶשְׁמֹר May I guard

יִזְכֹּר He will remember

יֹאמַר He might eat

נִשְׁפֹּט We would judge

יַעַמְדוּ May they stand

תִּמְלֹךְ You (m., s.) will rule

אֶקְרָא I usually call

יַעֲלֶה He will go up

תִּתְּנוּ You (m., pl.) will give

נֵרֵד We might go down

אֶקַּח I usually take

יִירָא May he fear

תִּשְׁפֹּט May you judge

תַּעֲשִׂי He will do

27.5 FRIDAY

1. List at least four ways that parallel lines of Hebrew poetry might be related to one another.

The relationship of parallel lines might be restatement with synonyms, a clarification and definition of first line, repetition with some additional information in the second line, opposites, cause and effect, statement and related request, or the first line may be a physical description with an abstract application in the parallel line.

2. Find three other examples of parallelism in your Bible. Proverbs is a good place to look. Identify the relationship between the lines.

Answers will vary. Any pairs of lines that express one of the relationships above are suitable.

3. Parse these sentences, identifying each word's part(s) of speech and if applicable, its number, gender, person, and tense. Then translate.

הַבֵּן דָוִד יַעֲשֶׂה שָׁלוֹם בָּאָרֶץ כֻּלָּהּ וְיִמְלֹךְ הוּא לְעוֹלָם

the son: definite article plus m., s. noun
David: proper noun, m., s.
will make: imperfect tense verb, m., s., 3rd
peace: noun, m., s.
in the land/on the earth: preposition plus definite article plus f., s. noun
all of it: preposition plus pronoun suffix: f., s., 3rd
and will rule: conjunction plus imperfect tense verb: m., s., 3rd
he: pronoun, m., s., 3rd
to eternity: preposition plus m., s. noun

The son of David will make peace in all the land and he will rule forever.

בַּבֹּקֶר יָרְדוּ אֶל הַיָּם בָּעֶרֶב יַעַמְדוּ בָּהָר

in the morning: preposition plus definite article plus m., s. noun

went down: perfect tense verb: m., pl., 3rd

to: preposition

the sea: definite article plus m., s. noun

in the evening: preposition plus definite article plus m., s. noun

will stand: imperfect tense verb: m., pl., 3rd

on the mountain: preposition plus definite article plus m., s. noun

In the morning, they went down to the sea. In the evening, they will stand on the mountain.

REVIEW

CHAPTER TWENTY-EIGHT

28.1 MONDAY

Review week. Today, practice vocabulary words, work on fluently reading aloud Psalm 100:5, and pursue the suggestions from the text for Chapter 28.

כִּי־טוֹב יְהוָה לְעוֹלָם חַסְדּוֹ וְעַד־דֹּר וָדֹר אֱמוּנָת׃

because	כִּי־
good	טוֹב
the LORD	יְהוָה
forever/to eternity	לְעוֹלָם
his steadfast love	חַסְדּוֹ
and until	וְעַד־
generation	דֹּר
and generation	וָדֹר
His faithfulness	אֱמוּנָתוֹ׃

28.2 TUESDAY

In the list of words below,

1. Put a check mark by participles.
2. For the others, distinguish between perfect and imperfect tense.
3. Circle any first person verbs.
4. Translate the first three words in as many legitimate ways as possible.
5. Read and translate the entire list.

נָתַן perfect tense

תַּעֲבֹד imperfect tense

✔ אֲנַחְנוּ (הוֹלְכִים)

תָּסוּרוּ imperfect tense, You will turn aside.

✔ אֲנִי (עוֹלֶה) I am going up.

יַעֲבֹד imperfect tense, He/It will work/serve/worship.

✔ הוּא לוֹקֵחַ He/It is taking.

שָׁפְטָה perfect tense, She judged.

יִזְכְּרוּ imperfect tense, They will remember.

יֵשֵׁב imperfect tense, He/It will sit/dwell.

שָׂמָה perfect tense, She/It put.

✔ נוֹשֵׂא He/It is carrying/lifting.

תִּקְרְאוּ imperfect tense, You will call.

✔ (נֹאכַל) We will eat.

✔ שׁוֹתֶה He/It is drinking.

שָׁמְעָה perfect tense, She/It heard.

4.a. Possible Translations for נָתַן:

He gave. He has given. He did give. He was giving. He had given. It gave. It has given. It did give. It was giving. It had given.

4.b. Possible Translations for תַּעֲבֹד:

You will work/serve/worship. You usually work/serve/worship. You might work/serve/worship. May you work/serve/worship. You would work/serve/worship. She will work/serve/worship. She usually works/serves/worships. She might work/serve/worship. May she work/serve/worship. She would work/serve/worship.

4.c. Possible Translations for אֲנַחְנוּ הוֹלְכִים:

We are walking/going. We were walking/going. We soon will be walking/going. We walk/go. We continue to walk/go. We are walkers. We are ones who walk/go.

Translations for the rest of the list may include the above variations as appropriate to verb form, but the answer key will list only one basic translation.

28.3 WEDNESDAY

1. Translate this phrase in five possible ways: הַמֶּלֶךְ הַנּוֹתֵן

   the giving king, the king who was giving, the king who is giving, the king who gives, the king who will be giving

2. Define and give an example of each. Examples may be Hebrew or English. For *acrostic* and *parallelism*, you may cite a Scriptural example or compose an original in English or Hebrew.

   a. onomatopoeia

      formation of a word from a sound associated with what is named

      Answers will vary. Here are examples: swish, bang, click.

   b. alliteration

      poetic repetition of beginning sounds in adjacent or related words

      Answers will vary. Here are examples: Peter Piper picked a peck of pickled peppers, bouncing baby boy, smooth sailing.

   c. assonance

      poetic repetition of vowel sound(s)

      Answers will vary. Here are examples: "wedding bells," "Old age should burn and rave at close of day" (Dylan Thomas), "lazy days."

   d. idiom

      a phrase that means something besides what the words actually say that everyone understands anyway; or a language's characteristic mode of expression

      Answers will vary. Here are examples: hit the ceiling, stick one's head in the sand, broken-hearted.

e. acrostic
a poetical form in which the first letter of a recurring feature, such as a line or paragraph, comes in alphabetical order or spells out a word

Answers will vary. Here are examples: Lamentations 3; Proverbs 31:10-31; Psalm 119, 9, 10, 25, 34, 37, 112, 145.

f. parallelism
literary structure in which a meaning is stated, then repeated in similar or related form

Answers will vary. Many examples are given in 27.5, pages 198-201 of the textbook, and many more are easy to find in Proverbs.

3. Translate.

מִי הַכֹּהֲנִים הָאֵלֶּה עִמְּךָ Who are these priests with you?

מֶה עָשִׂיתָ What have you done?

מַדּוּעַ לֹא־אֲכַלְתֶּם לֶחֶם Why did you not eat bread/food?

לָמָּה תַּעֲמֹד Why do you stand there?

מָה־אֵלֶּה What are these?

אָן הֲלַכְתֶּם Where did you walk?

אַיֵּה אִשְׁתְּךָ רָחֵל Where is your wife Rachel?

הִנֵּה אִשְׁתְּךָ הִיא וְאֵיךְ אָמַרְתָּ אִמִּי הִיא Hey! She is your wife! How did you say (How could you have said), "She is my mother"?

28.4 THURSDAY

1. Translate into Hebrew. *

עַתָּה הוּא הוֹלֵךְ בַּדֶּרֶךְ Now he is walking in the road.

*Some teachers who use this exercise as an exam will expect students to spell Hebrew from memory; others will allow references for spelling. We have not stressed spelling memorization in the workbook. Students are probably unprepared to spell all of these correctly (particularly the vowel points) unless you have provided additional practice. Even with spelling references, this section tests/reviews grammar and vocabulary knowledge.

הוּא יַעֲשֶׂה שָׁלוֹם בָּאָרֶץ כֻּלָּהּ He will make peace in the land, all of it.

בַּיּוֹם הַהוּא הוּא יִשָּׂא עֲוֹן הָעָם On that day, he will carry the iniquity of the people.

2. Translate into English.

אִם תִּשְׁמְעוּ אֶת הַמִּשְׁפָּטִים הָאֵלֶּה אָז יִתֵּן אֶתְכֶם אֶרֶץ טוֹבָה לְעוֹלָם

(*to give* drops its first root letter in imperfect conjugations; יִתֵּן is the imperfect, masculine, singular, third person form of *to give*)

If you will listen to these judgements, then he will give you a good land forever.

כָּל־הַמִּצְוָה אֲשֶׁר אָנֹכִי אֲצַוְּךָ (I have commanded you) הַיּוֹם תִּשְׁמְרוּ אַתֶּם לְמַעַן בְּנֵיכֶם

All of the commandment which I have commanded you today you shall guard for the sake of your sons/children.

לֹא שָׁמְרוּ חַרְבּוֹ אֲשֶׁר נָתַן אוֹתְךָ בָּהָר

You did not guard his sword which he gave you on the mountain.

אַתֶּם עוֹבְרִים הַיּוֹם אֶת־הַנָּהָר לָבֹא (to go) לָרֶשֶׁת (to dispossess) אֲנָשִׁים גְּדֹלִים מִמְּךָ עִירִים גְּדֹלֹת וּבְצֻרֹת (and fortified) בַּשָּׁמַיִם עַם־גָּדוֹל בְּנֵי הַמֶּלֶךְ הָרָע אֲשֶׁר אַתֶּם יְדַעְתֶּם

Today you are crossing the river to go to dispossess men greater than you and big cities fortified to the sky, a great people, sons of the the evil king which you knew.

מִי יַעֲמֹד לִפְנֵי צְבָא הַמָּקוֹם הַזֶּה

Who will stand before the army of this place?

לֶחֶם לֹא אָכַלְתִּי וּמַיִם לֹא שָׁתִיתִי

I did not eat bread/food or drink water.

28.5 FRIDAY

1. What is chiasmus? Give an example.

Chiasmus is a literary device in which words or ideas are repeated in reverse order in the same or a related form.

Answers will vary. Several examples are given in 28.5, pages 204-208 of the textbook.

Note for exercise #2 below: These verses can be written in better English and students should be encouraged to do so. Answer key translations are quite literal to facilitate understanding and checking work.

2. Translate Scripture.[1]

אַתָּה עָשִׂיתָ עִם־עַבְדְּךָ דָוִד אָבִי חֶסֶד גָּדוֹל כַּאֲשֶׁר הָלַךְ לְפָנֶיךָ בֶּאֱמֶת וּבִצְדָקָה

1 Kings 3:6

You showed to your servant, my father David, great steadfast love as he walked before you in truth/faithfulness and righteousness.

נָתַתָּ לוֹ בֵן יֹשֵׁב עַל־כִּסְאוֹ (his throne) כַּיּוֹם הַזֶּה

1 Kings 3:6

You gave to him a son who sits on his throne as this day.

וְהִנֵּה חֲטָאתֶם לַיהוָה (to the LORD) אֱלֹהֵיכֶם (your God) עֲשִׂיתֶם לָכֶם עֵגֶל (a calf) מַסֵּכָה (cast metal) סַרְתֶּם מַהֵר (quickly) מִן־הַדֶּרֶךְ אֲשֶׁר־צִוָּה (commanded) יְהוָה (the LORD) אֶתְכֶם

Deuteronomy 9:16

And behold, you sinned to the LORD your God. You made for yourselves a cast metal calf. You turned aside quickly from the way which the LORD commanded you.

[1] The forms of a couple words have been changed from how they appear in Scripture to forms you can readily translate. The meanings are the same.

אֶתֵּן לְזַרְעֲךָ אֵת כָּל־הָאֲרָצֹת הָאֵלֶּה

Genesis 26:4

(*to give* drops its first root letter in imperfect conjugations; אֶתֵּן is the imperfect, singular, first person form of *to give*)

I will give to your descendants all these lands.

אֵין־כָּמוֹךָ...בַּשָּׁמַיִם וּבָאָרֶץ שֹׁמֵר הַבְּרִית (the covenant) וְהַחֶסֶד לַעֲבָדֶיךָ הַהֹלְכִים לְפָנֶיךָ בְּכָל־לִבָּם (their heart)

2 Chronicles 6:14

There is none like you...in Heaven and in earth, guarding the covenant and steadfast love to your servants, those who walk before you with all their heart.

VERBS WITH OBJECT PRONOUNS

CHAPTER TWENTY-NINE

29.1 MONDAY

To practice vocabulary, write out conjugations of this week's verbs in the following charts.

Lie down and *send* follow the XXX imperfect tense pattern. See if you can spell their conjugations with only your knowledge of the pattern.

plural	singular	**LIE DOWN perfect**
שָׁכַבְנוּ	שָׁכַבְתִּי	first person
שְׁכַבְתֶּם	שָׁכַבְתָּ	second person, m.
שְׁכַבְתֶּן	שָׁכַבְתְּ	second person, f.
שָׁכְבוּ	שָׁכַב	third person, m.
שָׁכְבוּ	שָׁכְבָה	third person, f.

LIE DOWN imperfect

plural	singular	
נִשְׁכַּב	אֶשְׁכַּב	first person
תִּשְׁכְּבוּ	תִּשְׁכַּב	second person, m.
תִּשְׁכַּבְנָה	תִּשְׁכְּבִי	second person, f.
יִשְׁכְּבוּ	יִשְׁכַּב	third person, m.
תִּשְׁכַּבְנָה	תִּשְׁכַּב	third person, f.

SEND perfect

plural	singular	
שָׁלַחְנוּ	שָׁלַחְתִּי	first person
שְׁלַחְתֶּם	שָׁלַחְתָּ	second person, m.
שְׁלַחְתֶּן	שָׁלַחַתְּ	second person, f.
שָׁלְחוּ	שָׁלַח	third person, m.
שָׁלְחוּ	שָׁלְחָה	third person, f.

plural	singular	**SEND imperfect**
נִשְׁלַח	אֶשְׁלַח	**first person**
תִּשְׁלְחוּ	תִּשְׁלַח	**second person, m.**
תִּשְׁלַחְנָה	תִּשְׁלְחִי	**second person, f.**
יִשְׁלְחוּ	יִשְׁלַח	**third person, m.**
תִּשְׁלַחְנָה	תִּשְׁלַח	**third person, f.**

Alefs in *find* and *gather* complicate things. The ה at the end of בנה falls away in its perfect tense conjugations. For these three verbs, copy from the verb charts in Appendix D of your text in the tense specified.

plural	singular	**FIND perfect**
מָצָאנוּ	מָצָאתִי	**first person**
מְצָאתֶם	מָצָאתָ	**second person, m.**
מְצָאתֶן	מָצָאת	**second person, f.**
מָצְאוּ	מָצָא	**third person, m.**
מָצְאוּ	מָצְאָה	**third person, f.**

plural	singular	**GATHER imperfect**
נֶאֱסֹף	אֶאֱסֹף	**first person**
תַּאַסְפוּ	תֶּאֱסֹף	**second person, m.**
תֶּאֱסֹפְנָה	תַּאַסְפִי	**second person, f.**
יַאַסְפוּ	יֶאֱסֹף	**third person, m.**
תֶּאֱסֹפְנָה	תֶּאֱסֹף	**third person, f.**

plural	singular	**BUILD perfect**
בָּנִינוּ	בָּנִיתִי	**first person**
בְּנִיתֶם	בָּנִיתָ	**second person, m.**
בְּנִיתֶן	בָּנִית	**second person, f.**
בָּנוּ	בָּנָה	**third person, m.**
בָּנוּ	בָּנְתָה	**third person, f.**

Create is used only of God, so you need to be able to recognize only the perfect tense third person masculine singular: בָּרָא, the perfect tense first person: בָּרָאתִי, perfect tense second person masculine: בָּרָאתָ, imperfect tense third person masculine singular: יִבְרָא, and participle: בּוֹרֵא.

Also work on examining and reading aloud Genesis 11:5.

וַיֵּרֶד יְהוָה לִרְאֹת אֶת־הָעִיר וְאֶת־הַמִּגְדָּל אֲשֶׁר בָּנוּ בְּנֵי הָאָדָם׃

and went down*	וַיֵּרֶד
the LORD	יְהוָה
to see	לִרְאֹת
(direct object marker)	אֶת־
the city	הָעִיר
and (plus direct object marker)	וְאֶת־
the tower	הַמִּגְדָּל
which	אֲשֶׁר
built	בָּנוּ
the sons of	בְּנֵי
man	הָאָדָם׃

*if you notice something funny here, refer to the footnote on page 196

29.2 TUESDAY

Translate.

יִשְׁכַּב הוּא He will lie down.

שָׁכְבָה הִיא She lay down.

יִשְׁלְחוּ הֵם They will send.

אָסַפְנוּ אֲנַחְנוּ We gathered.

בָּנִיתִי אֲנִי I built.

בָּרָה הוּא He created.

תִּמְצְאוּ אַתֶּם You will find.

תִּשְׁכַּב אַתָּה You will lie down.

תַּאַסְפִי אַתְּ You will gather.

בּוֹרֵא הוּא He is creating.

יִבְנֶה דָוִד David will build.

אֶשְׁכַּב אֲנִי I will lie down.

שָׁלַחְנוּ אֲנַחְנוּ We sent.

תֶּאֱסֹף הִיא She will gather.

בְּנִיתֶם אַתֶּם You built.

שָׁכַבְתָּ אַתָּה You lay down.

שָׁלוּחַ הוּא He/it is sent.

יַעֲקֹב יִמְצָא Jacob will find.

בָּנְתָה רָחֵל Rachel built.

אַתָּה תִּמְצָא You will find.

אֶשְׁכַּב אֲנִי I will lie down.

יִבְנֶה הוּא He will build.

אָסְפָה שָׂרָה Sarah gathered.

שָׁלַחְתִּי אָנֹכִי I sent.

מָצָאנוּ אֲנַחְנוּ We found.

אַתָּה תִּשְׁמֹר אוֹתָנוּ You heard us.

לֹא יִשְׁמֹר אוֹתִי יַעֲקֹב Jacob did not hear me.

29.3 WEDNESDAY

Translate.

שְׁלָחָם הַמֶּלֶךְ The king sent them.

שָׁלוּחַ הֵם They were sent.

הַמֶּלֶךְ שׁוֹלֵחַ צָבָא The king is sending an army.

הַמֶּלֶךְ שׁוֹלֵחַ אֵת הַנְּבִיאִים The king is sending the prophets.

אָן יִמְצְאוּ חָכְמָה הֵם Where will they find wisdom?

בַּבֹּקֶר אָסַף הוּא אֵת כָּל־הָעָם In the morning, he gathered all the people.

עָלָה הוּא כְּאִישׁ מִלְחָמָה He went up like a man of war.

דָּוִד יִמְצָאֵנְנִי David will find me.

יִשְׁמָרְךָ אָבִי My father will guard you.

יִשְׁלָחֲךָ עִם כָּל־מִשְׁפַּחַת יַעֲקֹב He will send you with all of Jacob's family.

יִשְׁתֵּהוּ הוּא He will drink it.

אֵין יוֹם כְּיוֹם הַשַּׁבָּת There is no day like the Sabbath day.

לֹא נֹאכַל הַיּוֹם We will not eat today.

לָמָּה יִבְנֶה אוֹתוֹ הוּא Why will he build it?

אַתָּה תִּשָּׂא עָוֹן הָעָם You will carry the guilt of the people.

שָׁלַח דָּוִד אֶת־יַעֲקֹב אֶל־רָחֵל David sent Jacob to Rachel.

תִּשָּׂאֵנִי אֶל־רוּחַ You lift me up to the wind.
(Job 30:22)

29.4 THURSDAY

1. Translate.

רֵעַ הָלַךְ אִתָּךְ A neighbor walked with you.

יִבְנֶה הוּא אִתָּךְ He will build with you.

יִבְנוּ הֵם אוֹתוֹ They will build it.

תֵּרֵד אַתָּה אִתָּם You will go down with them.

שׁוֹפְטִים אוֹתוֹ הֵם They are judging him.

לֹא נִירָא אֲנַחְנוּ אוֹתָהּ We will not fear her.

דָוִד יִשְׁמַע אוֹתָנוּ David will hear us.

עָמְדוּ אִתּוֹ הֵמָּה They stood with him.

הָלַכְנוּ אֲנַחְנוּ אִתְּכֶם We walked with you.

שָׂרָה הִיא שָׁמְרָה אֶת־בִּתָּהּ Sarah guarded her daughter.

לֹא שָׁמַר אֹתִי יַעֲקֹב Jacob will not guard me.

מִשְׁפָּחָה יָרְדָה אִתָּהּ A family went down with her.

2. Translate from Scripture. Compare answers with published Bible translations.

וַיָּבֹא (came) נֹחַ (proper name) וּבָנָיו וְאִשְׁתּוֹ וּנְשֵׁי־בָנָיו אִתּוֹ

Genesis 7:7

Noah came and his sons and his wife and his sons' wives with him.

וַאֲנִי הִנְנִי מֵקִים (I establish) אֶת־בְּרִיתִי (my covenant) אִתְּכֶם וְאֶת־זַרְעֲכֶם אַחֲרֵיכֶם

Genesis 9:9

And I, here I am, I establish my covenant with you and with your descendants after you.

29.5 FRIDAY

Translate from Scripture.[1]

יוֹצֵר (forming) אוֹר (light) וּבוֹרֵא חֹשֶׁךְ עֹשֶׂה שָׁלוֹם וּבוֹרֵא רָע אֲנִי יְהוָה (the LORD) עֹשֶׂה
כָל־אֵלֶּה

Isaiah 45:7

Forming light and creating darkness, making peace and creating bad/evil/calamity, I am the LORD who does all these.

כִּי־בָרָא יְהוָה (the LORD) חֲדָשָׁה בָּאָרֶץ

Jeremiah 31:22

because the LORD created something new on the earth

וְאִם רַע בְּעֵינֵיכֶם לַעֲבֹד (to serve: unfamiliar form , but familiar root עבד)
אֶת־יְהוָה (the LORD) בַּחֲרוּ (choose) לָכֶם הַיּוֹם אֶת־מִי תַּעֲבְדוּ אִם אֶת אֱלֹהִים (the gods)
אֲשֶׁר עָבְדוּ אֲבוֹתֵיכֶם אֲשֶׁר מֵעֵבֶר (figure it out? from across) הַנָּהָר וְאִם
אֶת־אֱלֹהֵי (the gods of) הָאֱמֹרִי (the Amorites) אֲשֶׁר אַתֶּם יֹשְׁבִים בְּאַרְצָם וְאָנֹכִי וּבֵיתִי
נַעֲבֹד אֶת־יְהוָה (the LORD)

And if it is bad in your eyes to serve the LORD, choose for yourselves *Joshua 24:15*
today who you will serve: if the gods from across the river which your fathers served and if the gods of the Amorites with whom you are dwelling in their land. But I and my house will serve the LORD.

אָמַר מֹשֶׁה תֹּאכְלוּ הַיּוֹם כִּי־שַׁבָּת הַיּוֹם לַיהוָה (to the LORD) הַיּוֹם לֹא תִמְצְאוּ בַּשָּׂדֶה

Exodus 16:25

Moses said, "You will eat today because today is a Sabbath to the LORD. Today you will not find in the field."

וְאֵדָעֲךָ לְמַעַן אֶמְצָא־חֵן בְּעֵינֶיךָ

Exodus 33:13

And I will know you for the sake of my finding grace in your eyes.

As usual, these translations are basic and overly literal to help with understanding and checking work. Students will learn much by comparing their answers to multiple Bible translations.

---

[1] Slight changes have been made to some words to facilitate your translation.

WEAK LETTERS

CHAPTER THIRTY

30.1 MONDAY

Learn this week's vocabulary words and read Genesis 9:6. You will see in this verse another word for man is אָדָם, hence the name of the fellow in the garden. You may also notice its similarity to the Hebrew word for blood. Both are connected to the idea of redness.

שֹׁפֵךְ דַּם הָאָדָם בָּאָדָם דָּמוֹ יִשָּׁפֵךְ כִּי בְּצֶלֶם אֱלֹהִים עָשָׂה אֶת־הָאָדָם׃

the one who pours out	שֹׁפֵךְ
the blood of	דַּם
man	הָאָדָם
by man	בָּאָדָם
his blood	דָּמוֹ
(figure this out from first word of verse) will	pour out יִשָּׁפֵךְ
because	כִּי
in the image of	בְּצֶלֶם
God	אֱלֹהִים
made	עָשָׂה

(direct object marker)	אֶת־
man	הָאָדָם:

30.2 TUESDAY

1. Which letters are weak letters? ה, ו, י

2. What characterizes weak letters?

They have been skipped over and slurred in speech over the years, resulting in their absence from some verb conjugations where one would normally expect them to be.

3. Which letter is not weak but has often dropped out of words anyway? נ

4. Just for fun, try pronouncing these words with the ancient pronunciation of ו, a *W* sound: מִצְוָה עָוֺן וְדָוִד

5. Translate from (slightly modified) Scripture.[1]

וַיִּשָּׂא עֵינָיו וַיַּרְא (and saw) אֶת־בִּנְיָמִין (proper name) אָחִיו בֶּן־אִמּוֹ וַיֹּאמֶר הֲזֶה (Is this?) אֲחִיכֶם הַקָּטֹן אֲשֶׁר אֲמַרְתֶּם אֵלָי אָמַר אֱלֹהִים יָחְנְךָ (be gracious to you) בְּנִי

Genesis 43:29

This phrase, וַיִּשָּׂא עֵינָיו, is a common Biblical idiom meaning *to look*. It is often followed by the verb *to see*, as in this verse.

He lifted his eyes and saw Benjamin his brother, the son of his mother, and he said, "Is this your brother, the little one, of which you spoke to me?" He said, "May God be gracious to you, my son."

מֵחֲטָא בִלְשׁוֹנִי אֶשְׁמֹר

Psalm 39:1

from sin in my speech I will guard

זֹאת עֶצֶם מֵעֲצָמַי וּבָשָׂר מִבְּשָׂרִי

Genesis 2:23

this is bone from my bone and flesh from my flesh

---

[1] A few changes have been made to facilitate your translation. You won't need such help for long!

מֶה עָשִׂיתָ קוֹל דְּמֵי אָחִיךָ צֹעֲקִים (calls) אֵלַי מִן־הָאֲדָמָה

Genesis 4:10

What have you done? The voice of your brother's blood calls to me from the ground.

בֵּן רָאָה אֶת־כָּל־חַטֹּאת אָבִיו אֲשֶׁר עָשָׂה וַיִּרְאֶה (but he will fear) וְלֹא יַעֲשֶׂה כָּהֵן

Ezekiel 18:14

A son saw all the sins of his father which he did, but he will fear and he will not do like them.

30.3 WEDNESDAY

Read aloud and translate, supplying a suitable pronoun in your translation.

נֵלֵךְ We will walk.

יִשָּׂא He will carry.

תֵּדַע She/You will know.

תִּקַּח She/You will take.

יֵרְדוּ They will go down.

אֵשֵׁב I will dwell.

תֵּלְכוּ You will walk.

תִּקְחִי You will take.

אֵדַע I will know.

נֵרֵד We will go down.

יֵשֵׁב He will dwell.

תֵּלֵךְ She/You will walk.

תֵּשֵׁב She/You will dwell.

יֵרֵד He will go down.

יֵדְעוּ They will know.

יִקַּח He will take.

נָשָׂאתִי I carried/lifted.

יָדַעְנוּ We knew.

לָקַחְתָּ You took.

30.4 THURSDAY

Translate.

אֹמַר לוֹ אֵין לֶחֶם וּבָשָׂר I will say to him, "There is no bread and no meat."

אָז אֹכַל הָעֲצָמוֹת הָאֵלֶּה Then I will eat these bones.

בֶּן דָּוִד יוֹשֵׁב לַיָּמִין הָאָב The son of David is sitting at the right hand of the father.

יִתֵּן מַיִם לִרְחֹץ (to wash) רַגְלָיו וְרַגְלֵי הָאֲנָשִׁים אֲשֶׁר אִתּוֹ
He will give water to wash his feet and the feet of the men/people who are with him.

הִשְׁחִית (had corrupted) כָּל־בָּשָׂר אֶת־דַּרְכּוֹ עַל־הָאָרֶץ
All flesh had corrupted their way on the earth.

אֵשֵׁב בְּתוֹכֵךְ I will dwell in your midst.

תֵּדַע כִּי־הַמֶּלֶךְ שְׁלָחַנִי אֵלָיִךְ You/She will know that the king sent me to you.

30.5 FRIDAY

Translate from (sometimes slightly modified for ease of translation) Scripture.
As usual, students should compare their work and these sometimes overly literal answers with a Bible translation or two.

יִקָּרֵא (will be called) אִשָּׁה כִּי מֵאִישׁ
לֻקֳחָה (was taken: unfamiliar conjugation but recognizable root) זֹּאת

Genesis 2:23

[She] will be called "woman" because from man this was taken.

וְהָעֹרְבִים (the ravens: recognize the same root as evening here? both are dark)
מְבִיאִים (brought) לוֹ לֶחֶם וּבָשָׂר בַּבֹּקֶר וְלֶחֶם וּבָשָׂר בָּעָרֶב וּמִן־הַנַּחַל יִשְׁתֶּה

1 Kings 17:6

The ravens brought him bread and meat in the morning and bread and meat in the evening and from the stream he will drink.

אֶתֵּן לָכֶם לֵב חָדָשׁ וְרוּחַ חֲדָשָׁה אֶתֵּן בְּקִרְבְּכֶם...אֶתֵּן לָכֶם לֵב בָּשָׂר

Ezekiel 36:26

I will give to you a new heart and I will give a new spirit in your inward part...I will give to you a heart of flesh.

אֹרֶךְ (length) יָמִים בִּימִינָהּ

Proverbs 3:16

length of days is in her right hand

אָמַר יוֹסֵף (proper name) אֶל־אָבִיו לֹא־כֵן אָבִי כִּי־זֶה הַבְּכֹר (the firstborn) שִׂים יְמִינְךָ
עַל־רֹאשׁוֹ

Genesis 48:18

Joseph said to his father, "Not so, because this is the firstborn. Place your right hand on his head."

וְלֹא תָחוֹס (pity) עֵינֶךָ נֶפֶשׁ בְּנֶפֶשׁ (life for life) עַיִן בְּעַיִן שֵׁן בְּשֵׁן (tooth for tooth)
יָד בְּיָד רֶגֶל בְּרָגֶל

Deuteronomy 19:21

And your eyes shall not pity a soul: life for life, eye for eye, tooth for tooth, hand for hand, foot for foot.

HOLLOW VERBS

CHAPTER THIRTY-ONE

31.1 MONDAY

Practice old and new vocabulary today and work on reading and examining Judges 5:31.

כֵּן יֹאבְדוּ כָל־אוֹיְבֶיךָ יְהוָה וְאֹהֲבָיו כְּצֵאת הַשֶּׁמֶשׁ בִּגְבֻרָתוֹ וַתִּשְׁקֹט הָאָרֶץ אַרְבָּעִים שָׁנָה׃

thus	כֵּן
will perish	יֹאבְדוּ
all	כָל־
enemies of	אוֹיְבֶיךָ
the LORD	יְהוָה
but the one who loves Him	וְאֹהֲבָיו
like the going out	כְּצֵאת
the sun	הַשֶּׁמֶשׁ
in his strength	בִּגְבֻרָתוֹ
and was quiet	וַתִּשְׁקֹט
the land	הָאָרֶץ

forty	אַרְבָּעִים
years*	שָׁנָה:

(*yes, this is a singular noun being modified by "forty", but that's OK in Hebrew)

31.2 TUESDAY

Translate, supplying an appropriate pronoun.

מֵת He/It died.

בָּאָה She/It came.

קַמְנוּ We arose.

שַׁבְתִּי I returned.

קָמוּ They arose.

בָּאתָ You (m., s.) came.

שַׁבְתֶּם You (m., pl.) returned.

בָּאת You (f., s.) came.

שָׁב He/It returned.

קַמְתָּ You (m., s.) arose.

בָּאתֶם You (m., pl.) came.

קָם He/it arose.

בָּאתִי I came.

בָּא He/It came.

מֵתוּ They died.

שַׁבְתָּ You (m., s.) returned.

שָׁבוּ They returned.

מֵתָה She died.

קַמְתִּי I arose.

קָמָה She/It arose.

31.3 WEDNESDAY

Translate.

שָׁב הוּא He/It returned/is returning.

בָּאִים הֵם They are coming.

יָקוּם הוּא He/It will arise.

תָּבוֹא הִיא She/It will come.

בָּאָה הִיא She/It is coming.

שָׁב אֲנִי I am returning.

נָשׁוּב אֲנַחְנוּ We will return.

יָשׁוּב יִשְׂרָאֵל Israel will return.

מֵתִים הֵם They are dying.

נָמוּת אֲנַחְנוּ We will die.

בָּא הוּא He/It came/is coming.

בָּאוֹת הֵן They (f.) are coming.

שָׁבִים הֵם They are returning.

תָּבוֹא אַתָּה You (m., s.) will come.

תָּקוּם אַתָּה You (m., s.) will arise.

תָּמוּת הִיא She/It will die.

יָשׁוּבוּ הֵם They will return.

יָמוּת יַעֲקֹב Jacob will die.

שַׁבְנוּ אֲנַחְנוּ We returned.

תָּשׁוּב אַתָּה You will return.

31.4 THURSDAY

Translate.

כִּי בִּמְקוֹם אֲשֶׁר־הִגְלוּ (they led) אֹתוֹ שָׁם יָמוּת וְאֶת־הָאָרֶץ הַזֹּאת לֹא־יִרְאֶה עוֹד (again)

Jeremiah 22:12

Because in the place to which they led him, he will die. And he will not see this land again.

שָׁבוּ הַמַּלְאָכִים אֵלָיו וַיֹּאמֶר (and said) אֲלֵיהֶם מַה־זֶּה שַׁבְתֶּם

2 Kings 1:5, slightly altered

The messengers returned to him. And he said to them, "What is this? You have returned?"

בְּשָׁלוֹם תָּמוּת כַּאֲבֹתֵיכֶם הַמְּלָכִים אֲשֶׁר עָשׂוּ חֶסֶד בָּאָרֶץ

In peace you will die like your fathers the kings who showed steadfast love in the land.

שָׁבוּ הֵם אֶל־בֵּיתָם אֶת־מִשְׁפַּחַת רָחֵל

They returned to their house with Rachel's family.

בָּאִים הַמֶּלֶךְ גָּדוֹל וְשַׂר־צְבָאוֹ מֵהַמִּדְבָּר

The great king and the captain of his army are coming from the desert.

בָּעִיר הַזֹּאת יֵשֵׁב הוּא עַד־מוֹת הַכֹּהֵן הַגָּדוֹל וְאַחֲרֵי מוֹת הַכֹּהֵן הַגָּדוֹל יָשׁוּב הוּא אֶל־אֶרֶץ אֲבוֹתָיו

In this city he will dwell until the death of the high priest. And after the death of the high priest, he will return to the land of his fathers.

31.5 FRIDAY

1. Translate.

לִפְנֵי מוֹתוֹ שָׁב יַעֲקֹב עִם בָּנָיו אֶל־הָאֲדָמָה אֲשֶׁר־נָתַתִּי לָהֶם וְלַאֲבוֹתֵיהֶם

Before his death, Jacob returned with his sons/children to the land which I gave to them and to their fathers.

שָׁבָה שָׂרָה אֶל־הָעִיר כִּי אַנְשֵׁי הַצָּבָא בַּדֶּרֶךְ

Sarah returned to the city because the men of the army were on the road.

בְּנִי אִם־חָכַם לִבֶּךָ אָמוּת בְּשָׁלוֹם

My son, if your heart is wise, I will die in peace.

רָאָה הַשֹּׁפֵט כִּי רַב רָע לֵב הָאִישׁ

The judge saw that great was the wickedness of the heart of the man.

תָּבוֹא אַתָּה אִתִּי כִּי אֹתְךָ רָאִיתִי חָכָם לְפָנַי בַּדּוֹר הַזֶּה

You will come with me because I have seen you are wise before me in this generation.

וְדַם אֲבִיהֶם לֹא רָאוּ

And the blood of their father they did not see.

2. Explain the connections between Hebrew words for oxen and morning, Yemen and right hand, month and new.

Oxen and morning share a root that carries the meaning of "to split." Morning splits light from dark; plowing oxen split the earth.

"Right hand" and "south" share a root, because when facing the primary direction of east, the south is on one's right hand. "Yemen" shares this root, too, because it is the southernmost country of the Arabian peninsula. (And why should Yemen have a Hebrew name, you ask? Really, Arabic is the language of Yemen. Arabic and Hebrew are closely related languages.)

The moon seems to be continually renewed with a new moon each month. The new moon is particularly important in Biblical worship, not only for New Moon celebrations, but because all yearly holy days are timed by the moon. So the words for "new" and "moon" share a root.

COMMANDS

CHAPTER THIRTY-TWO

32.1 MONDAY

This week's vocabulary words are nouns naming plants and animals.

Numbers 29:37 contains several of this week's vocabulary words.

מִנְחָתָם וְנִסְכֵּיהֶם לַפָּר לָאַיִל וְלַכְּבָשִׂים בְּמִסְפָּרָם כַּמִּשְׁפָּט׃

their offering	מִנְחָתָם
and their drink offering	וְנִסְכֵּיהֶם
for a bull	לַפָּר
for a ram	לָאַיִל
and for lambs	וְלַכְּבָשִׂים
in their number	בְּמִסְפָּרָם
as the judgement	כַּמִּשְׁפָּט׃

32.2 TUESDAY

Translate.

קַח הַלֶּחֶם Take the bread/food.

הָעִיר שׁוּב עִמָּנוּ Return to the city with us.

בּוֹא אֵלַי Come to me.

שָׂא עֵינֶיךָ Lift up your eyes. (or, Look!)

שְׁלַח יְמִינְךָ Send your right hand.
this is a Biblical Hebrew way of saying "apply your power"

שְׁכַב שָׁם Lie down there.

עַתָּה בְּנֵה אֵת הַבַּיִת Now build the house.

שֵׁב פֹּה לְעוֹלָם וָעֶד Dwell here forever and ever.

לֵךְ בַּדֶּרֶךְ Walk in the road.

דַּע כִּי מַלְכְּכֶם אֲנִי Know that I am your king.

עֲנֵה אֵת הַשֹּׁפֵט Answer the judge.

עֲלֵה אִתָּם Go up with them.

שִׁמְעוּ עַמִּים כֻּלָּם Listen, all peoples.

קַח עֶבֶד עִמְּךָ Take a servant with you.

שְׁמֹר אֵת הַנַּעֲרָה Guard the young woman.

עֲשֵׂה צְדָקָה Do justice.

יְרָא אֶת־מַלְכְּךָ Fear your king.

אֱכֹל אֵת הַלֶּחֶם הַזֶּה Eat this bread.

שְׁתֵה מַיִם אוֹ יַיִן Drink water or wine.

זִכְרוּ הַמִּצְוָה Remember the commandment.

32.3 WEDNESDAY

1. Is each command in the list below for one or for many?

זְכֹר one

דְּעוּ many

יְרָא one

עֲשׂוּ many

שׁוּבוּ many

קוּם one

2. Translate.

זָכְרֵנִי Remember me.

שָׂאֵהוּ אֶל־אִמּוֹ Carry him to his mother.

עֲנֵנִי Answer me.

3. Label each drawing with a Hebrew vocabulary word from this week.

כֶּבֶשׂ, אַיִל

פְּרִי

צִפּוֹר

עֵץ

פַּר, בָּקָר

צֹאן, כְּבָשִׂים, אֵילִים

יוֹחָנָן בֶּן דִּיר

John son of Deere

32.4 THURSDAY

Translate.

לֹא תֶּחֶטְאוּ Do not sin.

לֹא תַעֲשׂוּ מִלְחָמָה Do not make war.

לֹא תֵּלֵךְ אֶל־הָעִיר רָעָה Do not go to the evil city.

לֹא תָשׁוּבוּ פֹּה Do not return here.

לֹא תִקַּח אֵת אֵשֶׁת רֵעֶךָ Do not take the wife of your neighbor.

אַל תִּפְתַּח לוֹ אֶת־הָאֹהֶל Do not open the tent for him.

עִם יִקְרָא אַל תַּעֲנֵהוּ If he calls, do not answer him.

הַבֶּגֶד הַזֶּה אַל תִּשָּׂא Do not lift that garment.

אַל תַּעֲמֹד פֹּה הַיּוֹם Do not stand here today.

הַלֶּחֶם הַזֶּה אַל תָּשִׂים שָׁם Do not put that bread/food here.

32.5 FRIDAY

Translate from Scripture (carefully).

אֶת־הַצִּפֹּר הַחַיָּה (living) יִקַּח אֹתָהּ וְאֶת־עֵץ הָאֶרֶז (cedar)

Leviticus 14:6

[he] will take the living bird and the cedar wood

וְהָיָה (and he will be) כְּעֵץ שָׁתוּל (planted) עַל־פַּלְגֵי (streams of) מָיִם אֲשֶׁר פִּרְיוֹ יִתֵּן בְּעִתּוֹ
וְעָלֵהוּ (and his leaf) לֹא־יִבּוֹל (will wither) וְכֹל אֲשֶׁר־יַעֲשֶׂה יַצְלִיחַ (will prosper)

Psalm 1:3

And he will be like a tree planted on streams of water, which gives its fruit in its time. And his leaf will not wither. And all which he does will prosper.

תַּבְנִית (the likeness) כָּל־בְּהֵמָה אֲשֶׁר בָּאָרֶץ תַּבְנִית (the likeness) כָּל־צִפּוֹר כָּנָף אֲשֶׁר תָּעוּף (flies) בַּשָּׁמָיִם

Deuteronomy 4:17

the likeness of any of the animals which are on the earth, the likeness of any bird of the wing which flies in the sky

וְגַם־לְלוֹט (and also to Lot) הַהֹלֵךְ אֶת־אַבְרָם (proper name) הָיָה (there were, *that is* he had) צֹאן־וּבָקָר וְאֹהָלִים

Genesis 13:5

And also to Lot, the one who walked with Abram, there were flocks and cattle and tents

אַל־תִּשְׁלַח יָדְךָ אֶל־הַנַּעַר וְאַל־תַּעַשׂ לוֹ מְאוּמָה (anything) כִּי עַתָּה יָדַעְתִּי כִּי־יְרֵא אֱלֹהִים אַתָּה

Genesis 22:12

Do not send your hand against the young man and do not do to him anything, because now I know that you fear God.

מַה־יָּדַעְתָּ וְלֹא נֵדָע תָּבִין (you will understand) וְלֹא־עִמָּנוּ הוּא

Job 15:9

What do you know and we don't know? You will understand, but it is not with us?

There are many ways to improve the English of these answer key translations and students should try to do so. It will be very helpful for understanding Hebrew and translation to compare answers with Bible translations.

REVIEW

CHAPTER THIRTY-THREE

33.1 MONDAY

No new vocabulary this week, so practice the old and take up some of the suggestions for further study in your text. Work this week on reading Isaiah 55:1.

הוֹי כָּל־צָמֵא לְכוּ לַמַּיִם וַאֲשֶׁר אֵין־לוֹ כָּסֶף לְכוּ שִׁבְרוּ וֶאֱכֹלוּ וּלְכוּ שִׁבְרוּ בְּלוֹא־כֶסֶף וּבְלוֹא
מְחִיר יַיִן וְחָלָב׃

hey	הוֹי
all	כָּל־
thirsty ones	צָמֵא
walk	לְכוּ
to waters	לַמַּיִם
and which	וַאֲשֶׁר
there is no	אֵין־
for it	לוֹ
silver	כָּסֶף
walk	לְכוּ

buy	שִׁבְרוּ
and eat	וֶאֱכֹלוּ
and walk	וּלְכוּ
buy	שִׁבְרוּ
with no	בְּלוֹא־
silver	כֶסֶף
and with no	וּבְלוֹא
price	מְחִיר
wine	יַיִן
and milk	וְחָלָב׃

33.2 TUESDAY

Translate.

אָסַפְנוּ אֲנַחְנוּ We gathered.

בָּנִיתִי אָנֹכִי I built.

בָּרָא הוּא He created.

תִּמְצְאוּ אַתֶּם You will find.

תִּשְׁכַּב אַתָּה You will lie down.

נֵלֵךְ אֲנַחְנוּ We will walk.

יִשָּׂא יַעֲקֹב Jacob will carry.

תֵּדַע אַתָּה You will know.

תִּקַּח הִיא She will take.

יֵרְדוּ הֵמָּה They will go down.

מֵת הוּא He died.

בָּאָה רָחֵל Rachel came.

קַמְנוּ אֲנַחְנוּ We arose.

אֲנִי שַׁבְתִּי I returned.

קָמוּ הֵם They arose.

שִׁמְעוּ עַמִּים כֻּלָּם Listen, all peoples.

קַח אֵת הַבָּנִים עִמְּךָ Take the sons/children with you.

שְׁמֹר אֶת־בִּתִּי Guard my daughter.

עֲשֵׂה חֶסֶד Do steadfast love/Love steadfastly.

יְרָא אֵת קוֹלִי Fear my voice.

33.3 WEDNESDAY

1. Translate.

בָּעִיר מְצָאָתַם הַצָּבָא The army found them in the city.

אֵין יוֹם כְּהַיּוֹם There is no day like today.

לֹא יֹאכְלוּ לֶחֶם הַיּוֹם They will not eat bread/food today.

לָמָּה יִבְנֶה בַּיִת דָּוִד Why will David build a house?

אַתָּה תִּשָּׂא אֵת עֲוֹן הָעָם You will carry the guilt of the people.

יִקַּח הוּא He will take.

אָנֹכִי אֶשָּׂא מַיִם I will carry water.

נֵדַע אֲנַחְנוּ We will know.

בָּא דָוִד David came/David is coming.

מוֹת יִמְצָא הוּא He will find death.

מֵתוּ הֵם They died.

הַכֹּהֵן שָׁב The priest returned/is returning.

בָּאוּ הָעֲבָדִים The servants came.

לֹא תַעֲשׂוּ מִלְחָמָה Do not make war.

אַל תַּעֲמֹד שָׁם הַיּוֹם Do not stand there today.

2. Which letters are weak and what difference does it make?

The weak letters are yud, hey, and vav. They have often dropped out of pronunciation and so create spelling irregularities in verb conjugation patterns.

33.4 THURSDAY

1. What is a hollow verb?

Hollow verbs are those with a yud or vav in the middle position of the three-letter root.

2. Hollow verbs lose a root letter as participles and in one tense. Which tense?

perfect tense

3. How are positive imperative statements formed?

by dropping the tav prefix from the second person imperfect tense conjugation

4. Distinguish between negative commands formed with לֹא and those formed with אַל.

Negative commands with לֹא express strong, perpetual prohibition. Those with אַל express less permanent negativity.

5. Which accent mark appears at the end of each verse?

the sof pasuk, which looks like a colon, separates verses; also, the silluq marks a verse's final syllable

6. What is the purpose of the etnachta?

to divide a verse into rough halves; it signals a pause in phrasing, like a comma

7. What was the pronunciation of vav way back when? "W"

8. A three-letter root's concrete meaning is often stretched into abstract/figurative meanings.

33.5 FRIDAY

1. Translate from Scripture. Some verbs forms have been modified.

אָמַר עֵלִי (proper name) לִשְׁמוּאֵל (to proper name) לֵךְ שְׁכָב וְהָיָה (and it will be) אִם־יִקְרָא אֵלֶיךָ תֹּאמַר דַּבֵּר (speak) יְהוָה (the LORD) כִּי שֹׁמֵעַ עַבְדֶּךָ הָלַךְ שְׁמוּאֵל (proper name) [and] שְׁכַב בִּמְקוֹמוֹ

1 Samuel 3:9

Eli said to Samuel, "Go lie down and it will be if He calls to you, you will say, 'Speak, LORD, because your servant is listening.'" Samuel went and lay down in his place.

שָׂם הָעֶבֶד אֶת־יָדוֹ תַּחַת יֶרֶךְ (the thigh of) אַבְרָהָם (proper name)

Genesis 24:9

The servant put his hand under the thigh of Abraham.

וְהָיוּ (and it will be) הַדְּבָרִים הָאֵלֶּה אֲשֶׁר אָנֹכִי מְצַוְּךָ (command you) הַיּוֹם עַל־לְבָבֶךָ

Deuteronomy 6:6

And these words which I command you today will be on your heart.

גַּם־ (also) לְשׁוֹנִי כָּל־הַיּוֹם תֶּהְגֶּה (will utter) צִדְקָתֶךָ כִּי־בֹשׁוּ (they are ashamed) כִּי־ חָפְרוּ (they are humiliated) מְבַקְשֵׁי (those who seek) רָעָתִי

Psalm 71:24

Also, all the day my tongue will utter your righteousness because they are ashamed, because those who seek my harm are humiliated.

הַדָּם הוּא הַנָּפֶשׁ (the life) וְלֹא־תֹאכַל הַנֶּפֶשׁ (the life) עִם־הַבָּשָׂר

Deuteronomy 12:23

The blood is the life. And you will not eat the life with the meat.

אִסְפוּ־עָם קַדְּשׁוּ (sanctify) קָהָל

sanctify is a verb with the same root as *holy*, it means *to make holy*
Joel 2:16

Gather a people. Sanctify a congregation.

2. What is chavruta learning?

Chavruta learning is an ancient Jewish tradition of Bible study undertaken with a partner in which the pair discuss and debate a passage, working together to understand and interpret it.

QUESTIONS

CHAPTER THIRTY-FOUR

34.1 MONDAY

Memorize and practice vocabulary.

Examine and work on the fluent reading of Genesis 22:2. Remember to continue to read it aloud this week, at least once a day.

וַיֹּאמֶר קַח־נָא אֶת־בִּנְךָ אֶת־יְחִידְךָ אֲשֶׁר־אָהַבְתָּ אֶת־יִצְחָק וְלֶךְ־לְךָ אֶל־אֶרֶץ הַמֹּרִיָּה וְהַעֲלֵהוּ
שָׁם לְעֹלָה עַל אַחַד הֶהָרִים אֲשֶׁר אֹמַר אֵלֶיךָ׃

said (if this strikes you as odd, see footnote on page 196)	וַיֹּאמֶר
take	קַח־
please	נָא
(direct object marker)	אֶת־
your son	בִּנְךָ
(direct object marker)	אֶת־
your only one	יְחִידְךָ
which	אֲשֶׁר־
you loved	אָהַבְתָּ

(direct object marker)	אֶת־
proper name: Isaac	יִצְחָק
and go	וְלֶךְ־
for yourself	לְךָ
to	אֶל־
the land of	אֶרֶץ
proper name: Moriah	הַמֹּרִיָּה
(can you figure this out?) send him up as a sacrifice	וְהַעֲלֵהוּ
there	שָׁם
for a burnt offering	לְעֹלָה
on	עַל
one of	אַחַד
the mountains	הֶהָרִים
which	אֲשֶׁר
I will say	אֹמַר
to you	אֵלֶיךָ׃

34.2 TUESDAY

1. כתב is regular in its conjugations. Complete these charts.

plural	singular	WRITE active participles
כּוֹתְבִים	כּוֹתֵב	masculine
כּוֹתְבוֹת	כּוֹתֶבֶת	feminine

plural	singular	WRITE perfect tense
כָּתַבְנוּ	כָּתַבְתִּי	first person
כְּתַבְתֶּם	כָּתַבְתָּ	second person, m.
כְּתַבְתֶּן	כָּתַבְתְּ	second person, f.
כָּתְבוּ	כָּתַב	third person, m.
כָּתְבוּ	כָּתְבָה	third person, f.

plural	singular	WRITE imperfect tense
נִכְתֹּב	אֶכְתֹּב	first person
תִּכְתְּבוּ	תִּכְתֹּב	second person, m.
תִּכְתֹּבְנָה	תִּכְתְּבִי	second person, f.
יִכְתְּבוּ	יִכְתֹּב	third person, m.
תִּכְתֹּבְנָה	תִּכְתֹּב	third person, f.

כָּתוּב	passive participle
כְּתֹב	command, m. s.

2. Write a Hebrew sentence that includes one of the verbs above.

Answers will vary, of course.

34.3 WEDNESDAY

Translate.

הָאָב אָהַב אֶת־בְּנוֹ The father loved his son.

הֶאָהַב הַבֵּן אֵת אָבִיו Did the son love his father?

הֲלֹא הוּא כָתַב עָלֶיךָ Did he not write to you?

הֲלֹא הָאוֹר טוֹב Isn't the light good?

הֲכָרַתָּ לְךָ עֵצִים Did you cut trees for yourself?

הֲתֹאכַל אֵת הַלֶּחֶם Will you eat the bread/food?

הֲיִבְנוּ הֵם בַּיִת חָדָשׁ Will they build a new house?

הַפָּר שָׁב אֶל הַשָּׂדֶה The bull returned to the field.

הֲנָתְנוּ פִּרְיָם הָעֵצִים הָאֵלֶּה Did these trees give their fruit?

מָה הַבְּהֵמָה הַזֹּאת אֲשֶׁר שָׁמַרְתָּ What is this animal which you guarded?

הַרְאִיתֶם הָאִישׁ הָעֹלֶה הַזֶּה Did you see this man who is coming?
from 1 Samuel 17:25

הֲשׁוֹמֵר הָעִיר אָנֹכִי Am I the guardian of the city?

הַאַתָּה הַשֹּׁפֵט כָּל־הָאָרֶץ Are you the judge of all the earth?

הֲלוֹא יָדַעְתָּ מָה־אֵלֶּה Do you not know what these are?
from Zechariah 4:13

הֲיִרְשׁוּ בָּקָר הֵם Will they inherit cattle?

הֲלֹא הוּא כָתַב אֵת כָּל־הַדְּבָרִים אֲשֶׁר נָתַתִּי לָעָם Did he not write the words which I gave to the people?

34.4 THURSDAY

Translate.

הוּא הָלַךְ בַּדֶּרֶךְ הָעָם He walked on the road to the sea.

הָהָרָה לְכוּ Go to/toward the mountain.

לֹא אֲנִי הָלַכְתִּי שָׁמָּה I will not go thither.

דָוִד בָּה הַבַּיְתָה David is coming homeward.

הַהוֹלְכִים אַרְצָה הֵם Are they going landward?

הַצָּבָא עוֹבֵר הַמִּדְבָּרָה The army is crossing over toward the desert.

הָאֹהֱלָה הוֹלְכִים כָּל־הָעָם All the people are going toward the tent.

בְּהֵמוֹת יוֹרְדוֹת הָעִירָה Animals are going down toward the city.

הֶאָסַפְתָּ צִפֳּרִים Did you gather birds?

הֲמִן־הָעֵץ הַזֶּה אָכַלְתָּ Have you eaten from this tree?

הוּא נְתָנָנוּ אֵת הַדְּבָרִים כָּתוּב בַּתּוֹרָה He gave us the words that are written in the Torah/Law.

לֹא תִכְרֹת אֶת־כָּל־הָעֵץ Do not cut every tree.

אִם לֹא יָבוֹא הַבֵּן יַעֲקֹב יִירַשׁ אֵת הַשָּׂדֶה If the son does not come, Jacob will inherit the field.

לֹא אָהַבְתִּי הָאִישׁ הַזֶּה I did not love this man.

גַּם תֵּלֵךְ הַמִּדְבָּרָה Also you (or, she) will go toward the desert.

קַח פְּרִי שָׁמָּה Take the fruit thither.

34.5 FRIDAY

1. Name at least six practices that can make Bible study effective and vibrant.

   Answers include, but are not limited to: Ask God for wisdom and understanding. Read regularly with a plan. Read widely in all of Scripture. Learn the context of a passage. Consider the author's questions, purpose, and audience. Read history. Read authors who write about the Bible. Listen to the sermon. Memorize verses; collect significant quotes. Summarize passages in a journal. Record your questions then seek out the answers. Pray Scripture. Learn in order to obey; constantly apply Scripture to daily life. Discuss with friends. Teach someone else.

2. Which word do you guess would be simpler to define, translate, and interpret: *expiation* or *for*? expiation

3. Translate from Scripture. Some verbs forms have been modified.

כֹּה (thus) אָמַר יְהוָה (the LORD) אֱלֹהֵי (the God of) יִשְׂרָאֵל לֵאמֹר (to say) כְּתָב־לְךָ אֵת
כָּל־הַדְּבָרִים אֲשֶׁר־דִּבַּרְתִּי (I spoke) אֵלֶיךָ אֶל־סֵפֶר (a book)

Jeremiah 30:2

Thus said the LORD, the God of Israel, "Write for yourself all the words which I spoke to you in a book."

רָאָה אֱלֹהִים (God) אֶת־הָאוֹר כִּי־טוֹב וַיַּבְדֵּל (and separated) אֱלֹהִים (God) בֵּין הָאוֹר וּבֵין
הַחֹשֶׁךְ (the darkness)

and separated: if you know the word *havdalah*, the ceremony that separates Sabbath from the coming week, you will see the same root in this verb

Genesis 1:4

God saw that the light was good and God separated the light from the darkness.

וְלֹא־יִכָּרֵת (will be cut off) כָּל־בָּשָׂר עוֹד (again) מִמֵּי הַמַּבּוּל (the flood)

Genesis 9:11

And all flesh will not be cut off again by the waters of the flood.

וַיְבִאֶהָ (and brought her) יִצְחָק (proper name) הָאֹהֱלָה שָׂרָה אִמּוֹ [and] לָקַח אֶת־
רִבְקָה (proper name) וַתְּהִי־ (and she became) לוֹ לְאִשָּׁה [and] אֲהֵבָהּ

Genesis 24:67

And Isaac brought her to the tent of Sarah his mother. He took Rebecca and she became his wife and he loved her.

אָמַר אַבְרָם (proper name) הֵן (behold) לִי לֹא נָתַתָּ זָרַע וְהִנֵּה בֶן־בֵּיתִי יוֹרֵשׁ אֹתִי

Genesis 15:3

Abram said, "Behold, You have not given me a descendant, and behold, a son of my house will inherit what is mine."

NUMBERS I

CHAPTER THIRTY-FIVE

35.1 MONDAY

This week's words are the cardinal numbers, one through ten. Practice counting!

1 Kings 7:27 includes several numbers, notice how they used in the sentence.

וַיַּעַשׂ אֶת־הַמְּכֹנוֹת עֶשֶׂר נְחֹשֶׁת אַרְבַּע בָּאַמָּה אֹרֶךְ הַמְּכוֹנָה הָאֶחָת וְאַרְבַּע בָּאַמָּה רָחְבָּהּ
וְשָׁלֹשׁ בָּאַמָּה קוֹמָתָהּ׃

made*	וַיַּעַשׂ
(direct object marker)	אֶת־
bases	הַמְּכֹנוֹת
ten	עֶשֶׂר
bronze	נְחֹשֶׁת
four	אַרְבַּע
cubits	בָּאַמָּה
the length	אֹרֶךְ
the base	הַמְּכוֹנָה
one	הָאֶחָת

and four	וְאַרְבַּע
cubits	בָּאַמָּה
width	רָחְבָּהּ
and three	וְשָׁלֹשׁ
cubits	בָּאַמָּה
height	קוֹמָתָהּ:

*Coming up in Chapter 40: Why does this mean *made* when it is in the imperfect tense? If you can't wait, here it is: The vav prefix changes the tense.

35.2 TUESDAY

Translate.

שְׁלֹשָׁה פָּרִים three bulls

שִׁבְעָה יָמִים seven days

אַרְבָּעָה עֵצִים four trees

עֲשָׂרָה כְּבָשִׂים ten lambs

חֲמִשָּׁה אֵילִים five rams

לָשׁוֹן אֶחָד one language

שִׁשָּׁה לֵילוֹת six nights

שְׁמֹנָה שָׂדוֹת eight fields

תֵּשַׁע עִירִים רָעוֹת nine evil cities

שְׁנַיִם שָׁנִים טוֹבִים two good years

אִישׁ אֶחָד לֹא יֶחֱטָא One man will not sin.

חֲמִשָּׁה צִפֳּרִים יֶאֱסֹף יַעֲקֹב Jacob will gather five birds.

שָׁבוּ שְׁלֹשָׁה בָּנִים Three sons returned.

כָּתַב הוּא אֵת שְׁלֹשָׁה דְּבָרִים עַל הָאֲדָמָה He wrote three words on the ground.

נָפְלוּ אַרְבָּעָה עֵצִים Four trees fell.

35.3 WEDNESDAY

Translate.

עֲשֶׂרֶת אֵילֵי דָוִד David's ten rams

אַרְבַּעַת עֵצִים four trees

תְּשַׁע עָרֵי הַמֶּלֶךְ הַגָּדוֹל the nine cities of the great king

שְׁמֹנָה מֶלֶךְ eight kings

חֲמִשָּׁה פָּרִים five bulls

אֲנִי מָצָאתִי שְׁלֹשֶׁת כְּבָשִׂים I found three lambs.

יִירַשׁ הוּא אֵת עֲשֶׂרֶת בָּתֵּי אָבִיו He will inherit the ten houses of his father.

שִׁשָּׁה עֶבֶד six servants

עַתָּה יֵשׁ שְׁבַע בְּהֵמוֹת שָׁם Now there are seven animals there.

עֲשֶׂרֶת הַדְּבָרִים the ten words/things (note: this phrase is what has been translated as "The Ten Commandments")

מִצְוָה אַחַת one commandment

שְׁנֵי בָנִים two sons

תּוֹרָה אַחַת one law

אַרְבָּעָה מָגֵן four shields

שְׁלֹשֶׁת צְבָאוֹת three armies

35.4 THURSDAY

Translate.

עֵינַיִם two eyes/eyes

רַגְלַיִם two feet/feet

יוֹמַיִם two days

שְׁנָתַיִם two years

יָדַיִם a pair of hands/hands

כְּנָפַיִם a pair of wings/wings

בְּעֵינֵי הָעָם in the eyes of the people

שְׁלֹשֶׁת עֵצִים זְקֵנִים three old trees

עֶשֶׂר נְשֵׁי יַעֲקֹב the ten wives of Jacob

אַרְבַּעַת אֲנָשִׁים חֲכָמִים בָּאוּ אֶל אַרְצֵנוּ Four wise men came to our land.

לֹא יִירַשׁ הוּא תִּשְׁעָה בָּתִּים He will not inherit nine houses.

הָאָב אָהַב אֵת חָמֵשׁ בְּנוֹתָיו וּשְׁלֹשֶׁת בָּנָיו The father loved his five daughters and three sons.

35.5 FRIDAY

1. What is an exhaustive concordance?

An exhaustive concordance lists every English word in the Bible in a particular translation and every verse in which it appears.

2. What is a Strong's number?

Dr. James Strong, a nineteenth century theology professor, produced an index for the words of the KJV and assigned a number to each of 8674 Hebrew words and 5624 Greek words from Scripture. These numbers, called "Strong's numbers" are often used by concordances and lexicons.

3. The words in the list below appear in the King James Version of the Bible. Each is used to translate several different Hebrew words. Find the Strong's numbers of those Hebrew words. Record the numbers next to each English word.

- stop 6113, 5640, 5462, 7092, 2629

- exalteth 7682, 7311, 1361

- caves 4631, 2356, 4247, 4631

- razor 8593, 4177, 8593

- fashion 4941, 1823, 3559, 8498

4. For each English word in the list above, look up at least one of the corresponding Hebrew words in a Hebrew dictionary. Write the Hebrew word, with a brief definition, beside its English translation.

Students should choose one of the Strong's numbers above for each word, look it up in a Hebrew dictionary organized by Strong's numbers (such as that in a Strong's Concordance, or an online concordance searchable by Strong's numbers, such as at http://www.biblestudytools.com/lexicons/Hebrew), write the Hebrew word listed there, and a brief definition.

NUMBERS II

CHAPTER THIRTY-SIX

36.1 MONDAY

This week's words are also about numbers, including some larger cardinal numbers and a few ordinals. Cardinal numbers are counting numbers; ordinals define something's position in a series. So רִאשׁוֹן and שֵׁנִי and שְׁלִישִׁי are Hebrew ordinal numbers.

You will see some of the larger cardinal numbers and many words you know in 2 Chronicles 1:2.

וַיֹּאמֶר שְׁלֹמֹה לְכָל־יִשְׂרָאֵל לְשָׂרֵי הָאֲלָפִים וְהַמֵּאוֹת וְלַשֹּׁפְטִים וּלְכֹל נָשִׂיא לְכָל־יִשְׂרָאֵל
רָאשֵׁי הָאָבוֹת׃

said*	וַיֹּאמֶר
Solomon	שְׁלֹמֹה
to all	לְכָל־
Israel	יִשְׂרָאֵל
to the captains of	לְשָׂרֵי
the thousands	הָאֲלָפִים
and the hundreds	וְהַמֵּאוֹת
and to the judges	וְלַשֹּׁפְטִים

and to every	וּלְכֹל
ruler	נָשִׂיא
and all	לְכָל־
Israel	יִשְׂרָאֵל
the heads of	רָאשֵׁי
the fathers	הָאָבוֹת׃

*If you are a devoted footnote reader, you already know that the vav prefix can change verb tense. That is why this looks like "and will say," but it is translated "said." More to come in Chapter 40.

36.2 TUESDAY

1. Write in Hebrew.

פַּעַם הוּא שָׁלַח אוֹתִי He sent me once.

עָשִׂיתָ אַתָּה לֶחֶם פַּעֲמַיִם You (m., s.) made bread twice.

חָטְאוּ הֵם שָׁלֹשׁ פְּעָמִים They sinned three times.

הַקָּהָל עָנָה חָמֵשׁ פְּעָמִים The congregation answered five times.

הָעָם עָלָה עֶשֶׂר פְּעָמִים The people went up ten times.

2. Translate.

יוֹם רִאשׁוֹן first day

מֵאָה מְלָכִים one hundred kings

אַרְבָּעִים יוֹם וְאַרְבָּעִים לָיְלָה forty days and forty nights

אֶלֶף הָרִים one thousand mountains

עֶשְׂרִים אֲנָשִׁים טוֹבִים twenty good men

חֲמִשִּׁים בְּהֵמוֹת fifty animals

36.3 WEDNESDAY

Translate.

דָּוִד בֶּן אַרְבָּעִים שָׁנָה David is forty years old.

אֲנִי בַּת עֶשְׂרִים שָׁנִים I am twenty years old.

לֹא יָבוֹא לַמִּלְחָמָה בֶּן מֵאָה שָׁנָה A man who is one hundred years old will not come to the war.

בִּשְׁנַת הַשֵּׁנִי in the second year

שָׂר־צְבָאוֹ הַשְּׁלִישִׁי the third captain of his army

פַּעַם יָמוּת אִישׁ A man will die once.

הָלַכְתִּי בַּדֶּרֶךְ אַרְבַּע פְּעָמִים I walked on the road four times.

שֶׁבַע שָׁנִים seven years

לֹא יִירַשׁ מֵאָה שָׂדֶה He will not inherit one hundred fields.

אֶלֶף אוֹרִים גְּדֹלִים בַּשָּׁמַיִם one thousand great lights in the sky

אֵין פֹּה חֲמִשִּׁים אֲנָשִׁים There are not fifty men here.

בָּאנוּ אֲנַחְנוּ עֶשְׂרִים פְּעָמִים We have come twenty times.

אַרְבָּעִים אֵילִים שָׁלַח הַמֶּלֶךְ אֶל אָחִיו The king sent forty rams to his brother.

אָכַלְתִּי אֶת־פִּרְיוֹ אַךְ־הַפַּעַם I ate his/its fruit only once.

36.4 THURSDAY

1. Biblically, the day begins at sunset, the week begins at sunset after Sabbath, the month begins with the new moon, and the new year begins civil calendar: Tishri/end of summer/Yom Teruah/Rosh Hashanah
ecclesiastical calendar: Nisan/spring

2. Find out which year this is since the Creation of the world, according to the Hebrew calendar. Be careful: remember the Hebrew year does not begin on January first.

Ask a rabbi for help, or check with www.hebcal.com/converter/.

3. Write 1914 as a Hebrew year. תרע"ד

(1914 + 3760 = 5674, 674 = 400 + 200 + 70 + 4)

4. In which Hebrew months and which season of the year are the Biblical pilgrimage festivals, the festivals for which all adult men of Israel came to the Temple in Jerusalem? See Exodus 23:14-17 and Leviticus 23 for help.

Passover: Nisan, spring
Shavuot: Sivan, early summer
Sukkot: Tishri, autumn

5. Translate from Scripture. As ever, students should strive for better English than these excessively literal answers and read these verses in a Bible when finished.

כִּי־לִי כָל־חַיְתוֹ־יָעַר (creatures of the forest) בְּהֵמוֹת בְּהַרְרֵי־אָלֶף

Psalm 50:10

because all the creatures of the forest are mine, animals on a thousand mountains

שַׂר הַצָּבָא הַשְּׁלִישִׁי לַחֹדֶשׁ הַשְּׁלִישִׁי בְּנָיָהוּ (proper name) בֶּן־יְהוֹיָדָע (proper name) הַכֹּהֵן
רֹאשׁ וְעַל מַחֲלֻקְתּוֹ (his division) עֶשְׂרִים וְאַרְבָּעָה אָלֶף

1 Chronicles 27:5

The third captain of the army, for the third month, Benaiah, the son of Jehoiada the head priest, and in his division were twenty-four thousand

36.5 FRIDAY

1. Translate from Scripture. Some verbs forms have been modified.[1]

נָשָׂאתִי עֵינַי [and] רָאִיתִי וְהִנֵּה שְׁתַּיִם נָשִׁים יוֹצְאוֹת (were going out) וְרוּחַ בְּכַנְפֵיהֶם וְלָהֵנָּה
כְנָפַיִם כְּכַנְפֵי הַחֲסִידָה (the stork) [and] תִּשֶּׂאנָה אֶת־הָאֵיפָה (the ephah, a measure of grain)
בֵּין הָאָרֶץ וּבֵין הַשָּׁמָיִם

Zechariah 5:9

I lifted my eyes (I looked) and behold, two women were going out and wind was in their wings. And to them were wings, wings like the stork, and they carried the ephah between the land and the sky.

[1] Footnote readers are aware that this is because the vav prefix can change tense. In the Bible, what looks like "and he walked" could mean "he will walk." I will use verb tenses in the familiar way and add *and* in brackets where necessary to avoid changing verb tense. In Chapter 40, we will get to the real deal. You may wish to look up these verses in your Hebrew Bible and compare. The meaning will be the same, but some verb forms different.

נָתַן יְהוָה (the LORD) אֶת־חֵן הָעָם בְּעֵינֵי מִצְרָיִם (Egypt) גַּם הָאִישׁ מֹשֶׁה גָּדוֹל מְאֹד בְּאֶרֶץ
מִצְרַיִם בְּעֵינֵי עַבְדֵי־פַרְעֹה (Pharaoh) וּבְעֵינֵי הָעָם

Exodus 11:3

The LORD gave the grace of the people in the eyes of Egypt. Also, the man Moses was very great in the land of Egypt, in the eyes of the servants of Pharaoh and in the eyes of the people.

עָלָה [and] שָׁכַב עַל־הַיֶּלֶד (the child) [and] שָׂם פִּיו (his mouth) עַל־פִּיו (his mouth) וְעֵינָיו
עַל־עֵינָיו וְכַפָּיו (the palms of his hands) עַל־כַּפָּו (the palms of his hands)
וַיִּגְהַר (and stretched) עָלָיו וַיָּחָם (became warm) בְּשַׂר הַיָּלֶד (the child)

2 Kings 4:34

[He] went up and he lay on the child and put his mouth on his mouth and his eyes on his eyes and the palms of his hands on the palms of his hands and stretched on him. The flesh of the child became warm.

פְּקַח־נָא (please) אֶת־עֵינָיו [and] יִרְאֶה [and] פְּתַח יְהוָה (the LORD) אֶת־עֵינֵי הַנַּעַר [and]
רָאָה וְהִנֵּה הָהָר מָלֵא (filled) סוּסִים (horses) וְרֶכֶב (chariots) אֵשׁ (fire) סְבִיבֹת (surrounding)
אֱלִישָׁע (proper name)

2 Kings 6:17

Open, please, his eyes and he will see. And the LORD opened the eyes of the young man and he saw. Behold! The mountain was filled with horses and chariots of fire surrounding Elisha.

2. Below is a diagram of the sources scholars search to determine Bible word meanings. At the center is any unknown word; each larger, concentric circle represents the next most closely related source of information. Finish the labeling by adding these terms to the appropriate rings: ancient translations, same sentence, same genre, cognate languages, same book, other books by same author, ancient Hebrew literature, whole Bible.

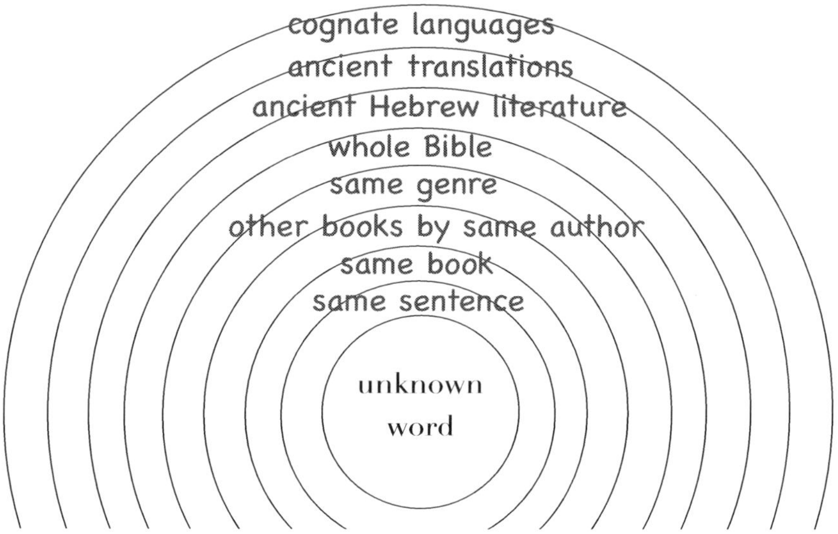

TO BE

CHAPTER THIRTY-SEVEN

37.1 MONDAY

This week: some important proper nouns from Scripture and one verb. Proper nouns mentioned less than 100 times in Scripture are printed in gray in *A Reader's Hebrew Bible*. Each of the names in this week's list appear more than 100 times.

Genesis 47:13 features two of them. Complete the chart below and practice fluently reading the verse this week.

וְלֶחֶם אֵין בְּכָל־הָאָרֶץ כִּי־כָבֵד הָרָעָב מְאֹד וַתֵּלַהּ אֶרֶץ מִצְרַיִם וְאֶרֶץ כְּנַעַן מִפְּנֵי הָרָעָב׃

and bread/food	וְלֶחֶם
there was not	אֵין
in all	בְּכָל־
the land	הָאָרֶץ
because	כִּי־
heavy (same root as *honor*)	כָבֵד
the famine	הָרָעָב
very (we might say "severe")	מְאֹד
and languished	וַתֵּלַהּ

the land of	אֶרֶץ
Egypt	מִצְרַיִם
and the land of	וְאֶרֶץ
Canaan	כְּנַעַן
literally, "from the face of" which could be translated as "because of the presence of"	מִפְּנֵי
the famine	הָרָעָב׃

37.2 TUESDAY

1. Translate this sentence in five equally legitimate ways: נָפַל שְׁלֹמֹה

Solomon fell. Solomon has fallen. Solomon had fallen. Solomon did fall. Solomon was falling.

2. Translate this sentence in three equally legitimate ways: שְׁלֹמֹה מֶלֶךְ׃

Solomon is a king. Solomon was a king. Solomon will be a king.

3. Translate into Hebrew.

These answers are given with subjects before verbs. It would be equally correct to write the verbs first.

Solomon was שְׁלֹמֹה הָיָה

Egypt was מִצְרַיִם הָיְתָה

Abraham and Moses were אַבְרָהָם וּמֹשֶׁה הָיוּ

they were הֵם הָיוּ

I was אֲנִי הָיִיתִי

we were אֲנַחְנוּ הָיִינוּ

אַתָּה הָיִיתָ you (*m., s.*) were

אַתְּ הָיִית you (*f., s.*) were

אַתֶּם הֱיִיתֶם You (*m., pl.*) were

אַתֶּן הֱיִיתֶן You (*f., pl.*) were

37.3 WEDNESDAY

Translate and read aloud.

עֶשְׂרִים אֲנָשִׁים הָיוּ בָּאִים בָּתִּים Twenty men were building houses.

יִצְחָק הָיָה נוֹתֵן מִצְוֹת לָעָם Isaac was giving commandments to the people/nation.

בְּאֶרֶץ־כְּנָעַן הָיָה יוֹשֵׁב אַהֲרֹן Aaron was dwelling in the land of Canaan.

וַיְהִי יָרַד יְהוּדָה מִצְרַיְמָה And it came to pass, Judah went down toward Egypt.

וְהָיָה יָבוֹאוּ אֶלֶף אֲנָשִׁים And it shall come to pass that a thousand men will come.

אַהֲרֹן הָיָה שׁוֹלֵחַ נְבִיאִים לְצִיּוֹן Aaron was sending prophets to Zion.

וְהָיָה שְׁלֹשָׁה מְלָכִים יִמְלְכוּ בְּאֶרֶץ יְהוּדָה And it shall come to pass that three kings will rule in the land of Judah.

וַיְהִי מֵת מֹשֶׁה And it was that Moses died.

וְהָיָה יִירַשׁ אַבְרָהָם אֵת הָאָרֶץ כְּנַעַן And it shall come to pass that Abraham will inherit the land of Canaan.

יְהוּדָה וְיִצְחָק הֵם הָיוּ נוֹתְנִים לֶחֶם לְיוֹשְׁבֵי מִצְרַיִם Judah and Isaac were giving bread/food to the residents of Egypt.

מִי הָיָה עוֹלֶה Who was going up?

הָיְתָה שׁוֹמֶרֶת אֵת הַבָּקָר הַמִּשְׁפָּחָה The family was guarding the cattle.

הָיוּ הוֹלְכִים יְרוּשָׁלַמָה הֵם They were walking toward Jerusalem.

37.4 THURSDAY

Translate.

וַיְהִי הָיִינוּ אֲנַחְנוּ עַבְדֵי הַמֶּלֶךְ And it came to pass that we were the servants of the king.

אָמַר יְהוּדָה אֵלַי מֹשֶׁה יִהְיֶה מֶלֶךְ גָּדוֹל Judah said to me, "Moses will be a great king."

עָנָה אַבְרָהָם אֹתוֹ הוּא אָמַר יְהִי־כֵן Abraham answered him. He said, "May it be so."

לֹא הָיִיתִי אִשְׁתְּךָ I will not be your wife.

וְהָיָה רָעָב בָּאָרֶץ There will be famine in the land.

וַיְהִי הַחֶרֶב בָּא עַל־הָאָרֶץ And it came to pass that the sword came on the land.

יִהְיֶה שְׁלֹמֹה שַׂר הַצָּבָא Solomon will be the captain of the army.

יִהְיוּ הֵם הַשֹּׁפְטִים They will be the judges.

הָיוּ נוֹתְנִים הַכֹּהֲנִים לֶחֶם לָעָם The priests were giving bread/food to the people.

נִהְיֶה אֲנַחְנוּ גֵּרִים We will be sojourners.

אָמְרָה שָׂרָה אֶל־שְׁלֹמֹה תִּהְיֶה אַתָּה אָב Sarah said to Solomon, "You will be a father."

יְהִי כֵן May it be so.

וְהָיָה יָמוּת יִצְחָק And it will come to pass that Isaac will die.

אַהֲרוֹן לֹא הָיָה בָּעִיר Aaron was not in the city.

37.5 FRIDAY

Translate from Scripture. (Some verbs have been modified, but very soon they will not need to be for you to read them!) Be sure to translate into better English and to compare with an English Bible or two.

כִּי־יֵצֵא עַמְּךָ לַמִּלְחָמָה עַל־אֹיְבוֹ (their enemy) בַּדֶּרֶךְ אֲשֶׁר תִּשְׁלָחֵם

וְהִתְפַּלְלוּ (and the people pray) אֶל־יְהוָה (the LORD) דֶּרֶךְ הָעִיר אֲשֶׁר בָּחַרְתָּ (you chose)

בָּהּ וְהַבַּיִת אֲשֶׁר־בָּנִתִי לִשְׁמֶךָ׃ (to Your Name) [and] תִּשְׁמַע הַשָּׁמַיִם
אֶת־תְּפִלָּתָם (their prayer) וְאֶת־תְּחִנָּתָם (their supplication) [and] תַּעֲשֶׂה מִשְׁפָּטָם׃

1 Kings 8:44-45

because (when) your people go down to war against their enemy on the path which you will send them and the people pray to the LORD [in] the way of the city which you chose and the house (temple) which I built to Your Name, and You will hear [from] Heaven their prayer and their supplication and You will do justice.

אָמַר אֱלֹהִים (God) יְהִי אוֹר וַיְהִי־אוֹר

Genesis 1:3

God said, "There will be light," and there was light.

קָרָא אֱלֹהִים (God) לָרָקִיעַ (the expanse) שָׁמָיִם וַיְהִי־עֶרֶב וַיְהִי־בֹקֶר יוֹם שֵׁנִי

Genesis 1:8

God called the expanse sky. And it was evening and it was morning, the second day.

אָמַר קַיִן (proper name) אֶל־הֶבֶל (proper name) אָחִיו וַיְהִי בִּהְיוֹתָם (came) בַּשָּׂדֶה [and] קָם
קַיִן (proper name) אֶל־הֶבֶל (proper name) אָחִיו וַיַּהַרְגֵהוּ (and killed him)

Genesis 4:8

Cain said to Abel his brother. And it came to pass that they came in a field and Cain arose against Abel his brother and killed him.

חָלִלָה (far be it) לְּךָ מֵעֲשֹׂת (to do: unfamiliar form, recognizable root) כַּדָּבָר הַזֶּה
לְהָמִית (to slay) צַדִּיק עִם־רָשָׁע וְהָיָה כַצַּדִּיק כָּרָשָׁע חָלִלָה (far be it) לָּךְ הֲשֹׁפֵט כָּל־הָאָרֶץ
לֹא יַעֲשֶׂה מִשְׁפָּט

you know words for *righteousness* and *wickedness*, here those same roots refer to people who exhibit those qualities

Genesis 18:25

Far be it from you to do like this thing, to slay the righteous person with the wicked person. And it will be that as the righteous person, so also the wicked one? Far be it from you that the Judge of all the earth will not do justice!

וְהָיָה אִם־לֹא יַאֲמִינוּ (will believe: notice the same root as truth and faithfulness?) לָךְ וְלֹא
יִשְׁמְעוּ לְקֹל הָאֹת (the sign) הָרִאשׁוֹן וְהֶאֱמִינוּ (may believe) לְקֹל הָאֹת
הָאַחֲרוֹן

Can you figure out the last word, הָאַחֲרוֹן, based on אַחַר? It means *the one that comes after*, in this case a second sign.

Exodus 4:8

And it will be that if they will not believe you and will not listen to the voice of the first, they may believe the voice of the one (the sign) that comes after.

TO HAVE

CHAPTER THIRTY-EIGHT

38.1 MONDAY

Notice how the noun נַחֲלָה is built on the same root as the verb *inherit*.

Memorize this week's nouns and read Deuteronomy 4:8.

וּמִי גּוֹי גָּדוֹל אֲשֶׁר־לוֹ חֻקִּים וּמִשְׁפָּטִים צַדִּיקִם כְּכֹל הַתּוֹרָה הַזֹּאת אֲשֶׁר אָנֹכִי נֹתֵן לִפְנֵיכֶם הַיּוֹם׃

and who	וּמִי
nation	גּוֹי
great	גָּדוֹל
which	אֲשֶׁר־
are to it	לוֹ
statutes	חֻקִּים
and judgements	וּמִשְׁפָּטִים
(adjective form of familiar root) righteous	צַדִּיקִם
like all	כְּכֹל
the teaching/law/instruction	הַתּוֹרָה

the this (this teaching)	הַזֹּאת
which	אֲשֶׁר
I	אָנֹכִי
am giving	נֹתֵן
before you	לִפְנֵיכֶם
today	הַיּוֹם׃

38.2 TUESDAY

Translate.

לִשְׁלֹמֹה בָּנִים רַבִּים בְּמִצְרָיִם Solomon has many sons in Egypt.

יֵשׁ לוֹ בָּשָׂר וְלֶחֶם He has meat and bread.

יֵשׁ לַאֲנָשִׁים מָגִנִּים The men have shields.

לִי עֲצֵי הַשָּׂדֶה I have fruit trees.

לֹא יִהְיֶה לַכֹּהֲנִים נַחֲלָה עִם יִשְׂרָאֵל There will not be an inheritance with Israel for the priests.

לָנוּ בָּקָר We have cattle.

שָׁלֹשׁ צִפּוֹר לְרָחֵל Rachel has three birds.

עֶשְׂרִים עִיר לַגּוֹי The nation has twenty cities.

לְאַהֲרֹן כְּלִי טוֹב Aaron has a good tool/implement/vessel.

אַשְׁלִכֵהוּ בָאֵשׁ I will throw it in the fire.

כתוב הַדְּבָרִים הָאֵלֶּה בַּסֵּפֶר שְׁלֹמֹה These words are written in the book of Solomon.

עֲשֵׂה צְדָקָה לְמַעַן שְׁמֶךָ Do righteousness for the sake of your name.

נָתַן לוֹ אֶבֶן אַתָּא You gave him a stone.

דָּוִד בָּא בְּשַׁעֲרֵי יְרוּשָׁלַםִ David came/is coming through the gates of Jerusalem.

יֵדְעוּ כָּל־הַגּוֹיִם כִּי מַלְכֵּנוּ הוּא All nations will know that he is our king.

וְלֹא תַעֲשׂוּ מִכֹּל הַתּוֹעֵבֹת הָאֵלֶּה אַתֶּם Do not do all these abominations.

38.3 WEDNESDAY

Translate.

אֵין לוֹ נַחֲלָה He does not an inheritance.

אֵין לָנוּ אֶלֶף סְפָרִים We do not have a thousand books.

יִשְׂרָאֵל עֹשֶׂה חָיִל Israel is doing valiantly.

דָּוִד בֶּן חַיִל David is a son of valor/valiant/strong/courageous.

אֵין לְיִצְחָק אֵשׁ Isaac does not have fire.

אֵין לָעִיר שְׁעָרִים The city does not have gates.

אֵין לַמִּשְׁפָּחָה כֵּלִים The family does not have tools/implements/vessels/pots and pans.

אֵין לְאַבְרָהָם אֶבֶן Abraham does not have a stone.

יֵשׁ לָעָם אֶרֶץ טוֹבָה The people have a good land.

אֵשֶׁת־חַיִל מִי יִמְצָא Who can find a strong/courageous/valiant woman/wife?
Proverbs 31:10

אֵין לִיהוּדָה אִשָּׁה Judah does not have a wife.

אֵין לָנוּ כְּבָשִׂים כִּי מֵתוּ הֵם We do not have lambs because they died.

גַּם אֵין לָנוּ פָּרִים Also, we do not have bulls.

אָהַב צְדָקָה הַמֶּלֶךְ הַטּוֹב The good king loved righteousness.

קָרָא לְמֹשֶׁה הוּא מִתּוֹךְ הָאֵשׁ He called to Moses from the midst of the fire.

אָמַר מֹשֶׁה הִנֵּנִי Moses said, "Here I am!"

38.4 THURSDAY

1. Translate.

הָיָה לָנוּ לֶחֶם We had bread/food.

יִהְיֶה לָנוּ לֶחֶם We will have bread/food.

לֹא הָיָה לָנוּ לֶחֶם We will not have bread/food.

לֹא יִהְיֶה לָנוּ לֶחֶם לְעוֹלָם וָעֶד We will not have bread/food forever and ever.

יֵשׁ לָנוּ לֶחֶם We have bread/food.

אֵין לָנוּ לֶחֶם We do not have bread/food.

הָיְתָה לְיַעֲקֹב אִשָּׁה Jacob had a wife.

תִּהְיֶה לְיַעֲקֹב אִשָּׁה Jacob will have a wife.

יֵשׁ לְיַעֲקֹב אִשָּׁה Jacob has a wife.

אֵין לְיַעֲקֹב אִשָּׁה Jacob does not have a wife.

לֹא תִּהְיֶה לְיַעֲקֹב אִשָּׁה Jacob will not have a wife.

2. Write Hebrew sentences that convey the same meaning as these English ones. Follow the pattern of the Hebrew sentences above.

אֵין לִיהוּדָה בַּיִת Judah lacks a house.

לֹא תִּהְיֶה לוֹ אִשָּׁה לְעוֹלָם וָעֶד He will never marry.

אֵין לָהֶם אֲבָנִים They do not have stones.

יִהְיֶה לְדָוִד נַחֲלָה David will have an inheritance.

38.5 FRIDAY

For each circled word in the verses below, find out its Strong's number with a concordance and a basic definition with a Biblical Hebrew dictionary. Write them next to the verse. If the circled word is a verb, record its lexical form, as well.

טָבְחָה טִבְחָהּ מָסְכָה יֵינָהּ אַף עָרְכָה שֻׁלְחָנָהּ

Proverbs 9:2

2873, to slaughter, טָבַח

וַיִּרְאוּ אֹתוֹ הָעָם וַיְהַלְלוּ אֶת־אֱלֹהֵיהֶם

Judges 16:24

1984, to shine/boast/praise, הָלַל

וַיֵּבְךְּ אֹתוֹ אָבִיו

Genesis 37:35

1058, to weep, בָּכָה

מָה הַבִּטָּחוֹן הַזֶּה אֲשֶׁר בָּטָחְתָּ

2 Kings 18:19

982, to trust, בָּטַח

מָלַךְ חִזְקִיָּה בֶן־אָחָז

2 Kings 18:1

2396, Hezekiah

וּמִקְדָּשִׁי תִּירָאוּ

Leviticus 19:30

4720, holy place/sanctuary

REVIEW

CHAPTER THIRTY-NINE

39.1 MONDAY

Review week: no new vocabulary. Check the text suggestions for further research and work on 2 Chronicles 7:3 today.

וְכֹל בְּנֵי יִשְׂרָאֵל רֹאִים בְּרֶדֶת הָאֵשׁ וּכְבוֹד יְהוָה עַל־הַבָּיִת וַיִּכְרְעוּ אַפַּיִם אַרְצָה עַל־הָרִצְפָּה
וַיִּשְׁתַּחֲוּוּ וְהוֹדוֹת לַיהוָה כִּי טוֹב כִּי לְעוֹלָם חַסְדּוֹ׃

and all	וְכֹל
the sons of	בְּנֵי
Israel	יִשְׂרָאֵל
were seeing	רֹאִים
the descent of	בְּרֶדֶת
the fire	הָאֵשׁ
and the glory of	וּכְבוֹד
the LORD	יְהוָה
on	עַל־
the house (the Temple)	הַבָּיִת

and they bowed	וַיִּכְרְעוּ
noses	אַפַּיִם
towards the earth	אַרְצָה
on	עַל־
the pavement	הָרִצְפָה
and worshipped	וַיִּשְׁתַּחֲווּ
and gave thanks	וְהוֹדוֹת
to the LORD	לַיהוָה
because	כִּי
is good	טוֹב
because	כִּי
to eternity is	לְעוֹלָם
His steadfast love	חַסְדּוֹ׃

39.2 TUESDAY

1. Rewrite these interrogative sentences as declarative Hebrew sentences.

הֲיִבְנוּ בַּיִת חָדָשׁ הֵם　　יִבְנוּ בַּיִת חָדָשׁ הֵם

הֲרָאִיתָ אַתָּה הַכְּסִיל　　רָאִיתָ אַתָּה הַכְּסִיל

הַהוֹלְכִים הֵם הָעִירָה　　הוֹלְכִים הֵם הָעִירָה

הֲלֹא אַתָּה אָמַרְתָּ כֵּן　　לֹא אַתָּה אָמַרְתָּ כֵּן

הַאַתָּה מֶלֶךְ כָּל־הָאָרֶץ　　אַתָּה מֶלֶךְ כָּל־הָאָרֶץ

2. Rewrite these declarative statements as imperative Hebrew statements.
Teachers using these exercises for testing, please see note on page 282.*

תִּכְתֹּב הַדְּבָרִים הָאֵלֶּה אַתָּה　　כְּתֹב הַדְּבָרִים הָאֵלֶּה אַתָּה

אַתָּה כָּרַתָּ אוֹתוֹ   כְּרָת אוֹתוֹ

מָצָא אַתָּה אֵת שְׁלֹמֹה בִּמְקֹמוֹ   מְצָה אֵת שְׁלֹמֹה בִּמְקֹמוֹ

אַתָּה תִּשְׁפֹּט אֵת הָאֲנָשִׁים בֶּאֱמֶת   שְׁפָט אֵת הָאֲנָשִׁים בֶּאֱמֶת

אֶת־עֲוֹנָם תִּשָּׂא אַתָּה   שָׂא אֶת־עֲוֹנָם

39.3 WEDNESDAY

Translate.

מֵאָה הָרִים one hundred mountains

יוֹם רִאשׁוֹן first day

אַרְבָּעִים יוֹם וְאַרְבָּעִים לָיְלָה forty days and forty nights

אֶלֶף נְבִיאִים one thousand prophets

גַּם הוּא יֵלֵךְ הָעִירָה Also, he will walk/go towards the city.

יִצְחָק לֹא יִירַשׁ שִׁבְעָה בָּתִּים Isaac will not inherit seven houses.

אֲבָנִים נָתַן אָחִיו His brother gave him stones.

עֶשֶׂר פְּעָמִים בָּא אַהֲרוֹן Aaron has come ten times.

לֶחֶם הָיָה נוֹתֵן יְהוּדָה לַגּוֹיִם Judah was giving bread/food to the nations.

לֹא אֶהְיֶה עַבְדְּךָ I will not be your servant.

עָנָה אַהֲרוֹן יְהִי כֵן Aaron answered, "May it be so."

וַיְהִי בִּשְׁנַת אַרְבַּע לְדָוִד הַמֶּלֶךְ הַגּוֹיִם עָשׂוּ מִלְחָמָה And it came to pass in the fourth year of King David, the nations made war.

אֵין לוֹ יַיִן He does not have wine.

לֹא יִהְיֶה לָנוּ נַחֲלָה We will not have an inheritance.

אֵין לוֹ כְּלִי He does not have an implement/vessel.

כָּתוּב הַדָּבָר הַזֶּה בְּסִפְרָתֶךָ This word is written in your book.

39.4 THURSDAY

Translate.

יַעֲשֶׂה חַיִל הוּא לְמַעַן שְׁמוֹ For the sake of his name, he will do valiantly.

אֵין לוֹ שֵׁם He/It does not have a name.

יֵשׁ אֵשׁ בִּירוּשָׁלַםִ There is a fire in Jerusalem.

הָיָה עוֹלֶה אֶל צִיּוֹן אַבְרָהָם Abraham was going up to Zion.

שָׁלֹשׁ פְּעָמִים בָּאוּ הֵם They have come three times.

הָיוּ לִשְׁלֹמֹה אֶלֶף נָשִׁים Solomon had one thousand wives.

לֹא יִכְרֹת אֵת הָעֵצִים יְהוּדָה Judah will not cut the the trees.

יֵשׁ לָהּ כְּלִי She has an implement/vessel.

בְּסֵפֶר מֹשֶׁה כָּתַב הוּא אֵת שְׁמֹתָם He wrote their names in Moses' book.

יִתְּנוּ בְּנֵי אַהֲרֹן הַכֹּהֵן אֵשׁ עַל־הַמִּזְבֵּחַ The sons of Aaron the priest will give fire on the altar.

לֹא יִהְיוּ לְמֹשֶׁה חֲמִשָּׁה פָּרִים טוֹבִים Moses will not have five good bulls.

יִהְיוּ לְיִצְחָק שְׁנֵי כְּבָשִׂים Isaac will have two lambs.

יִהְיוּ לָאָרֶץ שִׁשָּׁה מֶלֶךְ The land will have six kings.

יְהִי כֵן May it be so.

תִּהְיֶה לוֹ אִשָּׁה He will have a wife.

39.5 FRIDAY

1. What is a lexicon?
   a dictionary, especially of Hebrew, Greek, Syriac, or Arabic

2. Write and explain the acronyms of the two leading Biblical Hebrew lexica.

BDB: Brown, Driver, and Briggs (A Hebrew and English Lexicon of the Old Testament by Francis Brown, S.R. Driver, and Charles Briggs)

HALOT: The Hebrew and Aramaic Lexicon of the Old Testament by Ludwig Koehler and Walter Baumgartner

3. Translate from Scripture. Some verb forms have been modified, but this is the last week that will be necessary!

שַׂמְתִּי שָׁם אֶת־הָאָרוֹן אֲשֶׁר־שָׁם בְּרִית (the covenant) יְהוָה (of the LORD) אֲשֶׁר כָּרַת עִם־בְּנֵי יִשְׂרָאֵל

2 Chronicles 6:11

I have put there the ark in which is the covenant of the LORD which He made with the sons/children of Israel.

תּוֹעֲבַת יְהוָה (the LORD) דֶּרֶךְ רָשָׁע (wicked) וּמְרַדֵּף (and pursuit) צְדָקָה
יֶאֱהָב (unfamiliar conjugation, recognizable root)

Proverbs 15:9

A wicked way is an abomination to the LORD but He loves the pursuit of righteousness.

וּבֹעַז (and proper name) עָלָה הַשַּׁעַר [and] יָשַׁב שָׁם וְהִנֵּה הַגֹּאֵל (the redeemer) עֹבֵר אֲשֶׁר
דִּבֶּר־ (spoke) בֹּעַז [and] אָמַר סוּרָה שְׁבָה־ (unfamiliar conjugation, but familiar root) פֹּה
פְּלֹנִי אַלְמֹנִי (peloni almoni is basically Hebrew for "Mr. So-and-So". Be sure to say it aloud!)
סָר [and] יָשַׁב

Ruth 4:1

And Boaz went up to the gates and sat there, and behold, the redeemer was crossing over. Boaz spoke and said, "Turn aside, sit down here, Peloni Almoni." He turned aside and sat.

כִּי־יִקַּח אִישׁ אִשָּׁה וּבְעָלָהּ (and marries her) וְהָיָה אִם־לֹא תִמְצָא־חֵן בְּעֵינָיו כִּי־מָצָא בָהּ
עֶרְוַת (indecent) דָּבָר יִכְתֹּב לָהּ סֵפֶר כְּרִיתֻת (of divorce: recognize the same root as in *cut*?)
יִתֵּן בְּיָדָהּ [and] יְשַׁלְּחָהּ מִבֵּיתוֹ

and marries her: See the pronoun ending? The root is baal, like the Canaanite god, meaning *husband.*

Deuteronomy 24:1

When a man takes a wife and marries her, and it comes to pass that she does not find grace in his eyes because he found in her an indecent something, he will write for her a document of divorce and give it to her and send her from his house.

וַיְהִי בִּשְׁנַת אַרְבַּע לְדָרְיָוֶשׁ (of proper name) הַמֶּלֶךְ הָיָה דְבַר־יְהוָה (the LORD) אֶל־
זְכַרְיָה (proper name) בְּאַרְבָּעָה לַחֹדֶשׁ הַתְּשִׁעִי בְּכִסְלֵו (in the month of Chislev)

Zechariah 7:1

And it came to pass in the fourth year of Darius the King there was a word of the LORD to Zechariah on the fourth of the ninth month, in Chislev.

*Note for teachers testing with these exercises regarding 39.2.2 on page 278:

Unless you have been requiring students to memorize complete conjugation spellings, they may not be able to spell the vowels of the command forms in the first three on page 279. They should be able to provide the consonants if you are testing. For review purposes, the students can consult the verb charts in Appendix D of the textbook.

VAV

CHAPTER FORTY

40.1 MONDAY

Memorize vocabulary words and practice reading Genesis 44:18. Notice the Hebrew ear and nose idioms.

וַיִּגַּשׁ אֵלָיו יְהוּדָה וַיֹּאמֶר בִּי אֲדֹנִי יְדַבֶּר־נָא עַבְדְּךָ דָבָר בְּאָזְנֵי אֲדֹנִי וְאַל־יִחַר אַפְּךָ בְּעַבְדֶּךָ כִּי
כָמוֹךָ כְּפַרְעֹה׃

approached	וַיִּגַּשׁ
to him	אֵלָיו
Judah	יְהוּדָה
and said	וַיֹּאמֶר
please, excuse me,	בִּי
my lord	אֲדֹנִי
will speak	יְדַבֶּר־
please	נָא
your servant	עַבְדְּךָ
a word	דָבָר

in the ears of	בְּאָזְנֵי
my lord	אֲדֹנִי
and not	וְאַל־
will burn	יִחַר
your nose (please don't be angry)	אַפְּךָ
with your servant	בְּעַבְדֶּךָ
because	כִּי
as you	כָמוֹךָ
so also Pharaoh	כְּפַרְעֹה׃

40.2 TUESDAY

1. Explain these terms and how they differ from one another.

- Vav Conversive

  This term describes the vav prefix as a verb tense converter.

- Vav Consecutive

  This term emphasizes that the vav prefix connects a narrative.

- Wayyiqtol

  This is a way of referring to the vav prefix plus an imperfect tense verb without describing the function.

- Weqatal

  This is a way of referring to the vav prefix plus an perfect tense verb without describing the function.

- Vav Relative

  This term emphasizes that the vav prefix relates verbs in a story to one another.

2. Translate.

וַיִּפֹּל אַבְרָהָם And Abraham fell.

Though the vav prefix is always connecting ideas, it is not always necessary to include an "and" in an English translation. We have other ways to continue a tale, such as more use of dependent clauses and punctuation. The answers for this exercise will include "and," but not all future ones will. Student answers would be correct with or without including "and" in the translation.

וַיֶּאֱהַב יִצְחָק אֶת־שָׂרָה אִשְׁתּוֹ And Isaac loved Sarah, his wife.

וְאֶכְתֹּב אֲנִי עַל־סֵפֶר מַלְכֵי־יִשְׂרָאֵל וִיהוּדָה And I wrote in the book of the kings of Israel and Judah.

וַיִּכְרֹת שְׁלֹמֹה אֶת חַסְדּוֹ מֵעִם בֵּיתִי עַד־עוֹלָם And Solomon cut off his steadfast love from my house (family) forever.

וַיָּמֻתוּ הֵם לִפְנֵי הַמֶּלֶךְ And they died in the presence of the king.

וְשָׁב מֹשֶׁה לְאַרְצוֹ And Moses will return to his land.

וַיֶּאֱסֹף דָּוִד אֶת־כָּל־אַנְשֵׁי הַמָּקוֹם And David gathered all the men of the place.

וְשָׁכַבְתָּ אַתָּה בַּמָּקוֹם הַהוּא And you will lie down in that place.

וַיִּשְׁפֹּט מֹשֶׁה אֶת־יִשְׂרָאֵל שֵׁשׁ שָׁנִים And Moses judged Israel six years.

וַיֵּרֶד מֹשֶׁה אֶל־הָעָם וַיֹּאמֶר אֲלֵהֶם אִכְלוּ And Moses went down to the people and said to them, "Eat!"

רֵד וְשָׁמַרְתָּ אֵת הַצֹּאן Go down and guard the flock!

זָכֹר וְעָשִׂיתָ אֶת־כָּל־הַמִּצְוָה הַזֹּאת Remember and do all this commandment.

40.3 WEDNESDAY

1. Translate.

הוּא בַשָּׁנָה הָרִאשׁוֹנָה לְמָלְכוֹ (figure this out from the root and context) בַּחֹדֶשׁ הָרִאשׁוֹן פָּתַח אֶת־שַׁעֲרֵי הָעִיר

In the first year of his reign, in the first month, he opened the gates of the city.

וַיִּרְאֶה אַהֲרֹן רָאשֵׁי הֶהָרִים

Aaron saw the tops of the mountains.

וַתַּעֲמֹדְנָה הַנָּשִׁים עַל־שְׂפַת הַנָּהָר

The women stood on the bank of the river.

יָדַעְתִּי כִּי אַתָּה אָבִי אֶרֶךְ (long) אַפַּיִם וְרַב חֶסֶד

I knew that you are my father, patient and faithfully loving.

וְשַׂמְתִּי אֶת־הַדְּבָרִים בְּפִיו

I will put words in his mouth.

הַאָהַבְתָּ אוֹתוֹ בְּכָל־לְבָבְךָ וּבְכָל נַפְשְׁךָ

Did you love him with all of your heart and with all of your soul?

וַיִּקְחוּ אָזְנֵינוּ דְּבַר־פִּיו

And our ears took the word of his mouth. (We listened to him.)

וַיֵּלֶךְ מֹשֶׁה אֶל־בֵּיתוֹ וּפְנֵי הַמֶּלֶךְ לֹא רָאָה
Moses walked to his house and did not see the king's face.

2. Convert the tense of these verbs by adding the vav prefix. All of these will be spelled with וְ for perfect tense verbs or וַ with-a-dagesh-in-the-next-letter for imperfect tense verbs. Then write the translation of the new word.

נָפַל וְנָפַל and he will fall

אָהַבְתָּ וְאָהַבְתָּ and you will love

כָּתַבְתִּי וְכָתַבְתִּי and I will write

יָמוּת וַיָּמוּת and he died

יִשְׁלַח וַיִּשְׁלַח and he sent

שָׁכַב וְשָׁכַב and he will lie down

יִתֵּן וַיִּתֵּן and he gave

40.4 THURSDAY

Translate.

עָנְתָה רָחֵל Rachel answered.

וַתַּעַן רָחֵל Rachel answered.

יַעֲשֶׂה מִלְחָמָה אַהֲרֹן Aaron will make war.

וַיַּעַשׂ מִלְחָמָה הַמֶּלֶךְ The king made war.

יִהְיֶה רָעָב בָּאָרֶץ הַהִיא There will be famine in that land.

וַיְהִי רָעָב בָּאָרֶץ הַהִיא There was famine in that land.

יִרְאֶה הוּא עִיר He will see a city.

וַיַּרְא יְהוּדָה עִיר Judah saw a city.

וַיַּעַשׂ חֶסֶד דָּוִד עִם הַמִּשְׁפָּחָה David showed steadfast love to the family.

וַיַּעַל מֹשֶׁה אֶל־יְרוּשָׁלַםִ Moses went up to Jerusalem.

שָׂרָה הָיְתָה פּוֹתַחַת אֹהֶל Sarah was opening a tent.

וְיָרַשׁ שָׂדֶה יִצְחָק Isaac will inherit a field.

וַיִּשְׁפֹּט שְׁלֹמֹה אֶת־יִשְׂרָאֵל עֶשֶׂר שָׁנִים Solomon judged Israel ten years.

וְיִכְתֹּב מֹשֶׁה אֵת סֵפֶר הַתּוֹרָה Moses wrote the book of the Torah/law.

אַהֲרֹן יָשׁוּב וְיִבְנֶה עָרֵי יְהוּדָה Aaron will return and build the cities of Judah.

40.5 FRIDAY

Translate from Scripture.

וַיֹּאמֶר יְהוָה (the LORD) הֵן (behold) עַם אֶחָד וְשָׂפָה אַחַת לְכֻלָּם וְזֶה הַחִלָּם (they began)
לַעֲשׂוֹת (to do) וְעַתָּה לֹא־יִבָּצֵר (will be inaccessible) מֵהֶם כֹּל אֲשֶׁר יָזְמוּ (they will purpose)
לַעֲשׂוֹת (to do: infinitive form, coming up in Chapter 41)

Genesis 11:6

The LORD said, "Behold one people, and all of them have one language. And this is what they began to do. And now nothing of all which they will purpose to do will be inaccessible to them."

וְהִנֵּה שֶׁבַע פָּרוֹת אֲחֵרוֹת (other) עֹלוֹת אַחֲרֵיהֶן (after them) מִן־הַיְאֹר (the Nile) רָעוֹת
מַרְאֶה (appearance) וְדַקּוֹת (and thin) בָּשָׂר וַתַּעֲמֹדְנָה אֵצֶל (beside) הַפָּרוֹת עַל־שְׂפַת
הַיְאֹר (the Nile)

Genesis 41:3

And behold! Seven other bulls came up after them from the Nile, bad in appearance and thin flesh. And they stood beside the bulls on the bank of the Nile.

אַךְ בָּשָׂר בְּנַפְשׁוֹ דָמוֹ לֹא תֹאכֵלוּ

Genesis 9:4

But meat with its life, its blood, do not eat.

וְאָהַבְתָּ אֵת יְהוָה (the LORD) אֱלֹהֶיךָ (your God) בְּכָל־לְבָבְךָ וּבְכָל־נַפְשְׁךָ וּבְכָל־מְאֹדֶךָ

Deuteronomy 6:5

And you shall love the LORD your God with all your heart, and with all your soul/life, and with all your "very."

כִּי־זֶה שְׁנָתַיִם הָרָעָב בְּקֶרֶב הָאָרֶץ וְעוֹד (and yet) חָמֵשׁ שָׁנִים אֲשֶׁר אֵין־חָרִישׁ (plowing) וְקָצִיר (and harvesting)

Genesis 45:6

Because this was two years of the famine in the midst of the land and there will be yet five years in which there will be no plowing and no harvesting.

וִידַעְתֶּם כִּי בְקֶרֶב יִשְׂרָאֵל אָנִי וַאֲנִי יְהוָה (the LORD) אֱלֹהֵיכֶם (your God) וְאֵין עוֹד (beside) וְלֹא־יֵבֹשׁוּ (will be ashamed) עַמִּי לְעוֹלָם

Joel 2:27

You might have noticed that **עוֹד** was translated as *yet* in Genesis 45:6 and as *beside* in Joel 2:27. It can also mean *circling*, *continuance*, *still*, *again*, *anymore*, *since*. Be ready for it in the verse below.

And they will know that I am in the midst of Israel and that I am the LORD your God. And there is none beside. And my people will not be ashamed, ever.

וְלֹא־קָם נָבִיא עוֹד בְּיִשְׂרָאֵל כְּמֹשֶׁה אֲשֶׁר יְדָעוֹ יְהוָה (the LORD) פָּנִים אֶל־פָּנִים

Deuteronomy 34:10

A prophet still has not risen in Israel like Moses, who knew the LORD face to face.

INFINITIVES I

CHAPTER FORTY-ONE

41.1 MONDAY

Memorize vocabulary and work on reading Genesis 9:17.

וַיֹּאמֶר אֱלֹהִים אֶל־נֹחַ זֹאת אוֹת־הַבְּרִית אֲשֶׁר הֲקִמֹתִי בֵּינִי וּבֵין כָּל־בָּשָׂר אֲשֶׁר עַל־הָאָרֶץ׃

said	וַיֹּאמֶר
God	אֱלֹהִים
to	אֶל־
Noah	נֹחַ
this	זֹאת
sign of	אוֹת־
the covenant	הַבְּרִית
which	אֲשֶׁר
I established (a form of *arise*)	הֲקִמֹתִי
between me	בֵּינִי
and between	וּבֵין
all	כָּל־

flesh	בָּשָׂר
which	אֲשֶׁר
on	עַל־
the earth	הָאָרֶץ׃

41.2 TUESDAY

Translate.

עָפָר תֹּאכַל כָּל־יְמֵי חַיֶּיךָ You will eat dust all the days of your life.

You probably recognize these words from Genesis 3:14 and can guess that the last word means *your life*. Notice its similarity to the verb *to live* and the adjective *alive*.

וַיִּקַּח שֵׁשׁ־מֵאוֹת רֶכֶב And he took six hundred chariots.

שְׁלֹמֹה הַיֹּשֵׁב עַל־כִּסְאוֹ Solomon is the one who sits on his throne.

שֵׁשֶׁת יָמִים תַּעֲשֶׂה מְלָאכָה Six days you will do work.

אֶת הַמַּלְכוּת נָתַן הַמֶּלֶךְ לְדָוִד כִּי־הוּא אִישׁ חָיִל The king gave the kingdom to David because he is a valiant man.

לֹא יִחְיֶה הָאִישׁ הָרָשָׁע הַזֶּה This wicked man shall not live.

וְזָכַרְתִּי אֶת־בְּרִיתִי אֲשֶׁר בֵּינִי וּבֵינֵיכֶם וּבֵין כָּל־נֶפֶשׁ חַיָּה בְּכָל־בָּשָׂר
And I will remember my covenant which is between me and you and every living being of all flesh.

אֲדֹנִי שְׁמָעֵנִי
Hear me, my lord.

וַיִּשְׁלַח הַמֶּלֶךְ וַיִּקְרָא לְמֹשֶׁה וּלְאַהֲרֹן וַיֹּאמֶר אֲלֵהֶם חָטָאתִי הַפָּעַם וַאֲנִי וְעַמִּי הָרְשָׁעִים
The king sent and called for Moses and Aaron and said to them, "I have sinned this time. I and my people are wicked."

וְעַל־חַרְבְּךָ תִחְיֶה וְאֶת־אָחִיךָ תַּעֲבֹד
By your sword you shall live and you shall serve your brother.

כִּסְאֲךָ דָוִד עוֹלָם וָעֶד Your throne, David, is forever and ever.

וַיִּתֵּן אֲדֹנִי לְדָוִד כִּסֵּא כָבוֹד My lord gave David a seat of honor.

אֶעֱבֹד אֵת אֲדֹנִי אַבְרָהָם בֶּאֱמֶת I will serve my lord Abraham in truth/with faithfulness.

לֹא יַעֲשׂוּ שָׁלוֹם יְדֵי רְשָׁעִים The hands of the wicked will not make peace.

וְכָרַתִּי לָהֶם בְּרִית שָׁלוֹם בְּרִית עוֹלָם יִהְיֶה אִתָּם I made with them ("cut for them") a covenant of peace. It will be an eternal covenant with them.

41.3 WEDNESDAY

1. Identify the infinitives amongst the verbs below.

זְכֹר ✔ to remember

עֲבֹר ✔ to cross over

עוֹלָה going up

to judge ✔ שְׁפֹט

שְׁמֹעַ ✔ to hear

תִּשְׁתּוּ will drink

יוֹרֵד going down

to drink ✔ שְׁתוֹת

שְׁלֹחַ ✔ to send

רָאוּ saw

עֲמֹד ✔ to stand

to find ✔ מְצֹא

מוֹלֵךְ ruling

חְיוֹת ✔ to live

to guard ✔ שְׁמֹר

נוֹתֵן giving

to eat ✔ אֱכֹל

קְרֹא ✔ to call

וְשָׁפַט and will judge

to rule ✔ מְלֹךְ

בּוֹנֶה building

וַיִּקַּח and he took

אֱכוֹל eat!

שְׂאֵת ✔ to lift/carry

to build ✔ בְּנוֹת

עֲשׂוֹת ✔ to make

to see ✔ רְאוֹת

עֲלוֹת ✔ to go up

עָלָה went up

דַּעַת ✔ to know

רֶשֶׁת ✔ to inherit

2. Translate the words above: Hebrew into English and English into Hebrew.

41.4 THURSDAY

1. Translate.

הָלַכְתָּ לִרְאוֹת אֵת הַמֶּלֶךְ You went to see the king.

לְכוּ אֶל בֵּיתֵנוּ לֶאֱכֹל וְלִשְׁתּוֹת Go/Come to our house to eat and drink.

הוּא נָתַן לָהֶם חָכְמָה לָדַעַת לַעֲשׂת אֶת־כָּל הַמְּלָאכָה He gave them wisdom to know, to do all the work.

אֲנִי עָבַדְתִּי לִמְצֹא־חֵן בְּעֵינֵי אֲדֹנִי I worked to find grace/favor in the eyes of my lord.

בָּא מֹשֶׁה לִמְלֹךְ עַל הָאָרֶץ Moses is coming/came to rule over the land/earth.

אַנְשֵׁי חַיִל יָרְדוּ לִשְׁמֹר אֵת הַבַּיִת כִּי שָׁבוּ הָרְשָׁעִים
Men of valor went down to guard the house because the wicked ones returned.

וַיֹּאמֶר שְׁלֹמֹה אֵלַי לֵאמֹר לֵךְ מְצָא רִכְבִּי Solomon said to me, "Go, find my chariot."

יֵשׁ לוֹ רֶכֶב־אֵשׁ He has a chariot of fire.

לֹא תִכְרְתוּ לָהֶם בְּרִית Do not make a covenant with them.

2. Translate from Scripture.

הוּא־יִבְנֶה בַיִת לִשְׁמִי וְהוּא יִהְיֶה־לִּי לְבֵן וַאֲנִי־לוֹ לְאָב וַהֲכִינוֹתִי (and I will establish) כִּסֵּא
מַלְכוּתוֹ עַל־יִשְׂרָאֵל עַד־עוֹלָם

1 Chronicles 22:10

He will build a house to my name (a temple for me) and he will be a son to me, and I will be a father to him. I will establish the throne of his kingdom over Israel until eternity.

וַיְכַל (and completed) אֱלֹהִים (God) בַּיּוֹם הַשְּׁבִיעִי מְלַאכְתּוֹ אֲשֶׁר עָשָׂה וַיִּשְׁבֹּת (and rested)
בַּיּוֹם הַשְּׁבִיעִי מִכָּל־מְלַאכְתּוֹ אֲשֶׁר עָשָׂה

Genesis 2:2

And on the seventh day God completed his work which He did. And He rested on the seventh day from all his work which He did.

41.5 FRIDAY

Translate from Scripture.

As usual, answer key translations may be overly literal and poor English. Students should try to produce better translations, and compare theirs with one or more English Bibles.

בְּזֵעַת (in the sweat) אַפֶּיךָ תֹּאכַל לֶחֶם עַד שׁוּבְךָ אֶל־הָאֲדָמָה כִּי מִמֶּנָּה לֻקָּחְתָּ (you were taken)
כִּי־עָפָר אַתָּה וְאֶל־עָפָר תָּשׁוּב

Genesis 3:19

With the sweat of your nose you will eat bread/food until you return to the ground, because from it you were taken, because you are dust and to dust you will return.

וְשַׂמְתִּי אֶת־זַרְעֲךָ כַּעֲפַר הָאָרֶץ

Genesis 13:16

I will put your seed like the dust of the earth.

וְאִלּוּ (and though) חָיָה אֶלֶף שָׁנִים פַּעֲמַיִם וְטוֹבָה לֹא רָאָה הֲלֹא אֶל־מָקוֹם אֶחָד הַכֹּל הוֹלֵךְ

Ecclesiastes 6:6

And though one lived a thousand years twice, and did not see good, does not everything go to one place?

יְבֹאוּנִי רַחֲמֶיךָ וְאֶחְיֶה כִּי־תוֹרָתְךָ שַׁעֲשֻׁעָי (my delight)

Psalm 119:77

May your compassion come to me and I will live because your Torah/teaching/instruction/law is my delight.

וַיֹּאמֶר יְהוָה (the LORD) אֱלֹהִים (God) הֵן (behold) הָאָדָם (the man) הָיָה כְּאַחַד מִמֶּנּוּ לָדַעַת טוֹב וָרָע וְעַתָּה פֶּן־יִשְׁלַח יָדוֹ וְלָקַח גַּם מֵעֵץ הַחַיִּים וְאָכַל וָחַי לְעֹלָם

Genesis 3:22

The LORD God said, "Behold! The man will be like one from us to know good and evil. Now lest he send his hand and take also from the tree of life and eat and he will live forever..."

וַיָּקֻמוּ הָאֲנָשִׁים וַיֵּלֵכוּ וַיְצַו (and commanded) יְהוֹשֻׁעַ (proper name) אֶת־הַהֹלְכִים לִכְתֹּב אֶת־הָאָרֶץ לֵאמֹר לְכוּ וְהִתְהַלְּכוּ (walk: unfamiliar stem: recognizable root) בָאָרֶץ וְכִתְבוּ אוֹתָהּ וְשׁוּבוּ אֵלַי וּפֹה אַשְׁלִיךְ (I will cast) לָכֶם גּוֹרָל (lots) לִפְנֵי יְהוָה (the LORD) בְּשִׁלֹה (in proper name)

Joshua 18:8

The men arose and went and Joshua commanded the ones who were going to write the land, "Walk in the land and write it and return to me. And here I will cast lots before the LORD in Shiloh."

INFINITIVES II

CHAPTER FORTY-TWO

42.1 MONDAY

Practice vocabulary and read 1 Kings 20:7.

וַיִּקְרָא מֶלֶךְ־יִשְׂרָאֵל לְכָל־זִקְנֵי הָאָרֶץ וַיֹּאמֶר דְּעוּ־נָא וּרְאוּ כִּי רָעָה זֶה מְבַקֵּשׁ כִּי־שָׁלַח אֵלַי
לְנָשַׁי וּלְבָנַי וּלְכַסְפִּי וְלִזְהָבִי וְלֹא מָנַעְתִּי מִמֶּנּוּ׃

called	וַיִּקְרָא
the king of	מֶלֶךְ־
Israel	יִשְׂרָאֵל
to all	לְכָל־
the old ones (elders) of	זִקְנֵי
the land	הָאָרֶץ
and said	וַיֹּאמֶר
Know	דְּעוּ־
please	נָא
and see	וּרְאוּ
that	כִּי

evil	רָעָה
this	זֶה
is seeking	מְבַקֵּשׁ
because	כִּי־
he sent	שָׁלַח
to me	אֵלַי
for my wives	לְנָשַׁי
and for my sons	וּלְבָנַי
and for my silver	וּלְכַסְפִּי
and for my gold	וְלִזְהָבִי
and not	וְלֹא
I withheld	מָנַעְתִּי
any	מִמֶּנּוּ׃

Complete these charts for שׁבר which is regular in its conjugations.

plural	singular	**BREAK** perfect tense
שָׁבַרְנוּ	שָׁבַרְתִּי	first person
שְׁבַרְתֶּם	שָׁבַרְתָּ	second person, m.
שְׁבַרְתֶּן	שָׁבַרְתְּ	second person, f.
שָׁבְרוּ	שָׁבַר	third person, m.
שָׁבְרוּ	שָׁבְרָה	third person, f.

plural	singular	**BREAK** imperfect tense
נִשְׁבֹּר	אֶשְׁבֹּר	first person
תִּשְׁבְּרוּ	תִּשְׁבֹּר	second person, m.
תִּשְׁבֹּרְנָה	תִּשְׁבְּרִי	second person, f.
יִשְׁבְּרוּ	יִשְׁבֹּר	third person, m.
תִּשְׁבֹּרְנָה	תִּשְׁבֹּר	third person, f.

שְׁבוֹר	infinitive
שְׁבֹר	command, m. s.

42.2 TUESDAY "While," "when," and "during" are essentially interchangeable in today's translation exercises.

Translate.

בִּזְכֹר when remembering

בִּשְׁמֹר while guarding

כַּעֲלוֹת when going up

כִּרְאוֹת when seeing

בִּקְרֹא while calling

בֶּאֱכֹל during eating

בְּתֵת when giving

כִּשְׁכַּב when lying down

כַּעֲבֹד while crossing over

בִּשְׁלֹחַ when sending

כִּקְרֹא when calling

וַיֹּאמֶר he said

וַיֵּצֵא he went out

וָאֶשְׁבֹּר I broke

זְכֹר to remember

לְבֹשׁ to wear

יָלַדְתָּ you begot

42.3 WEDNESDAY

1. Translate.

וַיֵּצְאוּ הֵם They went out.

דָּוִד הַמֶּלֶךְ יָלַד אֶת־שְׁלֹמֹה King David begot Solomon.

וּנְתַתֶּם אַתֶּם לִי בֶּגֶד אֲשֶׁר לָבַשׁ־בּוֹ הַמֶּלֶךְ And you will give to me a garment which the king has worn.

כְּלִי זָהָב שָׁבַר אִישׁ הֶחָיִל The strong man broke a golden vessel.

רַק בְּאֶרֶץ כְּנַעַן יֵשׁ כֶּסֶף Only in the land of Canaan is there silver.

אֵין לְאַרְצוֹ זָהָב רַב His land does not have much gold.

2. Match phrases with their translations.

a. when they eat	e. בְּשִׁבְתְּךָ
b. while you were doing	h. בִּהְיוֹתוֹ
c. as he saw	g. בְּזָכְרֵנוּ
d. when you go out	b. בַּעֲשׂוֹתְךָ
e. while you sit	d. בְּצֵאתְךָ
f. during your crossing over	f. בְּעָבְרְכֶם
g. when we remembered	a. בְּאָכְלָם
h. while he was	i. בַּעֲלוֹתוֹ
i. while he went up	c. כִּרְאוֹתוֹ

42.4 THURSDAY

Translate.

מִתִּתִּי לֶחֶם from my giving bread/food

מִזְּכֹּר אֵת הָרֶכֶב from remembering the chariot

עָלַי לִשְׁמֹר אֵת הַזָּהָב I must guard the gold.

עָלֵינוּ לִשְׁמֹעַ אֵת נְאֻם מֹשֶׁה We ought to hear the declaration of Moses.

עָלָיו לַעֲשׂוֹת שָׁלוֹם He ought to make peace.

עָלֶיךָ לִכְתֹּב אֶת־דִּבְרֵי הַתּוֹרָה־הַזֹּאת עַל־סֵפֶר It is on you to write the words of this teaching/law/Torah in a book.

עָלָיו לָשׁוּב אֶל צִיּוֹן He ought to return to Zion.

עָלֵינוּ לִמְצֹא הַצֹּאן We must find the flock.

תֵּן לָהֶם רַק זָהָב לֹא תִּתֵּן כֶּסֶף Give them only gold. Do not give silver.

וַיֵּצֵא יִצְחָק Isaac went out.

לֹא תִלְבַּשׁ הַבֶּגֶד הַהוּא פֹּה Do not wear that garment here.

יְהוּדָה יָלַד אֶת־אַהֲרוֹן Judah will beget Aaron.

יַאַסְפוּ פְּרִי הַגָּפֶן They will gather the fruit of the vine (grapes).

מִצִּיּוֹן תֵּצֵא תוֹרָה The Torah/teaching/law will go forth from Zion.

עָלֶיךָ לֶאֱסֹף אֵת הַכְּבָשִׂים הַיּוֹם You ought to gather the lambs today.

42.5 FRIDAY

Translate from Scripture.

וְאָמַרְתָּ אֲלֵהֶם כֹּה (thus) אָמַר יְהוָה (the LORD) צְבָאוֹת שׁוּבוּ אֵלַי נְאֻם יְהוָה (the LORD)
צְבָאוֹת וְאָשׁוּב אֲלֵיכֶם אָמַר יְהוָה (the LORD) צְבָאוֹת

Zechariah 1:3

And you will say to them, "Thus said the LORD of armies, 'Return to me,' declares the LORD of armies, 'And I will return to you,' said the LORD of armies.'"

וַיִּקְרָא רָעָב עַל־הָאָרֶץ כָּל־מַטֵּה־לֶחֶם שָׁבָר

Psalm 105:16

[He] called a famine on the land and broke every staff of bread.

בַּיּוֹם הַהוּא נְאֻם יְהוָה (the LORD) צְבָאוֹת תִּקְרְאוּ אִישׁ לְרֵעֵהוּ אֶל־תַּחַת גֶּפֶן וְאֶל־תַּחַת
תְּאֵנָה (fig tree)

Zechariah 3:10

"In that day," declares the LORD of armies, "You will call, each man to his neighbor, to [come] under a vine and under a fig tree."

וַיְדַבֵּר (and spoke: same root letters as *word*) אֶל־עֶפְרוֹן (proper name) בְּאָזְנֵי עַם־הָאָרֶץ
לֵאמֹר אַךְ אִם־אַתָּה לוּ (oh, please) שְׁמָעֵנִי (will listen to me) נָתַתִּי כֶּסֶף הַשָּׂדֶה קַח מִמֶּנִּי
וְאֶקְבְּרָה (and I will bury) אֶת־מֵתִי שָׁמָּה

Genesis 23:13

And he spoke to Ephron, in the ears of the people of the land, saying, "But if you, oh, please, will listen to me, I will give the silver of the field. Take it from me and I will bury my dead there."

הַשֶּׁמֶשׁ יָצָא עַל־הָאָרֶץ וְלוֹט (proper name) בָּא צֹעֲרָה (toward proper name)

Genesis 19:23

The sun went out over the land and Lot came toward Zoar.

נִבְחָר (chosen) שֵׁם מֵעֹשֶׁר (from riches) רָב מִכֶּסֶף וּמִזָּהָב חֵן טוֹב

Proverbs 22:1

Chosen a name from abundant riches. (A good character/reputation is better than wealth.) Grace/favor is better than silver and gold.

וַיִּדַּר (and vowed) יַעֲקֹב נֶדֶר (a vow: notice same root letters as the verb *to vow*) לֵאמֹר אִם־
יִהְיֶה אֱלֹהִים (God) עִמָּדִי (with me) וּשְׁמָרַנִי בַּדֶּרֶךְ הַזֶּה אֲשֶׁר אָנֹכִי הוֹלֵךְ וְנָתַן־לִי לֶחֶם לֶאֱכֹל
וּבֶגֶד לִלְבֹּשׁ: וְשַׁבְתִּי בְשָׁלוֹם אֶל־בֵּית אָבִי וְהָיָה יְהוָה (the LORD) לִי לֵאלֹהִים (for God)

Genesis 28:20-21

Jacob made a vow, "If God will be with me and will guard me in this way which I am going and give to me food to eat and a clothes to wear and I return in peace to my father's house, the LORD will be my God."

INFINITIVES III

CHAPTER FORTY-THREE

43.1 MONDAY

Read the textbook vocabulary notes, memorize vocabulary, and work on Genesis 45:3.

וַיֹּאמֶר יוֹסֵף אֶל־אֶחָיו אֲנִי יוֹסֵף הַעוֹד אָבִי חָי וְלֹא־יָכְלוּ אֶחָיו לַעֲנוֹת אֹתוֹ כִּי נִבְהֲלוּ מִפָּנָיו׃

said	וַיֹּאמֶר
proper name Joseph	יוֹסֵף
to	אֶל־
his brothers	אֶחָיו
I am	אֲנִי
proper name Joseph	יוֹסֵף
Is still?	הַעוֹד
my father	אָבִי
living	חָי
and not	וְלֹא־
they were able	יָכְלוּ

his brothers	אֶחָיו
to answer	לַעֲנוֹת
him	אֹתוֹ
because	כִּי
dismayed	נִבְהֲלוּ
from his face (in his presence)	מִפָּנָיו׃

43.2 TUESDAY

Translate.

אֲדוֹנִי נָתַן לָנוּ לִשְׁמֹר אֵת כַּסְפּוֹ My lord allowed us to guard his silver.

אִמּוֹ נָתְנָה לוֹ לַעֲלוֹת לִירוּשָׁלַםִ His mother allowed him to go up to Jerusalem.

הֵם נָתְנוּ לִי לִשְׁכַּב They allowed me to lie down.

יָצְאוּ בֵּית מֹשֶׁה וְאֶחָיו וּבֵית אָבִיו רַק צֹאנָם וּבְקָרָם יָשְׁבוּ בְּאֶרֶץ כְּנַעַן

The house of Moses, and his brothers, and his father's house went out. Only their flocks and their cattle dwelt in the land of Canaan.

לֹא נָתַן הַמֶּלֶךְ לִי לִשְׁבֹּר רִכְבּוֹ

The king did not allow me to break his chariot.

וַתִּפֹּל עַל־רַגְלָיו וַתֹּאמֶר שְׁמַע נָא אֲדֹנִי אֵת נְאֻם הַנָּבִיא

And she fell at his feet and said, "Listen, please, my lord, to the prophet's declaration!"

אוֹכֵל הוּא פְּרִי הַגָּפֶן

He is eating the fruit of the vine (grapes).

לֹא לָבְשָׁה רָחֵל אֵת הַבֶּגֶד הַזֶּה Rachel did not wear that garment.

צְאוּ מִשָּׁם צְאוּ מִתּוֹךְ הָעִיר לִשְׁבֹּר כְּלֵי הַמֶּלֶךְ Go out from there! Go out from the midst of the city to break the vessels of the king!

אֵין אֲנָשִׁים רְשָׁעִים פֹּה

There are no wicked men here.

וְהָיָה כְשִׁבְתּוֹ עַל כִּסֵּא מַלְכֻתוֹ וְכָתַב לוֹ אֶת־מִשְׁנֵה (a copy: like *Mishnah*) הַתּוֹרָה הַזֹּאת עַל־סֵפֶר מִלִּפְנֵי הַכֹּהֲנִים

And it shall be when he sits on the throne of his kingdom, he will write for himself a copy of this Torah/teaching/law in a book, in front of the priests.

הַמֶּלֶךְ יָלַד בֵּן

The king begot a son.

עֵינֶיךָ פְּתַח לִרְאוֹת Open your eyes to see.

וַתִּשָּׂא אַתָּה אֵת הַזָּהָב מֵעָפָר You lifted the gold from the dust.

בַּעֲלוֹתוֹ אֲנִי יָרַדְתִּי While he was going up, I went down.

כְּשָׁמְעוֹ אֵת נְאֻם הַנָּבִיא הוּא שָׁב When he heard the prophet's declaration, he returned.

43.3 WEDNESDAY

Translate.

תּוּכַל לַעֲשׂוֹת שָׁלוֹם You will be able to make peace.

יָכֹל לִסְפֹּר הַצֹּאן He was able to count the flocks.

אוּכַל לִפְתֹּחַ אֲנִי אֵת שַׁעֲרֵי הָעִיר I will be able to open the city gates.

מֹשֶׁה יוּכַל לִכְתֹּב לוֹ אֵת כָּל־הַדְּבָרִים הָאֵלֶּה אֶל־סֵפֶר Moses will be able to write all these words in a book.

יָכֹלְנוּ לָרֶשֶׁת שָׂדוֹת וּבָקָר We were able to inherit fields and cattle.

יוּכַל לִשְׁמֹעַ אֶת־קוֹלְךָ He will be able to hear your voice.

הַמֶּלֶךְ יָכֹל לִשְׁפֹּט אוֹתָם The king was able to judge them.

תּוּכַל לָדַעַת אֶת־קוֹלִי You will be able to know my voice.

הָעָם יָכֹל לָרֶדֶת The people were able to go down.

הַכֹּהֵן יוּכַל לִזְבּוֹחַ אֶת־צֹאנְךָ The priest will be able to slaughter your sheep/goats.

רַק אַחֲרֵי עֶשֶׂר שָׁנָה יוּכַל לָשׁוּב שְׁלֹמֹה Only after ten years will Solomon be able to return.

תּוּכַל לַעֲשׂוֹת לִי מִקְדָּשׁ You will be able to make a holy place for me.

הוּא יָכֹל לִלְבֹּשׁ אֵת בִּגְדִי He was able to wear my garment.

תּוּכַל לָשֶׁבֶת עַל־כִּסֵּא אֲדֹנִי־הַמֶּלֶךְ You will be able to sit on the throne of my lord, the king.

הוּא יָכֹל לִרְאוֹת אֵת הָאֵשׁ He was able to see the fire.

43.4 THURSDAY

Translate.

אִם שָׁמוֹעַ תִּשְׁמְעוּ אֵת דְּבָרַי תִּהְיֶה חָכָם אַתָּה If you will really hear my words you will be wise.

רָאֹה רָאִיתָ אֵת אָבִי You have surely seen my father.

אָמֹר אָמַר כִּי שְׁלֹמֹה שִׁמְךָ He has surely said that your name is Solomon.

נָפוֹל יִפֹּל הָעֵץ הַהוּא That tree will surely fall.

שׁוּב אָשׁוּב אֵלֶיךָ I will surely return to you.

אָסֹף יֶאֱסֹף כָּל־הַצֹּאן He will surely gather all the flocks.

נָשׂוֹא נָשָׂא עֲוֹנֵנוּ He has surely carried our guilt.

עָלֹה יַעֲלֶה אִתָּנוּ דָוִד David will surely go up with us.

הֵם עָשֹׂה יַעֲשׂוּ חֶסֶד They will surely love steadfastly.

עָשֹׂה תַּעֲשֶׂה שָׁלוֹם שָׂרָה Sarah will surely make peace.

פָּתֹחַ יִפְתְּחוּ אֵת הַשְּׁעָרִים They will surely open the gates.

הוּא שָׁפוֹט יִשְׁפֹּט אוֹתְךָ He will surely judge you.

הַדְּבָרִים הָאֵלֶּה יָצֹא יֵצְאוּ These words will surely go forth.

43.5 FRIDAY

The Bible studies from your textbook are good work for today and may take more than one day to complete.

Complete answers will not be given for these independent studies because a book could probably be written on each one. Ideally, Teacher, you will do the studies, too, and assess the effort and the understanding of the process that your student shows, then discuss conclusions together. But, 43.5.1 should include learning that the Hebrew words translated "fool" are not the same. There are several sorts of fools, encompassing the silly, stupid, wicked, impious, and perverse. 43.5.2 should reveal that the Hebrew word for fear includes feelings of awe, reverence, and wonder, whereas "fear" probably has mostly negative connotations of dread and terror in our modern English.

VERB STEMS

CHAPTER FORTY-FOUR

44.1 MONDAY

Practice vocabulary and fluent reading of 1 Kings 18:24. Remember that the name of the LORD is read as *Adonai*.

וּקְרָאתֶם בְּשֵׁם אֱלֹהֵיכֶם וַאֲנִי אֶקְרָא בְשֵׁם־יְהוָה וְהָיָה הָאֱלֹהִים אֲשֶׁר־יַעֲנֶה בָאֵשׁ הוּא
הָאֱלֹהִים וַיַּעַן כָּל־הָעָם וַיֹּאמְרוּ טוֹב הַדָּבָר׃

and call	וּקְרָאתֶם
on the name of	בְּשֵׁם
your god	אֱלֹהֵיכֶם
and I	וַאֲנִי
will call	אֶקְרָא
on the name of	בְשֵׁם־
the LORD	יְהוָה
and it will be	וְהָיָה
the god	הָאֱלֹהִים
who	אֲשֶׁר־

will answer	יַעֲנֶה
with the fire	בָאֵשׁ
He is	הוּא
the God	הָאֱלֹהִים
and answered	וַיַּעַן
all	כָּל־
the people	הָעָם
and said	וַיֹּאמְרוּ
good is	טוֹב
the word	הַדָּבָר׃

44.2 TUESDAY

Translate from Scripture.

וַיּוֹצֵא ([God] brought out) אֹתוֹ הַחוּצָה (outside) וַיֹּאמֶר הַבֶּט־ (look) נָא הַשָּׁמַיְמָה וּסְפֹר
הַכּוֹכָבִים (the stars) אִם־תּוּכַל לִסְפֹּר אֹתָם וַיֹּאמֶר לוֹ כֹּה (thus) יִהְיֶה זַרְעֶךָ

Genesis 15:5

God brought him outside and said, "Look, please, toward Heaven and count the stars if you are able to count them." And he said, "Thus will be your descendants."

וַיַּךְ (and struck) לֵב־דָּוִד אֹתוֹ אַחֲרֵי־כֵן סָפַר אֶת־הָעָם וַיֹּאמֶר דָּוִד אֶל־יְהוָה חָטָאתִי מְאֹד
אֲשֶׁר עָשִׂיתִי וְעַתָּה יְהוָה הַעֲבֶר־נָא אֶת־עֲוֹן עַבְדְּךָ כִּי נִסְכַּלְתִּי (I have acted foolishly) מְאֹד

2 Samuel 24:10

David's heart struck him after he counted the people. David said to the LORD, "I have sinned greatly in my actions and now, LORD, will you please pass over your servant's guilt because I have acted very foolishly."

מִזְבַּח אֲדָמָה תַּעֲשֶׂה־לִּי וְזָבַחְתָּ עָלָיו אֶת־עֹלֹתֶיךָ וְאֶת שְׁלָמֶיךָ (peace offerings) אֶת־צֹאנְךָ
וְאֶת־בְּקָרֶךָ בְּכָל־הַמָּקוֹם אֲשֶׁר אַזְכִּיר (I cause to be remembered) אֶת־שְׁמִי אָבוֹא אֵלֶיךָ
וּבֵרַכְתִּיךָ (and bless you)

Exodus 20:24

You will make an earthen altar for me and offer for sacrifice on it your whole burnt offerings and peace offerings of your flock and your cattle in every place where I cause to be remembered my name. I will come to you and bless you.

וַיֹּאמֶר יְהוָה אֶל־קָיִן (proper name) לָמָּה חָרָה לָךְ וְלָמָּה נָפְלוּ פָנֶיךָ

Genesis 4:6

The LORD said to Cain, "Why are you angry and why did your face fall?

לֹא־תַעֲשֶׂה כֵן לַיהוָה אֱלֹהֶיךָ כִּי כָל־תּוֹעֲבַת יְהוָה אֲשֶׁר שָׂנֵא (hates) עָשׂוּ לֵאלֹהֵיהֶם כִּי גַם אֶת־בְּנֵיהֶם וְאֶת־בְּנֹתֵיהֶם יִשְׂרְפוּ (they burn) בָאֵשׁ לֵאלֹהֵיהֶם

Deuteronomy 12:31

You will not do thus to the LORD your God because every abomination which the LORD hates they have done for their gods, because even their sons and their daughters they burn with fire for their gods.

רַק בְּכָל־אַוַּת (desire) נַפְשְׁךָ תִּזְבַּח וְאָכַלְתָּ בָשָׂר כְּבִרְכַּת (as a blessing) יְהוָה אֱלֹהֶיךָ אֲשֶׁר נָתַן־לְךָ בְּכָל־שְׁעָרֶיךָ הַטָּמֵא וְהַטָּהוֹר יֹאכְלֶנּוּ כַּצְּבִי (as gazelle) וְכָאַיָּל (and as deer)

Deuteronomy 12:15

Only (however), in every desire of your soul (whenever you want), you may slaughter and eat meat as a blessing of the LORD your God which he has given to you in all your gates. The unclean and the clean may eat as of a gazelle or a deer.

44.3 WEDNESDAY

1. Consider how you can continue to use and study Hebrew in everyday life. Do at least one of these today: sing songs or pray blessings found in *Biblical Hebrew: A Homeschool Primer*, get an Israel guidebook from the library and start planning a trip, or pick a psalm to pray and start memorizing it in Hebrew.

2. Explain aspect and voice.

Aspect can be of three sorts. 1. Simple action. Example: He tore. 2. Intensive action. Example: He shredded the thing to bits. 3. Causative action. Example: He caused it to be torn.

Voice relates the relationship between subject and verb. In active voice, the noun did the verb. Example: I kicked. In passive voice, the verb got done to the subject. Example: I was kicked. The middle voice relates reflexive action: the noun both acted and received the action of the verb. Example: I kicked myself.

3. Translate from Scripture.
Then consult English translations.

לֹא תֹאכַל כָּל־תּוֹעֵבָה

Deuteronomy 14:3

Do not eat any abomination.

כָּל־צִפּוֹר טְהֹרָה תֹּאכֵלוּ

Deuteronomy 14:11

You will eat every clean bird.

וַיַּרְא כָּל־הָעָם וַיִּפְּלוּ עַל־פְּנֵיהֶם וַיֹּאמְרוּ יְהוָה הוּא הָאֱלֹהִים יְהוָה הוּא הָאֱלֹהִים

1 Kings 18:39

All the people saw and they fall on their faces and said, "The LORD is the God! The LORD is the God!"

4. In English, put the verb *to cut* into each of the Hebrew stems (as was done with *to kill* in your textbook).

- QAL, or PA'AL: simple action, active voice He cut it.
- NIFAL: simple action, passive voice He was cut.
- PIEL: intensive action, active voice He gashed it.
- PUAL: intensive action, passive voice He got gashed.
- HIFIL: causative action, active voice He caused it to be cut.
- HOFAL: causative action, passive voice He was caused to cut it.
- HITPAEL: intensive action, middle (reflexive) voice He gave himself a gash.

44.4 THURSDAY
Translate from Scripture.

Students should do their best, use these overly literal translations for checking work, then compare with English Bibles.

לֹא־טוֹב הַדָּבָר הַזֶּה אֲשֶׁר עָשִׂיתָ חַי־יְהוָה כִּי בְנֵי־מָוֶת אַתֶּם אֲשֶׁר לֹא־שְׁמַרְתֶּם עַל־אֲדֹנֵיכֶם
עַל־מְשִׁיחַ יְהוָה

1 Samuel 26:16

What you did is not good! The LORD's life that ("As the LORD lives") you are sons of death who did not keep watch over your lord, over the LORD's anointed.

וַיְהִי אַבְרָם בֶּן־תִּשְׁעִים שָׁנָה וְתֵשַׁע (ninety) שָׁנִים וַיֵּרָא (appeared) יְהוָה אֶל־אַבְרָם וַיֹּאמֶר
אֵלָיו אֲנִי־אֵל שַׁדַּי הִתְהַלֵּךְ ("walk" in hitpael) לְפָנַי וֶהְיֵה תָמִים (blameless)

Genesis 17:1

And it was that Abram was ninety-nine years old. The LORD appeared to Abram and said to him, "I am God Almighty. Walk before me and be blameless."

וּמַלְכִּי־צֶדֶק (and proper name: can you see what it means? *righteous king*) מֶלֶךְ
שָׁלֵם (proper name) הוֹצִיא (brought) לֶחֶם וָיָיִן וְהוּא כֹהֵן לְאֵל עֶלְיוֹן

brought, **הוֹצִיא**: this is the verb *go out* in a different stem, can you figure out which one? *hifil*

Genesis 14:18

Melchizedek, King of Salem, brought bread and wine. He was a priest of God Most High.

אַחֲרֵי יְהוָה אֱלֹהֵיכֶם תֵּלֵכוּ וְאֹתוֹ תִירָאוּ וְאֶת־מִצְוֹתָיו תִּשְׁמֹרוּ וּבְקֹלוֹ תִשְׁמָעוּ וְאֹתוֹ תַעֲבֹדוּ
וּבוֹ תִדְבָּקוּן (you shall cling)

Deuteronomy 13:4

After the LORD your God you shall walk, and fear Him, and guard His commandments, and listen to His voice, and work for/worship Him and cling to Him.

וְסָפַרְתָּ לְךָ שֶׁבַע שַׁבְּתֹת (sabbaths) שָׁנִים שֶׁבַע שָׁנִים שֶׁבַע פְּעָמִים וְהָיוּ לְךָ יְמֵי שֶׁבַע
שַׁבְּתֹת (sabbaths) הַשָּׁנִים תֵּשַׁע וְאַרְבָּעִים שָׁנָה

Leviticus 25:8

You will count seven sabbaths of years, seven years seven times, and you will have the days of seven sabbaths of years, forty-nine years.

וַתֹּאמֶר אֶל־אָבִיהָ אַל־יִחַר בְּעֵינֵי אֲדֹנִי כִּי לוֹא אוּכַל לָקוּם מִפָּנֶיךָ כִּי־דֶרֶךְ נָשִׁים לִי

Genesis 31:35a

And she said to her father, "Do not be angry, my lord, because I am not able to arise before you because I have the way of women."

44.5 FRIDAY

The Bible studies from your textbook are good work for today and may take more than one day to complete.

44.5.1: Students should read these phrases in Hebrew and follow the contextual word study process as practiced in Chapters 36 and 37. Possible translations of the given verses that do not use the word "heart:"

1 Kings 10:2: she told him what she was thinking
Job 34:10: thoughtful, intelligent men
Proverbs 7:7: a heedless young man
Isaiah 6:10: dull the people's minds
Isaiah 63:4: the day of vengeance was foremost in my thoughts
Psalm 101:4: a crooked mind
Isaiah 13:7: every man will be in terror
Psalm 12:2: they tell two different stories, they speak deceptively

Ecclesiastes 2:23: he stays up thinking and worrying
Psalm 22:26: may your purpose and attitude live forever; you will live forever
Jonah 2:3: in the middle of the sea
Ecclesiastes 1:13: I dedicated energy and attention

44.5.2: Many Bible translations do not distinguish these terms consistently. A search of the references in Hebrew will show a vast difference in these folks' attitude toward God, obligation to His commandments, and connection with the community of Israel. This study would be a good subject for a "contrast and compare" essay or list.

REVIEW

CHAPTER FORTY-FIVE

45.1 MONDAY

Review vocabulary from recent weeks well today. Since this is the last chapter, you will have fewer exercises with those words than with earlier ones.

Read this week two commandments that begin with the same word and on which Yeshua said hang all the Torah and the Prophets. These are wonderful to memorize.

The כָל's of Deuteronomy 6:5 are pronounced *cole*, rather than *coll*. In each, the kametz is followed by a letter without a dagesh and then a makkef. Further details of kametz pronunciation are available in Appendix B of your textbook.

וְאָהַבְתָּ אֵת יְהוָה אֱלֹהֶיךָ בְּכָל־לְבָבְךָ וּבְכָל־נַפְשְׁךָ וּבְכָל־מְאֹדֶךָ׃

Deuteronomy 6:5

וְאָהַבְתָּ לְרֵעֲךָ כָּמוֹךָ

Leviticus 19:18

and you shall love	וְאָהַבְתָּ
(direct object marker)	אֵת
the LORD	יְהוָה
your God	אֱלֹהֶיךָ
with all	בְּכָל־

your heart	לְבָבְךָ
and with all	וּבְכָל־
your soul	נַפְשְׁךָ
and with all	וּבְכָל־
your might	מְאֹדֶךָ׃
and you shall love	וְאָהַבְתָּ
your neighbor	לְרֵעֲךָ
as yourself	כָּמוֹךָ

45.2 TUESDAY

1. Explain how the vav prefix works and some of its various names.

A vav prefix is always a conjunction, but on verbs, it can also change the tense. Because this vav prefix connects a narrative, it is known as the vav consecutive. Because it converts the verb tense, it is also known as the vav conversive. Because it relates verbs to one another in a story, it is sometimes called the vav relative. To refer to it without reference to purpose or meaning, the terms wayyiqtol and weqatal are used.

2. What is the role of a vav prefix when spelled as follows and affixed to a verb?

- וְ join phrases and change the tense of a perfect tense verb; or act simply as a conjunction without changing tense on an imperfect tense verb
- וּ join phrases and change the tense of a perfect tense verb
- וַ with dagesh in next letter join phrases and change the tense of an imperfect tense verb

3. What happens when a vav consecutive is affixed to an imperfect tense verb that has a root ending with ה?

The final hey of the verb drops off.

4. What is an infinitive verb? Give an example in English and Hebrew.

a basic verb form without tense, gender, number, or person

In English, infinitives are in the form of "to ________," for example, "to ski," "to dance," or "to work."

Hebrew infinitives are listed in Appendix D of the textbook.

5. Translate.

וַיִּסְפֹּר שְׁלֹמֹה כָּל־הָאֲנָשִׁים הַגֵּירִים אֲשֶׁר בְּאֶרֶץ יִשְׂרָאֵל Solomon counted all the sojourning men in the land of Israel.

אַתָּה נָתַתָּ לוֹ לִשְׁכַּב You allowed him to lie down.

נָפוֹל יִפֹּל הַבַּיִת הַהוּא That house will surely fall.

45.3 WEDNESDAY

Translate words, phrases, and sentences.

בְּקִרְבָּהּ in her/its inward part

נַפְשׁוֹ his soul

עַל־פְּנֵי מַיִם on the surface of the water

עָפָר מִן־הָאֲדָמָה dust of the ground

וְנָתַתִּי רוּחִי בָכֶם וִחְיִיתֶם I will give you my spirit and you will live.

אֶלֶף וְאַרְבַּע־מֵאוֹת רֶכֶב one thousand four hundred chariots

יְהוָה אֱלֹהֵינוּ כָּרַת עִמָּנוּ בְּרִית The LORD our God made a covenant with us.

וּבָנִיתִי לְדֹר־וָדֹר כִּסְאֲךָ I will build, from generation to generation, your throne.

כִּסֵּא מַלְכוּתוֹ עַל־יִשְׂרָאֵל the throne of his reign/kingdom over Israel

פְּרִי הַגָּפֶן fruit of the vine, or grapes

אַל תְּשַׁבֵּר אוֹתוֹ Do not break it!

כֶּסֶף וְזָהָב silver and gold

יַעֲלֶה לִזְבֹּחַ He will go up to sacrifice.

וַיִּלְבַּשׁ בִּגְדֵי יִצְחָק And he wore Isaac's clothes.

הַכֹּהֵן הוּא יֵלֵד שְׁלֹשָׁה בָּנִים The priest will beget three sons.

וְעַתָּה יֵשֶׁב־נָא עַבְדְּךָ תַּחַת הַנַּעַר עֶבֶד לַאדֹנִי וְהַנַּעַר יַעַל עִם־אֶחָיו And now, please, your servant will remain, instead of the young man being a servant to my lord, and the young man will go up with his brothers.

אֱלֹהֵי מִצְרַיִם
the gods of Egypt

יֵשׁוּעַ הַמָּשִׁיחַ
Jesus Christ

לֹא אֵצֵא
I will not go out.

45.4 THURSDAY

1. Translate.

דָּוִד אָסֹף יֶאֱסֹף אֵת כָּל־הַבְּהֵמָה David will surely gather all the animals.

עָשׂה יַעֲשֶׂה שָׁלוֹם בָּאָרֶץ He will surely make peace in the land.

שְׁלֹמֹה יוּכַל לָשֶׁבֶת עַל כִּסֵּא אָבִיו Solomon will be able to sit on the throne of his father.

בְּאָכְלָם אֲנַחְנוּ שַׁבְנוּ While they were eating, we returned.

בְּהֵמָה טְמֵאָה unclean animal

הוּא יוּכַל לָדַעַת כִּי אֲנִי אָחִיו He will be able to know that I am his brother.

שָׁפוֹט יִשְׁפֹּט אוֹתָם בְּחָכְמָה He will surely judge them in wisdom.

יָכֹל לִרְאוֹת אֵת רֹאשׁ הָהָר He was able to see the mountaintop.

וָאֶשָּׂא עֵינַי וָאֶרְאֶה וְהִנֵּה רֶכֶב רַב־מְאֹד I lifted my eyes and looked, and behold! very many chariots!

שְׁמַעְנָה נָשִׁים דְּבַר־יְהוָה וְתִקַּח אָזְנְכֶם דְּבַר־פִּיו

from Jeremiah 9:20

Hear, women, the word of the LORD and let your ear take the word of his mouth! (Try converting this to English idiom.)

2. Explain aspect and voice.

Aspect can be of three sorts. 1. Simple action. Example: He tore. 2. Intensive action. Example: He shredded the thing to bits. 3. Causative action. Example: He caused it to be torn.

Voice relates the relationship between subject and verb. In active voice, the noun did the verb. Example: I kicked. In passive voice, the verb got done to the subject. Example: I was kicked. The middle voice relates reflexive action: the noun both acted and received the action of the verb. Example: I kicked myself.

3. What is the gender, number, person, aspect, voice, stem, and translation of this verb? יָצָא

gender: masculine
number: singular
person: 3rd
aspect: simple action
voice: active voice
stem: qal or pa'al
translation: He went out.

45.5 FRIDAY

Work on some good Hebrew Bible study today, and for the rest of your life! May God bless you in all your efforts to know and follow Him with joy, wisdom, and peace.

45.5.1: Vanity's primary meaning in modern English is excessive pride in appearance or accomplishments. This is not the meaning in Ecclesiastes at all. Studying the word in Ecclesiastes should reveal that Kohelet decries emptiness, meaninglessness, unsubstantiality, unfairness, incomprehensibility. The Hebrew word's root meaning is "vapor" or "breath."

45.5.2: This is a pretty tricky question that keeps people up at night. Examining the Hebrew words with context and a Hebrew dictionary will reveal why there has been some confusion. 31.5 touched upon the dragon/jackal word similarity. Some suggest "dinosaur" as the best translation. Exploring the Biblical words for owl and ostrich will reveal that Strong's #3284 has had multiple translations, probably because the bird's species was surmised from its attributes as described in Scripture. Read the occurrences of #3284 and see what you think. #3283 is a masculine plural bird word, #3284 is a feminine version, but the masculine singular version never appears in Scripture. About these translation choices, as with most topics concerning the Bible, you can find some heated debate. Hebrew knowledge may help you choose credible sources of information and come to informed conclusions.

31000631R00178

Made in the USA
San Bernardino, CA
29 February 2016